PERFECTLY NEGATIVE

How I Learned to Embrace
Life's ~~Lemons~~ Lessons

*For Kim —
always move forward with
courage.*

Linda Carvelli

*All the best,
Linda*

This book is a work of creative nonfiction. The events are portrayed to the best of the author's memory. Some names may have been changed to protect the privacy and/or confidentiality of the people who have lived these lives. Each of them has their own story of these events and none would be wrong.

The conversations in the book all come from the author's recollection, though they are not written to represent word-for-word transcripts. Rather, the author has retold them in a way that evokes the feeling and meaning of what was said and in all instances, the essence of the dialogue is accurate.

For more information, contact the publisher:
Linda Carvelli Enterprises, LLC
www.lindacarvelli.com
linda@lindacarvelli.com
Instagram: www.instagram.com/lindacarvelli/
Facebook: www.facebook.com/lindacarvellilifecoach/
Twitter: @Writes2Survive

ISBN: 978-1530670901

Printed in the United States of America

Cover design by Mirage Design (www.mirage-design.com)

For my parents and my sister, forever in my heart

To my husband, ti amo

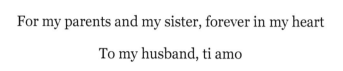

"It is in the whole process of meeting and solving problems that life has meaning..." ~ M. Scott Peck, *The Road Less Traveled*

Contents

Chapter 1

When Life Hands You Lemons, Get Married

"One slice of lemon meringue pie and three forks?" My sister looked at me as she ordered dessert from the waitress.

"Sure, why not?" I shrugged my shoulders.

"You girls can share it. I'm already too full," Mom said.

I looked at Lori. "Oh, then let's get it to go."

"No, no, I'll be fine. They'll enjoy it here." Mom looked at the waitress and tapped her hand on the table.

The three of us had just been to the House of Brides for our final dress fittings and I really had no business eating dessert, but when life handed me lemons, I guess I decided to order lemon pie. I thought I had been managing the stress of all the last-minute wedding details but none of us anticipated receiving the devastating news of my mother's illness.

"So what else is on your list of things to do before the big day?" my sister asked.

"The guys' tuxedos and then—Mom, you're still coming with me to the florist to finalize the flowers, right?" I stared across the table at my mother.

"Yes, I wouldn't miss that." Mom yawned.

I noticed Mom struggling to keep her eyes open so I kicked Lori's leg under the table and tilted my head toward Mom. "On second thought, let's get the pie to go. I'm pretty full myself."

Just last week we found out my mother's breast cancer had returned—this time, in her bones—after ten years of remission. Mom begged her doctor to postpone any treatments until after my wedding, but he insisted she start chemotherapy right away.

My mother apologized when she told me she had cancer again. "I'm sorry this is happening now . . . of all times."

I stared into my mother's sad eyes and placed my right hand on my heart. "Mom, I can't imagine how you're feeling right now, but we just need to focus on getting you better. You have to dance at the wedding."

I had no way of knowing that this devastating news would be the beginning of ten years filled with one tragedy after another: four cancer diagnoses, three deaths, two divorces, and a significant other turned not-so-significant. Nor would I have predicted that when I finally had some distance from all the pain and really took the time to witness my life—almost like watching a movie—I would realize that everything had happened for a reason and that each painful experience only helped me to survive the next.

Two weeks after her first chemotherapy treatment, with my wedding two weeks away, my mother's hair began to fall out. Of course, I had hoped she'd be the first chemo patient not to lose her hair, but Lori and I had encouraged Mom to pick out a wig, just in case. My mother smiled and acted with dignity, but I know she must have felt scared and defeated on the inside.

The morning of my wedding, I woke up with a bleeding cold sore on my lower lip and the sound of rain on my bedroom window. I mean, I know April showers, blah blah blah, but why did the weathermen have to be right today? I felt the chill in the air even before I leaned my forehead against the glass. I squinted through my thick-lensed wire eyeglasses and still couldn't see through the misty haze on my wedding day.

I inhaled and smelled coffee brewing. Dad buzzed around the kitchen fixing my favorite breakfast: scrambled eggs with white American cheese, toast with real butter, and his special seasoned home fries.

"Well, it's still here." I frowned.

"Good morning. What's still where?"

"This scabby cold sore." I pointed to the villain and pushed my face into his light blue eyes.

"You can't even see it. You're beautiful. Stop picking at it."

"Where's Mom, still sleeping?" I started to set the table.

"Yes. She needs to take it easy today."

As I ate the cheesy eggs, butterfly wings fluttered in my stomach, partly from my nerves but mostly because the wedding day I had dreamed of had arrived and my dream and my reality were like day and night. In the dream, my happy and healthy family made me the center of attention, danced all night to the big band music, and hung around the ballroom even after all the guests had left.

I took a long hot shower and as I walked back to my bedroom I saw my mom for the first time that morning. She sat alone at the dining room table, wearing her white terry cloth robe and a pink fleece head wrap. I watched her lift her coffee cup to her mouth with all four fingers except for that cute pinkie finger pointed to the ceiling, take a quick sip, and force herself to eat a bite of dry toast. I felt guilty that she had to wear a fancy dress, an itchy wig, and a forced smile all day.

"Good morning." Mom smiled without showing her teeth.

I pointed to my lower lip and pouted.

"Let me see." My mother put on her reading glasses. "Are you using the cream I bought you?"

I nodded and frowned.

"It'll be fine. Stop picking at it. What time will your sister be here?"

"I think around ten or eleven."

"Okay, well, let me get myself cleaned up then." Mom slowly rose from the table and picked up her dishes.

"I'll get those. You go ahead and get ready, Mom."

I took her dishes to the sink where Dad stood staring out the window at his huge garden of vegetables and flowers that surrounded the fish pond. Everything looked brown and dead, struggling to come alive after a long, cold winter.

"It won't be long before everything is back in bloom again."

"Do you think she'll be okay today, Dad?"

"She'll be fine. She just may need a nap or two, okay?" Dad rubbed my back.

"Sure," I answered, but the prima donna in me still hoped today would be the wedding I had always wanted.

When I first heard Mom's cancer had returned, I told my father we should postpone the wedding. Even given my mother's illness, my father never took me up on my offer and insisted Mom wanted to see her youngest of four children married, settled, and happy.

As I think back now, I wonder if my mother's health was really the primary reason I was so willing to reschedule the wedding. Dean and I had dated for seven years and marriage seemed like the next obvious step to me, even if my sister had not agreed. Shortly after our engagement, Lori had taken me out for what I thought would be a celebratory lunch. Instead, my sister treated me like a criminal, asking probing questions about my relationship with Dean. I had occasionally complained to Lori when Dean would go out with his friends on Friday nights and so she asked if I had finally accepted this routine. She asked if I thought it was normal that Dean's mother still did his laundry and cleaned his apartment. I answered yes to both questions, finding her questions silly. I mean, I assumed that after we were married Dean would go out with *me* on Friday nights and we would do our own laundry. It never even vaguely crossed my mind that maybe, with my sister's experience and maturity, she knew something that I was just too immature to recognize.

"I think your sister is here. I'm going to put on my monkey suit and check on your mother."

Lori arrived at the same time as my hairdresser. "Sorry, I'm late." She dropped her bags on the dining room floor. "I hope the sun makes an appearance." She carried her dress into my childhood bedroom and, as she closed the door, I heard, "I see you still have that cold sore, huh?"

I lifted my finger to my lip and mumbled, "Yeah, I guess I do." *Thanks for noticing, Sis.* I rolled my eyes at my hairdresser and she followed me into the bathroom where she worked her magic to secure my veil into my short blond hair. My sister helped me into my ivory silk and lace wedding gown before I made the final touches to my makeup.

Dad knocked on the door and popped his head in before entering the bathroom. He rarely wore a suit and always complained when he had to dress for anything other than golf or gardening, but today he didn't put up a fuss. I had forgotten how handsome he looked in a tuxedo.

"The photographer and florist are here," he announced as they both appeared in the doorway.

The photographer started snapping pictures of me getting ready for the big day. She took a picture of me staring into the bathroom mirror and then she followed me into the living room and asked me to stare out the window. I had never liked those silly staged pictures that always landed at the beginning of wedding albums. Maybe I should have had her taking photos while Dad made my cheesy eggs. I mean, that moment would have captured the real us.

Adele, my family's go-to florist, held up my bouquet. "What do you think?"

"It's perfect," I said as Lori walked in and agreed. "You remembered to use something unscented for my mom's bouquet, right?"

"Of course I did."

My mom entered the living room wearing a wide smile, a peach chiffon flowing skirt, and a fitted jacket with sequins and pearls. She wore her diamond earrings, diamond necklace, diamond bracelet, pearl bracelet, and diamond rings. It drove me crazy when she chose to wear all of her best jewelry all at the same time. I'd say, "Mom, wear diamonds or pearls." But today I said nothing.

She pointed her right toe and twirled around just enough to lift the skirt away and show off her toned legs. "Well, how do I look?"

"Be-you-tiful." I mimicked the way my mother always pronounced the word. I stood up and gave her a gentle hug. Her hair and makeup looked so natural.

"Remember to reapply your lipstick." I winked at her. The three girls shared this little beauty secret: even if we wore no other makeup, we always carried lipstick in our purse and used it on our lips and cheeks to provide extra color if we looked pale.

"Do you feel okay?" I asked.

"Yeah, I feel good," she replied, and I wondered if she had told me the truth.

The photographer led us to the family room and asked my parents to pose in front of the brick fireplace. My sister and I stood together and stared at our parents. "How cute they are," Lori said.

I remember thinking, I hope I'm blessed with a forty-six-year marriage just like theirs.

My mother fixed my father's cummerbund and asked him to button his jacket. He wrapped his arm around her waist and held her hand as if they were about to dance a waltz. As they looked into each other's eyes, I heard Dad whisper, "I love you, Annie."

After a few more formal pictures, Dad and I walked outside toward the antique car Dean and I had chosen. My sister drove my mother in my parents' car.

Although I had noticed all the cars in the church parking lot, when we entered the vestibule I froze at the sight of all the people staring at me.

I watched my brothers walk my mom to her seat and then turned to my niece and two nephews with both thumbs up. "Okay, munchkins, it's your turn."

My sister tugged at my train and patted my back, but her wink gave me the confidence I needed to follow her down the aisle. When the music switched to "Here Comes the Bride" Dad looked right into my eyes and patted my cold and sweaty hand.

"Ready?"

Without answering him, I bit my lip and shrugged my shoulders, "I guess so." We interlocked our arms and faced the crowd.

We took the tiniest steps on the red carpet toward the altar and I felt relief when I first saw my fiancé. I had called Dean just a few hours before the ceremony and he knew exactly what I wanted to ask him. Right then his eyes gave me his answer again: *See, I showed up.*

My father offered my hand to Dean. "Take good care of her."

"Yeah, I will, Frank." Dean held my hand just as the heavy rain collided with every stained glass window in the church.

The priest declared us husband and wife and we shared a quick peck on the lips before turning toward our families and friends. The rain turned to mist long enough for us to greet our guests and take some pictures outside. I stood on my tippy toes, searching for my mom and spotted her and my dad getting into their car. I figured she must have needed nap number one.

Mom and Dad missed the photos taken outside of the county club, too. The band announced Dean and I as "Mr. and Mrs."—omitting my last name for the first time in my life—as we entered the ballroom. I stood between Dean and his mother in the receiving line, but kept stealing glimpses of my mom. I noticed that she could use a little more lipstick.

Dean and I hardly sat at our dinner table for two and other than the quick kiss at the altar, I don't remember Dean ever kissing me at the reception. We danced the traditional first and last wedding dances and, although we had agreed to visit each guest table throughout the night, we had done that more separately than together.

Had Mom been feeling better, she would have visited each guest herself, too. Instead, one or more of my siblings stayed close by her side as guests walked to her table to say hello. Her smile and wide eyes lit up her face as she watched my father and I dance to the song she had helped me choose, "The Way You Look Tonight." Instead of dancing with my mother, my father escorted her to the small room adjacent to the ballroom and then I knew Mom needed nap number two.

Other than my immediate family, my parents had only shared my mother's cancer recurrence with a handful of their closest friends and relatives. My mother tried so hard to not overshadow my big day. But by the end of the evening, anyone who knew my mother well enough must have sensed something very different about her and the way my family doted on her more than me. The first day of my married life felt more like a funeral than a wedding.

Dean had built our duplex in the same town as his parents. My in-laws gave us a ride home from the reception and I think my husband may have gotten a bit confused about where he lived now that we were married. I thanked his parents while Dean helped me out of the car, but instead of following me he walked back toward his parent's car and sat in the backseat.

"Dean, where are you going?"

"Oh, I'm going to get my car."

"It's late. Let's just get it in the morning."

I never expected Dean to carry me over the threshold, but I never expected to walk into our new home alone on my wedding night either.

I stared out the front window as I plopped myself down on the living room carpet, surrounded by my wedding dress and its long train. As I look back now, I never worried that Dean's odd behavior might be a telling sign of our future together. In fact, the only person on my mind was my mother.

The next morning, I called my parents to check in. Mom sounded tired. I never said it out loud, but just like I had felt about the wedding, I wanted to postpone the honeymoon, too.

"I'll be fine. Go have fun. I'll be right here when you return."

Chapter 2

Are There Really Any Mistakes in Life?

I rested the phone on its cradle as I thought about my mother's advice. For as far back as I could remember, my mother had always been there whenever I returned to her—from anywhere. As a little girl, every morning, I would wake up in my cozy bedroom decorated with sheer white curtains, flowery bedspread, fluffy pillows, and crisp sheets and I'd find her sitting at the kitchen table right outside my door, sipping her morning coffee.

"Did you sleep well, doll?" Mom would always ask as she stood up to prepare whatever my little heart desired for breakfast. Now that I know what it's like to stock a kitchen for other people besides myself, I have no idea how my mother always had the right ingredients to cook anything I ever wanted.

From kindergarten through high school, when I stepped off the school bus Mom was always home and in the kitchen, ready to serve me any snack I craved. And she always knew what to do with whatever baggage I brought with me—backpack, homework, dirty clothes, or tears from the latest childhood drama.

Imagine my mother's surprise when, nine years after raising three kids with two years between each, at the age of thirty-seven she found out she was pregnant with me. My parents never made me feel like anything other than a blessing to them. Even when I misbehaved, my mother called me her bonus child. "You'll certainly keep me young, doll," she would say.

On the other hand, Lori and my oldest brother, Arthur, constantly told me I was a mistake and reminded me I was born exactly nine months after New Year's Eve—a night for careless lovers, apparently. My mother always corrected Arthur when she heard him call me a mistake, but that never stopped him from teasing me behind her back.

"Get out!" I yelled at Arthur when, for no reason, he barged into my bedroom and made fun of me while I played quietly with my Barbie dolls.

"Four eyes!" he whispered.

I threw my new eyeglasses across the hardwood floor and ran upstairs to find my brother Frankie in the bedroom he shared with Arthur. Frankie hadn't heard me crawl under his bed while he lay on top of it wearing huge headphones blaring rock music. And he never heard the heavy footsteps running up the stairs until my father and Arthur banged the bedroom door and startled him.

"What? What's going on?" Frankie asked.

"Where's the little brat?" Arthur asked as he bent down to look under his bed.

"She's not in here," Frankie answered.

Arthur rushed across the hall to search Lori's empty room and returned. He lifted Frankie's bedspread. "Here! Dad, she's right here!" He giggled as he grabbed my arm and dragged me from under the bed to hand me over to my father.

"Your mother and I paid good money for those glasses." My father spanked my bum. "You better learn to take better care of them. Now, go to your room."

Even without my glasses I saw Frankie mouth, "Sorry," while Arthur just grinned. At the age of ten, all I ever wanted was to hang out with my big brothers and sister. I never understood why Arthur preferred to pick on me by playing practical jokes instead of playing board games or cards.

Lori was nine years older than me and had her own way of tormenting me. She insisted my parents had adopted me. I was the only one of us with blond hair, fair skin, and light eyes. I thought I took after my father's northern Italian family, but it never stopped me from wondering if Lori had been telling the truth.

Honestly, most days I just felt like an only child, hanging out with my parents while the big kids were out with friends their own age. But one afternoon, I remember hanging out with Arthur's girlfriend, Cynthia, who actually was an only child. We sat at the kitchen table playing with my new Lite-Brite toy from Santa.

"Can we make the witch?" I asked.

We finished adding all the colored pegs and flipped the switch to light it up. Cynthia named the Halloween-colored witch Wanda and, just like that, all of my siblings began calling me Wanda. I felt so special to be named after my toy and relieved that they had stopped calling me a "mistake" and telling me I was adopted. Many years later, I realized how gullible I had been when I learned that my siblings thought of me as a witch and that "Wanda" was a code word for "brat" or "pest."

I never thought of myself as a brat . . . I mean, who does, really? Maybe I just never figured out how to be the perfect little sister. Being the youngest child all I ever wanted was to have everything my siblings had, regardless of our age difference. I begged for a bra when I turned six (as opposed to most girls who nagged their parents around the age of nine). And I never complained when I had to wear eyeglasses in the fourth grade because everyone else in my family wore them.

But the biggest thrill I wanted more than anything was to drive. Long before my foot could reach the gas pedal, I would sit alone for hours in one of my parent's cars parked in our driveway, pretending to go to the bank and the grocery store, just like my mother. After I turned fifteen I nagged everyone in the house until someone let me drive a car around the neighborhood. One night, my dad asked Frankie to run an errand and I pouted until my brother gave in. "All right, hurry up. Let's go."

As soon as we drove away from the house, I raised my eyebrows and smiled. "Can I drive?"

"Sure, but don't tell anyone."

I tried to park the car on a hill, but I jumped the curb and heard a crunch before I realized I had hit a telephone pole. Other than a tiny cut on my hand and heart palpitations, we were both fine. No one noticed the scratch on my hand or the small dent in the hood of Frankie's sports car and we kept the secret between us.

Another day, no one was home when the bus dropped me off from school and I convinced two of my girlfriends to take a joyride in my father's company van. I had driven five streets from my house when my sister's little red Fiat convertible appeared in the rearview mirror. I pressed the gas pedal to the floor, foolishly thinking Lori would forget the entire incident if I parked the van back in the driveway before she got home. She pulled in right behind me and never said a word until we were all sitting across from each other in the living room.

"Wanda, do you have any idea how much trouble you could have caused?" she asked me. "Dad could lose his company and we could all be out of jobs!"

Lori enjoyed embarrassing me in front of my friends. And, unlike Frankie, who never talked about me crashing his car, Lori threatened to use the neighborhood chase against me every chance she had. So much for "do unto others as you would have them do unto you."

Of all the lessons the Catholic nuns taught me in ten years of catechism, that Golden Rule has become the rule I remember most and it's how I strive to live my life. My parents raised all four of their children the same way; they instilled in us the same values, taught the same manners, and, for the most part, took us to church. As a kid, I attended mass because it was important to my mother. In high school, I sometimes went to church with my friends, basically so I could make my confirmation and, someday, get married in a church. I realized I liked the music and hearing the people singing around me. But mostly, church was like a fashion show. I loved to see what clothes, shoes, and jewelry women wore each week.

We lived outside of Providence, Rhode Island, in an area known as the Jewelry District. It was home to a large number of jewelry manufacturing companies. By the time I had turned ten, my dad owned his own jewelry manufacturing company—our family business. In middle school, while most of my friends earned their allowance taking out the garbage or mowing the lawn, I earned mine doing jewelry "homework." Some nights, Dad brought home loose earrings and, after I finished my school homework, Mom and I spent the night pushing earrings into gray or beige felt jewelry cards.

At some point, my father gave controlling interest of the business to Arthur, so my entire family worked there and reported to him. Dad and Cynthia designed the jewelry, Lori managed the finances and the front office, and Frankie ran the shipping and receiving department. Once I had started to drive—legally—Frankie offered me my dream job: I would assist his primary driver with deliveries when he needed some extra help. Some days I helped Lori in the front office, but given the choice I preferred to drive alone to avoid the office politics and sibling rivalry.

Because my entire family worked together, I assumed I would build my career at Dad's company—his legacy—but I always felt like a burden, the little baby sister no one ever wanted. My father had the most patience for me, but I had no talent or interest to design and create jewelry. I wanted to attend college. I hadn't been exposed to anything other than owning a business so I researched business schools.

With my parents' guidance and hard-earned money, I picked Bentley College in Massachusetts. Even though I was a little scared, for the first time I looked forward to living away from my siblings. They probably felt the same way.

I applied as an economics major, but during my very first computer class the professor recognized I had a knack for programming and he suggested I study computer science. In the mid-eighties, the technology industry was pretty new to me, but my father encouraged me to take a risk. I changed my major to computer science before my second semester.

The summer before my senior year, Dad said he had something to talk to me about and asked me to go for a ride with him. My mom had been diagnosed with breast cancer about six months earlier. They kept her illness private and, because I had been away at school, I hadn't witnessed most of her treatments. I was certain Dad had bad news about Mom. I never anticipated the discussion he wanted to have with me.

As we drove toward no specific destination he asked, "Do you think you'll work with the family after you graduate from college?"

Are you kidding me? No one will ever take me seriously there. I hesitated to give him an answer while I thought about the best way to say, "No way, Jose!" As much as I wanted to be involved with Dad's legacy, I knew I'd always be just the little baby sister. My father stared at me, waiting for my response.

"I don't think there's a place for me there, Dad."

He looked surprised.

I continued, "I'll have a degree in computers and you don't have a computer system installed."

"You could install them and manage them for us."

I paused for a breath. "Dad, I won't have the experience to manage that on my own right out of college. I mean, if you hire someone who has done this sort of thing then maybe I could work as an assistant or something."

I never wanted to disappoint my father, but he never made me feel that I had an obligation to work for him either. Having been blindsided with his question, I surprised myself with the choice I made. In high school I always assumed I would work with my family, but college opened my eyes to so many other possibilities. Deep down, though, I believed that even if I ventured away from the family business and made a mistake my family would be there to save the little sister.

Chapter 3

Getting Rid of the Pain

Lori had no patience for me working in her office, so I wondered what had motivated her to save me from failing my advanced accounting class. I figured my father must have told her that I'd decided not to work with the family and maybe Lori felt relieved. My entire life she watched me want— and mostly get—everything she had, so maybe she felt threatened by me. Or maybe she thought I was destined to do something bigger. After I had failed my accounting midterm, my professor suggested I hire a tutor. Lori volunteered to help me for free.

"I can't believe you actually majored in this crap," I said to her on the phone one night.

"My God, it's so easy, Wanda. Let me try to explain it this way." She begged me to listen to her while she thought of different ways to explain debits and credits, T-accounts, and assets and liabilities.

"This is so painful. How did you let me pick a college known for accounting? I hate accounting!"

"You can do this." I had no idea what made her so sure I would get it, but the passion in her voice made me trust her.

Lori never gave up on me, and I ended up passing the course.

After college, I accepted a job with a computer consulting firm in Boston and moved to a parent-subsidized apartment in Chestnut Hill, Massachusetts. Along with the firm's other new employees, my manager enrolled me in an intense two-month computer-training program at Boston University before assigning me to a client. I still cannot remember the exact moment when I felt the excruciating pain in my back and all the way down my right leg, but I do remember attending most of those BU classes in a horizontal position, lying down on the grungy carpet. I suffered through the entire training program and six months of work assignments before I headed home, for the first time since graduation, to spend Thanksgiving with my family. I stepped out of my parent-subsidized Honda Prelude and opened the trunk to get my laundry basket full of dirty clothes. My mother's mouth dropped open as she watched me walk toward her like an old lady without a cane.

"Linda, what happened?"

"Nothing new, Ma. It looks worse after driving for an hour. I'll straighten out in a few minutes."

Mom smiled as she grabbed the laundry basket. "Come on, let me make you something to eat."

My parents had listened to me complain about my back and leg pain over the phone, but neither knew how severe the injury was until they witnessed me walking at a forty-five degree angle. My mother and Frankie both had had back surgery to fix a ruptured disc several years earlier, and Mom was worried I may have the same problem. She made an appointment for me to see her surgeon and, after he reviewed my X-rays, he confirmed her fear.

"You have a herniated disc which is causing the pain in your leg."

He told us I needed surgery and I told my mother I wanted a second opinion. My parents left for Florida the day after Christmas, like they had every year since buying a condo in Fort Lauderdale, so Lori brought me to a neurologist for the second opinion—on New Year's Eve.

The surgeon gave me two options: a few months of traction or a laparoscopic discectomy to repair my ruptured disc.

"Is this hereditary?" I asked.

"Well, although you were born with a certain bone structure that can be hereditary, this type of injury can be from any number of things."

I remembered the day I had fallen off a horse during horseback riding lessons and the time my high school girlfriend crashed her parents' car into a telephone pole with me in the backseat. I probably aggravated my back each time I moved boxes in and out of my college dorm rooms, and maybe the last move into my first grown-up apartment caused something to snap, or slip, or—what had he said?—rupture?

I opted for the surgery. At twenty-three years old and with a lifetime ahead of me, I felt I had already experienced enough unbearable pain in the last six months despite ice packs, heating pads, and rest. I just wanted my back fixed so I could live the rest of my life pain-free.

Lori invited me to her New Year's Eve party that evening, but I decided to go home, take a pill, and fall asleep. After my sister dropped me off, I crawled into my parents' bed to avoid climbing the stairs to my bedroom and cried myself to sleep. Lori called several times to check on me, but I refused to have her pick me up. I appreciated my sister's concern, but I only wanted my mother. My parents assured me they would be home in time for the surgery—eight days from then—and since I nagged them to death about it, they probably wished they had never left me in the first place.

My mom and dad checked me into the hospital the afternoon before the surgery—in the late eighties, insurance companies paid for the night before surgery, too— and they stayed until visiting hours ended, promising to return in the morning. The doctor had scheduled my surgery for one o'clock and the nurse said she'd see me around eleven. When she walked into my room two hours early, I lost my temper.

"You said eleven," I yelled.

"I know. Your doctor had a cancellation and wants to take you earlier."

"Too bad for him! My parents aren't here yet! I'm not going early! I'm not ready!"

My dad walked into the room holding a medium-sized cardboard box.

"Dad!" I screamed. The nurse explained the situation to him and he smiled as he placed the box on the shelf next to my bed.

"Linda, it's okay. The pain will be gone a lot sooner." Dad patted my knee.

I knew my dad always spoke the truth, but I still sighed and pouted.

The nurse returned with a gigantic, bearded Neanderthal-looking guy and his gurney. She told me this man would take me to the operating area and the nurses there would prep me for surgery.

"No! I'm not getting on that thing with that man!" I screamed again as I limped across the room and pressed my back up against the closet. "I'm not going. Dad! Please!"

Dad walked toward me and reached for my hand. I stomped my feet, shook my head, and whined, "No! Daddy, please!"

He took my hand in his and escorted me to the gurney. "Come on, we all just want you to feel better."

"Linda, you'll be fine. We'll take good care of you. I promise. You'll need to remove your glasses," the nurse said.

"Why? I won't be able to see!"

We negotiated until she agreed to let me wear my glasses and she asked the Neanderthal to return them to her after he dropped me off in the OR.

Then she whispered, "Did you take off your panties?"

"Noooooooooo." I sighed, hoping she would break at least one of her senseless rules.

"You need to take off your panties before the surgery, Linda."

Besides being scared, I felt completely defeated. I never liked surprises—then or now. Just tell me what to expect, in almost any situation, and I'll behave. The nurse probably wished she had medicated me before the transporter wheeled me to the operating area. Then I realized that my father had filled the box with pieces of jewelry to give to the nurses to make up for my difficult behavior.

I can remember only three things from after I woke from the surgery: my dad's blue eyes staring at me and his hand holding mine, *Days of Our Lives* on the TV, and the fact that I felt no pain in my back or down my leg. I felt no pain at all.

Chapter 4

I Guess We Should Get Married

After the surgery, I decided to live closer to my parents. So I returned to work at the consulting firm and moved back home instead of my apartment. Naturally, I recovered faster with Mom's tender loving care.

By June I felt like new again. One Friday night, a friend asked a few of her single girlfriends to meet up with a few of her boyfriend's single friends to, as she put it, "see what happens."

So three girls and three guys met at the Hot Club—and that was when I first met Dan and . . . Dean. My eyes were immediately drawn to Dean's handsome Italian features. He had dark hair held back by a good amount of gel, dark eyes, and a bright smile showing off perfectly straight and white teeth. He held a cigarette in one hand and a cocktail in the other—the entire night. He also held everyone's attention with his loud voice and knack for telling jokes.

I placed my empty glass next to his on the bar and accepted his offer to buy me another vodka tonic. He lit another cigarette and the two of us moved away from the others and just talked. We were both twenty-four and the youngest kids in our families. Dean and I had graduated from high school the same year, but while I attended college, he worked at his dad's construction company. By the end of the night, although we hadn't kissed or exchanged phone numbers, I felt like we had hit it off.

Within a couple of weeks, Dean and I were set up on a double date with the couple who had introduced us. The four of us drove to Newport on a summer Sunday and spent the afternoon hanging outside on the sprawling lawn of a hilltop restaurant overlooking the harbor. I felt comfortable with Dean. He was always happy and generous, and he made me laugh. And he must have been a good kisser because our friends made fun of us for making out in the backseat all the way home.

We continued to date and eventually met each other's families. I don't remember the exact circumstances in either case, but if I had to guess, there was food involved. Lots of Italian food. Both of our moms were great cooks while Dean and I were great at picking a restaurant or ordering pizza.

Besides eating, drinking, and an occasional bike ride, we spent much of our time attending the weddings of our friends and cousins. I had always dreaded replying to a wedding invitation as a solo guest. Of course, I thought, everyone would ignore the bride and groom and only focus on the fact that I was without a date. The knowledge that I could rely on Dean as my "and guest" had improved my self-esteem—but never enough for me to actually broach the subject of our own wedding. I didn't want to scare him off for fear that I would be alone again. Plus, whenever anyone asked him when he would get married, he always repeated his rule: "Not until I'm at least thirty."

But I feared following in my sister's footsteps—thirty-three, unmarried, and considered an old maid. I had always wondered who my sister dreamt of meeting. She had a long-term boyfriend in high school and I thought they'd marry and be "high school sweethearts" forever. When they broke up, I never asked her why. In her early thirties, I thought she seemed serious with a guy because she had bought him an expensive cashmere sweater for Christmas. He gave her jumper cables, and when they broke up I never had to ask why.

In October 1990, Lori confessed to me that she had met a man at a bar. At first I thought, you go to bars? And then I wondered what quality man can she meet at a bar? Her face lit up when she talked about John. He had been divorced for a long time, had three sons, worked as a financial planner, and owned a sailboat. After just a few weeks, she asked me to meet him—even before he met our parents. When Lori requested that I meet John prior to anyone else in my family, it was the one moment in time when I realized that my sister respected me—respected me as an adult—finally.

I stared at John for the first time and thought, oh, he's older. He's much older. I wondered why Lori had never mentioned their age difference. Then, when he actually engaged me in the conversation, I realized he was a young old guy. John was a member of a sailing team and sailed every week. He loved to ski, and he traveled a lot. He sat on the boards of several organizations, led a yacht club, and worked as the general agent at a big life insurance company. He seemed very intelligent as he described his career as a financial advisor. As I watched the two of them smiling at each other I recognized respect—exactly what I had seen each time I stared at my parents. Lori and John listened to each other and they never talked over one another. Although Lori was younger—I still had no idea by how much at that point—she had always been very responsible, clear-headed, and right about a person's character.

Just four months later, on Valentine's Day, John asked Lori to marry him while dining at a romantic French restaurant in Providence. The story and accompanying photograph made the front page of the society section in the next morning's newspaper. Seeing Lori so happy made me happy and excited for her. She knew what she had been searching for in a husband and she had finally met her prince.

I had been a bridesmaid in both of my brother's weddings, but Lori asked me to be her maid of honor. It had been six years since Mom's mastectomy, but this upcoming wedding motivated her to pursue breast reconstruction. She had recovered nicely, and the three of us were inseparable while we planned the Newport wedding.

Like any bride getting married outdoors, Lori checked the weather forecast every day. The weathermen, unfortunately, were forecasting torrential rain on Lori's August wedding day. I tried to calm her down. "Don't worry about it. They're always wrong."

But I was wrong and the weathermen were right.

She called John the morning of their wedding. I had never heard her whine like a child before.

"Johnnie, it's raining awful."

The concierge knocked at the door to deliver the scotch I had ordered for my sister. It wasn't clear if it was the scotch or John that calmed her nerves, but she laughed her bubbly laugh soon after her first sip. I helped her get into her gown, stepped back to look at her, and smiled. Lori looked like a princess.

The rain stopped by the time the ceremony started, but the ground remained saturated with water and mud. Instead of walking her down the very steep and slippery hill leading to the dock where John waited, my dad delivered my sister to John in a golf cart. Lori and John exchanged wedding vows and were pronounced husband and wife at sunset, with the sky painted stunning shades of gray, purple, and pink after a perfect storm.

I witnessed my sister's love affair with John and became fixated on marrying Dean. I hoped he would break his ridiculous age rule and propose. Not everyone supported my obsession. No one in my family had ever been crazy about Dean. I mean, they liked him as a person—he was a fun guy to be around—but I now know they just never liked him as a husband for me.

I loved Dean because he was handsome, funny, polite, respectful of my parents (and his), and generous. I thought Dean loved me because he always bought me expensive jewelry for every occasion and in Providence that's what people do! As I look back now, I'm ashamed to have measured his love for me this way, and I also wonder if he gave me these gifts only because my dad owned a jewelry company. I never thought about whether Dean would be a good husband. But I never thought about whether I'd be a good wife either. Sure, we fought sometimes, but mostly because I got tired of him always going out with his friends on Friday nights. I accepted his choice because I assumed he would stop this tradition once we were married. I trusted Dean and believed he and I would always love each other, just like the wedding vows stated: for better or worse, richer or poorer, in sickness and in health.

Throughout the first four years of our relationship, Dean and I had only experienced the good, the richer, and the healthy. But in 1993, two years after Lori's wedding, my family faced the first health crisis since my mother's first breast cancer diagnosis in 1985.

I remember sitting at my office desk and staring at my screen, struggling to fix a computer "bug" when my phone rang. I picked up the handset and placed it on my shoulder, holding it in place with my right ear. You know, the position that later promised to give me a stiff neck. I heard my mom's upbeat voice on the other end of the phone.

"Hi, doll, how are you? How was your day?"

After a ten-second recap of my day, she told me the results of my father's blood test from the day before.

She whispered, "Dad has lymphoma."

The doctors wanted to start him on chemotherapy right away. Incidentally, maybe two or three years earlier, my father had become hooked on a radio talk show doctor who promoted alternative medicine and was obsessed with using only homeopathic remedies. Naturally, my father refused his doctor's recommendation to start chemotherapy treatment.

"Is he there? Can I talk to him?"

"He's on the deck having a glass of his wine. Hang on."

I pictured him surrounded by his colorful flower garden, and I could hear the water flowing from the fish pond in the backyard. When he spoke into the phone, he sounded optimistic, as he always did, and announced that he had already spoken with his homeopathic "doctor," who had recommended he try a regimen of organic carrot juice and garlic, mixed with other natural ingredients I had never heard of, to make some liquid concoction. I rolled my eyes as I listened to him defend his medical choices, but then I remembered how he cured the worst sore throat of my life with onion and honey juice. And then I thought about some of the other mechanical-type tools he had invented or fixed in the past. He once made a kitchen gadget—that I've since seen for sale in stores—out of scrap metal and wood, which he used to fry an egg into a perfect circle. He tinkered in his greenhouse fixing shovels and rakes instead of buying new ones. And he made several jewelry-related tools and models to help with the mass production of his creative designs. Basically, my father could create or fix anything—like MacGyver. I considered him nothing short of a genius, but come on, cancer? I wanted to say, Dad, this isn't a simple sore throat!

Instead I said, "Dad, so I hear everything you're saying and I'm okay with your decision, but you have to promise me something."

"Sure, what is it?"

I cleared my throat. "Well, if there is no improvement in your next blood test, you need to have the chemotherapy."

"I know."

I knew my father well enough to know he needed to feel in control of his own choices. I also admired that he really believed the natural concoction would save his life. I loved my dad for his determination and perseverance. I mean, even when faced with a life threatening disease, he needed to fight it—his way. Otherwise, how else would he know if his way could have worked? This may have been the first time I understood the value of making a choice based on my own beliefs and the value of being responsible for the outcome of the choice—good or bad. I think this may have been the first time I realized I wanted to live my own life in a way that meant having zero regrets.

Within three months, Dad started chemo. The doctors were pleased with his subsequent tests and felt they had the disease under control—for the time being. Dad's lymphoma was called chronic lymphocytic leukemia. His type of cancer was known to progress slowly, but he would live with it, and some form of treatment, for the rest of his life.

I don't remember Dean's reaction to the initial news of my dad's diagnosis. Nor do I remember how or if he supported me when I felt nervous or scared. It may have been that once my father's health had stabilized, we all felt like we had averted a major tragedy and just moved on.

A year later, in early August, on the weekend before Dean's twenty-ninth birthday, he and I took a road trip to Ogunquit, Maine. We had packed a small cooler with snacks and booze for our two-night stay at a quaint bed and breakfast. Dean would have preferred a typical hotel, but once I assured him I booked a private room with our own bathroom, he was okay with the choice I had made. On Saturday, we skipped the beach for a day of walking the oceanfront path called the Marginal Way, eating lunch at an indoor café, and visiting most of the shopping tourist traps.

That night, we had reservations at an Italian restaurant to celebrate Dean's birthday. I remember that we drank cocktails before, during, and after dinner and vaguely remember our meal being yummy. But what I remember for sure is that we ended up naked, in bed, talking about our future. I mentioned we needed at least a year to plan a wedding and, by then, he'd be thirty years old. I reminded him that I had my grandmother's wedding ring set so he wouldn't have to buy one. My mom's stepmother had recently given me—the only unmarried granddaughter—her engagement and wedding rings because she wanted to keep the rings in my grandfather's family. Dean and I talked about the duplex he wanted to build on the land his parents were giving to him. He would live in one apartment and rent the other one out. He knew he couldn't afford a mortgage on his own and since all his friends were already married, he needed a roommate. I offered to help him buy part of the land and building materials for the house.

I connected all the dots for Dean. He'd be turning thirty soon, we had the ring, and we had a plan for a place to live. I can't recall which one of us brought up the fact that our parents would be disappointed if we just lived together. I can't recall which one of us suggested we get married. Then we both fell asleep.

The next morning, I woke up and leaned on the wall to guide me to the bathroom. I walked toward the bed and Dean grinned at me. I turned my head to look at him out of the corner of my eye and bit my lower lip.

"So, do you remember what we talked about last night?" I asked.

"Yeah, do you?"

"Yes. Does this mean we are getting married?"

"Yeah, I guess so."

I admit this proposal had no similarities to the one of my dreams. There was no candlelight. No moonlight. No man on one knee. No flowers, except maybe the ugly blue and yellow flowers on the comforter covering our naked and hungover bodies. At twenty-nine years old, I just felt happy— or maybe relieved—that I was getting married.

As we drove back to Rhode Island I asked, "Are we going to tell our parents?"

"Yeah, I think we should, don't you?"

"Yeah, probably," I agreed.

We arrived at his parents' house and saw Dean's dad, John, standing in the middle of his garden. We waved him into the house. Dean's mother, Marie, stood up from the couch and met us at the kitchen counter. The back door opened and his dad walked into the kitchen.

"What's up?" his mother asked. "Did you have a good birthday?"

"Yeah. So, we think we're going to get married," Dean replied.

"Oh, wow, really? That's great," Marie said.

My future father-in-law looked at me with his eyes wide open and gave me a hug. "Sorry, I'm all sweaty from working outside. This is great."

"Have you told your parents yet?" Marie asked me.

"No, we just drove home and came here first. I guess I'll head there now." I said good-bye to Dean's parents and stared at Dean, hoping he would offer to come with me, but he continued to talk with his parents. Maybe I should have just asked Dean to come with me or maybe I thought it was no big deal that I'd be alone when I told my parents I was getting married. "Well, bye," I said to Dean. "I guess I'll talk to you later.

"Call you later," he said as he walked me to the door.

I walked into my parents' house alone, tossed my tote bag in the dining room, and rushed through the kitchen. "Mom, I'm home! Where are you? Mom!"

I found her in the living room sitting quietly in her favorite blue recliner with her reading glasses down low on her nose. She was reading the book I had finished the previous week. My mother, Lori, and I had an informal sort of mother-daughter book club—though maybe "book exchange" is a better term for it considering we just passed books around without engaging in any real conversation or discussion about them.

I blushed and grinned as I sat on the couch across from her. I had never thought to ask my parents for permission to go away alone with Dean. My mother knew I had planned the trip for Dean's birthday, but neither of us mentioned it to my father. Even now, I have no idea how my dad would have felt about it, but somehow telling him I was going to a bed and breakfast with my boyfriend seemed a little disrespectful.

"How was your trip?" she asked.

"It was nice. Dean and I are getting married."

"Married?" She removed her glasses and placed the book on the glass-top side table. "Linda, are you sure you want to marry him? I mean . . . he's so attached to his mother."

"Yes, Mom. I know he's close to his mother, and I don't see why that's such a bad thing." The fact was, I admired that Dean had a close friendship with his mother and I believed, after we were married, I would be my husband's best friend and he would treat me with the same respect he treated her.

I don't remember my mother explaining her comment any further. Instead, she asked my sister to talk to me—Lori's so-called "deposition luncheon." Despite the doubts of the two most important women in my life, I believed Dean and I were a good match. I believed that Dean and I would always be there for each other, no matter what life had in store for us.

Chapter 5

Just How Bumpy Will This Be?

I only needed to defend my decision to marry Dean that one time with Lori because for the next year and a half no one tried to change my mind. So the big, fat Italian wedding planning began. Lori agreed to be my matron of honor, Arthur made a phone call to his private country club for the reception, both of my brothers said yes when Dean asked them to be ushers, and Dean's sister and mother offered to make Italian wedding cookies. That meant cookies for almost two hundred people, especially if all their plus-ones attended. Holy butter balls!

About a year before the wedding, in the spring, I had my first appointment at The House of Brides. I remembered this fun tradition from when Cynthia and Lori got married, and I was excited to finally follow in their footsteps and have the same experience. I must have tried on at least ten dresses, but we all agreed the first one was the one. And then Mom treated us to lunch—salads and lemon meringue pie—one piece, three forks.

That summer, Dean and I rode our bikes together for exercise. He regularly used his gym membership and played golf often, but back then I hadn't been bitten by the exercise bug. I sporadically visited the gym when I had an immediate goal to reach—like fitting into a wedding dress. Together we also chose a Frank Sinatra–style big band for the wedding and agreed to take a few ballroom dance lessons. I felt confident and relaxed since all of the plans were falling into place for our big day.

In the fall, with much of the wedding prep under control, my parents started their snowbird ritual again: two weeks in Florida followed by three or four weeks in Rhode Island. Dad dreamed of staying in the warm sun, golfing every day, all winter long, but Mom never liked that much distance from her kids and grandkids for more than two weeks at a time. And although Dad's health had remained stable and the side effects from the chemo were mild, I think she liked the security of being close to Dad's doctors in Rhode Island in case they were needed.

That winter I decided to take advantage of some unused vacation time to visit my parents and relax a little before the wedding. My mother's friend's daughter lived nearby and she treated me to a Panthers hockey game. One day, my dad surprised me by skipping golf to come to the beach with me and my mom. I must have been in my early teens the last time I had seen my dad on a beach . . . in a bathing suit. I followed my parents to their beach spot and received an even bigger surprise when I realized all of my parents' friends had planned a bridal shower on the beach. And then, another day, my mother and I golfed together for the first time. That was the first day I noticed my mother limping.

"Mom, what's wrong with your leg?" I asked.

"It's my ankle. I may have twisted it. I'll be fine," she said.

I headed home a day or two after our golf outing. My parents were due in Rhode Island the first week of March so Mom would not miss my bridal shower. My father wore the biggest pout as he entered the house.

"Ya know, a June wedding would have been really nice." He winked and grinned at me.

I stared at my mother as she limped across the family room, sat in a dining room chair, and released a big sigh.

"Mom, I thought you felt better when I last talked to you."

"I did. I think it's just stiff from sitting on the plane and walking through the airport. I'll make an appointment to see my doctor. It'll be all fixed by your shower. I promise."

It snowed a couple of days before my shower and the ground was still a bit slushy. Dad insisted on driving Mom and me to the country club. Mom's slacks hid the Ace bandage she wore around her ankle. The doctor had taken an X-ray, and a week after my shower I learned what was wrong with my mother's ankle.

Four weeks before our wedding, Dean and I drove with my parents to finalize the wedding menu. We had all tasted small amounts of two entrée options and enough of the side dishes to decide on the potato and vegetable.

"Well, that was great. I don't know about you two, but we're still hungry. How about dinner?" my dad asked.

We ate at a restaurant down the road from the country club. I can't recall if we had just ordered our meals or if our dinner plates had just been cleared, but at some point during the meal my dad said, "Your mother and I have something we need to tell you."

I looked at Dean and he looked at my parents.

"We saw Mom's doctor for the results of the X-ray."

I stared at my mother.

"It's cancer," Mom said.

I blinked, dropped my head to stare at the table, and then looked at my mom again.

"Where?" I asked.

Mom explained what they had heard at the doctor's office. She would have more tests to confirm, but he seemed certain that my mom's breast cancer had returned . . . in her bones.

"My ankle, for sure, and my wrist. That had been bothering me, too." She shrugged her shoulders.

My mom raised her loose-fitting long-sleeved jacket to reveal another Ace bandage around her wrist.

"We had an appointment with my oncologist yesterday. He's still around from ten years ago, believe it or not." Mom smiled. "Anyway, we would have waited until after the wedding to tell you two . . . and everyone . . . but he wants me to start chemo right away. I asked him if I could wait just four weeks, but he didn't recommend that option. My first treatment is next week."

Shifting in his seat, Dean focused on the glass in front of my mom and said, "Anne, I'm so sorry."

I remained quiet. I squinted at my father and then I stared back at my mother. I wondered if they were telling me the whole story.

"Are you telling me everything?" I asked.

"Everything we know now, yes," Dad replied.

The next four weeks were solemn to say the least. I no longer cared whether we served snap peas or broccoli, or if I carried roses or orchids, or, God forbid, if my dress was too tight from that extra bite of pie. None of those trivial details mattered anymore. I only worried about my mom and whether she'd be well enough to witness my wedding day.

Mom lost her hair two weeks after her first chemo treatment. Lori and I helped her choose a wig very similar to her own hair color, and my mother's longtime hairdresser styled it perfectly. Despite how she must have felt, Mom looked beautiful at the wedding. And although she wasn't her usual energetic self, she wore a smile. I will always be grateful that my mother lived to see her bonus child married, settled, and happy.

As I look back now, I realize my mother definitely saw me married. And she definitely saw me happy, but I wonder if she knew that it was she who made me happy—beyond happy—blessed—because she attended my wedding. Most of all, I realize that my mother definitely saw me settle(d) and only now do I wonder if she knew I had been settling with the wrong guy.

Dean and I returned from our honeymoon and my attention returned to my mother. My sister had organized my mother's busy medical calendar. The doctor appointments, various scans, blood draws, and chemotherapy treatments repeated week after week, month after month. Lori coordinated and assigned all of Mom's rides, meals, and medications. She kept us all focused; we were in a groove.

And then Dad contracted a respiratory infection and was admitted to the hospital. His doctor reminded us that, over time, my father's immune system may need help to fight the side effects of the disease. The doctor was confident that, with fluids and antibiotics, Dad would recover from this infection. He cautioned my dad, though, that in the future, at the first sign of any small symptom—a cough, a sniffle—to check his body temperature immediately and often. Getting ahead of a fever would be key to beating an infection and staying out of the hospital.

For so many years before this episode, the side effects from Dad's cancer treatments were mild and never held him back from living his life. If I hadn't known he took a chemotherapy pill on a daily basis, I never would have guessed he had cancer. But it seemed the shock and stress of Mom's recent diagnosis may have started to catch up to all of us.

I struggled to find my own new normal. It's now clear to me that other than sleeping, eating, and showering in a different house, Dean's routine remained the same. I, on the other hand, was the new wife who tried to keep it all together—taking care of my husband and our home, taking care of my mother and father, working full-time, and studying for my MBA.

Or maybe studying provided me with the distraction I needed at that time in my life. Being the only one in my family to earn a master's degree, I often wondered if my siblings would finally take me seriously. On my graduation day, my father's health kept him home, but my mother felt great and brought enough pride for the both of them. Her hair had grown to the length of a military crew cut by then, and we both wore big smiles when Dean took our picture after I received my diploma.

I gained a ton of spare time after graduation and, at one point, I thought Dean and I might even consider having a baby, but neither of us brought it up. Within four months of my graduation, as if she had waited to witness my latest accomplishment, my mother's health nose-dived like an airplane that had suddenly run out of fuel. She landed in the hospital on Thanksgiving and my family seemed like one big fish out of water, especially Dad. He had dinner with all of us at Lori's house and left before dessert—his favorite course—to eat a second dinner with my mom at the hospital. I don't remember if any of us ate dessert that day.

For the first year and a half of my marriage, I watched my mother struggle through chemotherapy and its side effects. Even as it worked against the cancer, it damaged everything else—her lungs, her heart, and her overall quality of life. On Christmas Eve, she asked her oncologist to stop all the treatments because she couldn't stand being tired, weak, and nearly bald any longer. I remember I was at work when my sister called to tell me what my mother had decided. I never needed my sister to tell me what would happen next, but I still called the oncologist to ask him what my mother's decision really meant. Maybe I hoped he would surprise me and tell me my mother had been cured. Maybe I just wanted to scream at him for not changing her mind or for not being able to save her life. When I asked him if he had clearly explained to my mother—and my father—what her decision meant, he assured me he had. Whether she continued the treatment or not, she had to fight a terminal cancer that, one way or another, would end her life. I hung up the phone, held back the tears as I gathered my things, and then sobbed uncontrollably as I walked to my car. I sobbed as I realized my mom was the bravest woman I had ever known. She knew her life would end and decided she wanted to feel alive before she died.

Dean and I usually had Christmas Eve dinner with his family, but I insisted our tradition be broken that year. We visited his family after we had dinner with mine at Frankie's house, but only after my entire family had left. I needed to fully experience what I knew would be the last Christmas Eve with my mother—the last Christmas Eve with my family together—the way it had been my entire life.

The next day, Dean and I ate dinner with my family at Arthur's house and left to have dessert with my in-laws.

At five thirty the next morning, the sound of the phone ringing startled me. I opened my eyes and thought what everyone thinks when the phone rings at that hour.

I assumed I would hear my sister's voice telling me Mom had been rushed to the hospital again. I rolled over and hesitated before I picked up the phone. One part of my assumption proved correct—I heard my sister's voice—but my mother was not the one who had been rushed to the hospital by ambulance, my father was.

"They think he may have had a stroke. Can you meet me at the hospital?"

"What? You have to be kidding me!" I sat up in the bed.

"I know. What the fuck, right?" Then we both laughed at the same time. Not a happy laugh, a nervous laugh. It seemed too insane to be true. What family endured these kinds of health issues in such a short period of time? I mean, sure, it had been ten years since Mom's first breast cancer diagnosis. But within the past four years Dad had received his lymphoma diagnosis and endured constant chemotherapy treatments, and then Mom received her second terminal cancer diagnosis four weeks before my wedding. For the past six months, it was my mother who had been in and out of the hospital much too often. And now, Dad had had a stroke! A stroke? Isn't that what parents threaten to have when their kids are acting up or staying out past their curfew?

I repeated the phone conversation to my husband as I jumped out of bed and got dressed. I expected Dean to come with me to the hospital, but he never offered and I never asked. I just rushed to the hospital on my own.

I met my sister outside the door of my father's room. Her arms were crossed in front of her chest and she had her head cocked toward Arthur.

"He's a fucking idiot," she whispered, but I could tell she wanted to scream.

Arthur, the first one to Dad's rescue, took care of the admissions paperwork and Dad was placed in a room with three other patients. We were not being snobs, believe me, but Dad's immune system could be compromised because of the lymphoma and the chemotherapy so Lori and I had always insisted in the past that he be in a private room.

Barely conscious, Dad could not talk, walk, or swallow. I stood beside him, touched his hand, and let him know Lori and I would take care of everything.

"Hi, Daddy." I pouted. "Everything will be okay," I whispered.

And then I followed Lori as she stomped past Arthur to the admissions desk to demand a private room.

Within a week, the doctors had inserted a feeding tube, given us instructions to bypass our father's mouth and feed him through his stomach, and sent him to a rehabilitation facility to relearn how to walk, talk, and eat. Taking care of my sixty-nine-year-old father reminded me what it was like to babysit for my niece and nephews when they were babies. He resisted the rehab facility as much as he resisted the hospital (and holiday celebrations and birthday parties), but he had always fought against any situation he had not chosen himself. After he had had time to process the situation, he immersed himself in it and ended up being the "life of the party."

One Saturday afternoon I suggested that Dean and I could visit my father together.

"You know I play cards with the guys on Saturday afternoons." Dean reminded me how he met his seventy- to eighty-year-old friends to play High Low Jack, an activity I once admired him for, but lately made me wonder when he might spend more time with me. I thought Dean would offer to make an exception to his Saturday card game, but I never mentioned it and neither did he.

I expected to find my father in his room, but the nurse pointed me to the recreation room down the hall. As I entered, I saw my father twirl around in his wheelchair in front of the window overlooking the parking lot.

"I was looking out the window waiting for you." He mumbled a little bit, but his speech had improved so much I could understand every syllable.

"I want to show you something." He wheeled his chair ahead of me and waved me back to his room. He proudly held up a small painting he had finished earlier that day in a community art class. Life could be so ironic—my father could have taught the art class considering the dozens of oil paintings he had created on his own with few lessons, and now he acted like a little kid learning to paint for the first time. I smiled when I realized he hadn't lost any of his artistic talent.

Dad made quicker progress than any of us expected and the doctors discharged him after two weeks. Over the course of the next month, being at my parents' house was like people watching at Grand Central Station. Between all the health care providers, visitors, and family members, the house was buzzing with chaos.

As I watched my dad progress in his speech and ability to walk, I never ceased being amazed by his will. He couldn't yet eat through his mouth or play a round of golf so I never understood why he would torment himself by watching the Food and Golf channels. By the time his seventieth birthday rolled around that March, his recovery strategy had hit me in the face as he proved he could talk, walk, eat normally, and golf again! Dad proved that where there was a will, there was a way, and he had more will than any man I had ever known.

I wondered if I—or Dean—had the will to stay married. Maybe it was maturity that we lacked, especially during the bad times. As I look back now, it's so easy to admit that, during the first two years of my marriage, my husband ranked last on my list of priorities. While I thought he should understand—and accept—why my family had become my first concern, perhaps he thought I was ignoring him or purposely being mean. What is also very obvious now is that we never talked about any of these issues. I continued to take care of my family and Dean continued on his merry, bachelor-like way.

Chapter 6

My Angel

It seemed that just when Dad's health had stabilized, Mom's sped downhill. On April Fools' Day, less than four months after my mom had stopped her chemotherapy treatments, her doctor delivered the words no one ever wants to hear. Mom was nearing the end of her life. I waited for him to add "just kidding," but instead he confirmed she would likely live only another few days. Not one day, not a couple of days, but a few. I should have asked him to be more specific. Does "a few days" mean three days, four days, five days? Would he have said "a week" if he meant seven days?

I walked into my mom's room and stared at her resting in the hospital bed we had moved closer to the windows. When we first admitted her, I wondered why my mother had been given a private room. After hearing the doctor's words, I guessed I had my answer. I thought about what it must feel like for patients whose hospital roommates, complete strangers, died in the bed next to theirs. Do the admissions coordinators strive to place two dying patients together? Do the coordinators actually know which patients will die during that visit? If one patient dies, does the living one already know she could be next? Or does the living patient have no idea she may die, but she witnesses her roommate's death and all the hubbub that occurs afterward and becomes scared to death— for real? The scheduling and coordination of hospital room assignments seemed very complicated to me, so I assumed all terminally ill patients just automatically received private rooms for the sole purpose of having privacy . . . to die.

Being Italian, my family found the private room very handy for another reason: the empty bed became a table filled with massive amounts of comfort food—eggplant parmesan, meatballs, crusty bread, and wine and pepper biscuits. Lori and I had vowed never to leave Mom alone—with anyone— except one of us. We took turns going home to shower, but I found it extremely difficult to be anywhere else but by my mother's side.

It doesn't matter how long anyone has been ill, when the doctor finally tells you there is nothing else they can do for your loved one except keep them comfortable (also known as doped up on morphine) I beg you to keep from beating yourself up for not being better prepared when your loved one dies. I'm sure there are books on the subject, but I never read them because I never truly accepted that my mother was dying, and by the time the reality of the situation had actually hit me, it was too late to read the "how to" book anyway.

For the previous six months, Mom had been in and out of the hospital every other month. Aside from the fact that the cancer had broken her bones and caused her to wear a cast on her left arm, she had difficulty breathing, which happened when her heart slowed down and her lungs filled up with fluid. The doctors would drain the fluid and she'd bounce right back. Every time she bounced back, it became harder for me to believe she was dying. Some days the urgency surrounding her care in the emergency room freaked me out and I thought she'd die that day. Other days, when I stared at her—her rosy complexion (even without lipstick on her cheeks), her smile, and her bubbly personality—I convinced myself she would come home from the hospital for good. This roller-coaster ride—in and out of hospitals, up and down energy levels— constantly played with my emotions. Maybe I refused to accept her illness, or maybe I really believed she could live forever. I just never imagined, or allowed myself to imagine, the rest of my life without my mom in it.

On the fourth day of this hospital stay, a Saturday afternoon, Lori had returned to the hospital after spending some time with her husband.

"Wand, why don't you go home for a little while now?"

Mom and I had been watching *Wheel of Fortune* and I couldn't bring myself to leave her side—not even to have a much needed shower. Plus, I loved to play *Wheel of Fortune*. So I stayed and I forced myself to keep quiet so my mom could solve the puzzle before me. If not this game show, Mom would ask to watch *The Lawrence Welk Show* and, sometimes, Lori and I were blessed to hear Mom sing along.

Since she'd been admitted to the hospital, Mom met with a social worker and a priest every day. After just a couple of sessions with the therapist, my mother had reached a milestone. But "milestone" suggests it was a desired achievement so maybe it makes more sense to call it a turning point. I don't know, I only remember when my mother told us she was dying and that she asked for private time with each of us. The social worker had told me my mother accepted her death and it was okay for me to give her permission to leave this earth.

I sat on the edge of my mother's hospital bed and held her fragile but soft hand—the one without any needles stuck in it. I stared into her glossy wide-open eyes and, as I felt my throat closing, I pressed my lips together, hoping to stop the tears from pouring from my eyes.

"Doll, you know I'm not going to get better this time?"

I sniffled and wiped my nose. "Mom, I love you so much. You are the bravest woman I have ever known." She gently squeezed my hand and I knew what I had to tell her. "It's okay for you to go. I'll be fine. We'll all be okay."

Those words were the hardest thing I've ever had to say to someone, but I loved my mom too much to not give her what I knew she needed to hear. People say when you love something you should set it free and, if it's meant to be, it'll come back to you. I wondered how that could be true in this situation.

"You are and will always be the apple of my eye. Be happy," Mom said to me. And then she sang "You Are the Sunshine of My Life" and all I could think about were the times my mom sang this song to comfort me through a bad experience with a girlfriend or a boyfriend or a teacher or a sibling. I thought she was my personal magician—making all the bad stuff disappear.

When she finished singing, I leaned over and kissed her forehead and she asked me to get Dean. I guided my husband to my mother's deathbed, worried that he wouldn't be able to handle how she looked or the overall reality of the situation.

My mother stared at Dean. "You better take good care of her."

Dean wiped a tear from his eye. "I will, Anne, I promise."

And then Mom blurted out, "You two need to go make a baby. Make a baby . . . right there . . . in that bed." She pointed to the empty bed behind the curtain. She had no idea that the bed had been covered with obscene amounts of Italian food, such as wine biscuits and pizzelle cookies. Neither Dean nor I made any deathbed promises to my mother.

Everyone except Lori and I went home that night.

Mom seemed more restless than usual so the nurses came in and increased her morphine. Alone with her again, Lori and I sat on opposite sides of her bed and Mom started to babble—about sex. Sex with my father! Come on, no one admits their parents actually have sex—we are all immaculate conceptions! Although I blushed a little while I heard about my own parents' sex lives, many years later it made me happy to know they had a healthy sex life. I blushed more when my mother turned to me, grinning, and asked if I had sex with my first boyfriend—the boyfriend I'd been dating when my mother received her first breast cancer diagnosis. I grimaced and lied,

"No. Mom, no." I remembered when she had found my diaphragm in my underwear drawer while putting away my clean laundry, but I also had flashbacks of the special times we spent in church together and, for some reason, I couldn't tell her the truth, not even on her deathbed. She asked my sister the same question about her high school boyfriend and Lori gave the same answer I had given. I never asked Lori if she had lied, too. My sister and I had talked about many things, but sex was not one of them.

Mom looked up and stared at the ceiling. She murmured, pressing her arms down by her side. She tapped the white sheets, repeating, "I'm straight and narrow . . . I'm straight and narrow . . ." Lori and I said good-bye to Mom that night and she thought we left the hospital, but like all the nights before, we gave her privacy as we slept on the other side of the curtain—after we removed the food from the bed, of course.

That night, Lori tossed and turned in the bed. I tossed and turned in the recliner. When I woke up at four o'clock the next morning, I drew the curtain back a little and stared at my mom. Her breath had been getting fainter and fainter each day and that day, as I squinted to see her, I couldn't see her chest rising or falling. With a scared look in my eyes, I tapped my big sister's arm and pointed toward Mom. We both rose to our feet, still dressed in the clothes we had worn the day before, and walked to one side of our mother's bed. Lori bent down and put her ear up to my mother's nose and then squeezed my hand. She looked at me and I knew. I knew heaven had gained an extraordinary angel—my angel.

Chapter 7

Can We Still Be Friends?

The tragedy of watching my mother slip away from me was replaced by the fact that I had to relive the worst event of my entire life every single time I woke up—whether it was several times during a restless night or after the many daytime naps I indulged in to escape my sadness. Each time I opened my eyes I believed I had just lived through an awful nightmare, but after blinking a few times, I would lose my mother all over again. I adopted a habit of raising the covers over my head, rolling over into a fetal position, and wishing I never had to leave my bed again. With my eyes squeezed shut, I wondered how I could exist without ever again hearing my mother sing to me, seeing her smile, or feeling her rub my back.

Everyone said I would feel better once I returned to my normal routine but I just thought, Normal? Life can never be normal for me again—not without my mother. I resented everyone around me for moving forward as if nothing had happened. I felt angry and just wanted to be left alone. I wanted to scream at the top of my lungs, stomp my feet, and slam the doors. But instead I pretended to be happy—normal—and hid my anger and sadness, especially around my jovial husband. How could he know how I really felt? And why should I make him feel sad, too?

I pretended to be okay around my family, too. My dad seemed like a lost soul without his wife of forty-eight years and

I thought it best to stay positive to help him get on with the rest of his life. Lori and I even shielded him from the horrible job of cleaning out Mom's clothing and other personal items.

I rummaged through an entire bureau drawer dedicated to me. "I can't believe she kept all of this," I said to Lori.

My mother saved every elementary school report card and the receipts from my college tuition. She even preserved the hair from my first dramatic haircut—a foot-long blond ponytail—in a plastic bag.

Dad stood in the doorway of his bedroom and told us to divvy up Mom's jewelry between us.

"Dad, are you sure?" I asked.

"Of course. She wanted you girls to have it."

Lori and I sat on my parents' bed with five of my mother's jewelry boxes between us. Some boxes were filled with silk pouches holding rings, necklaces, and bracelets made of real gold, diamonds, and pearls. And many other boxes contained the costume jewelry my mother had collected over the years—much of it created or designed by my dad. I never realized it then, but the process of sorting through a loved one's belongings after they have passed away—and talking through the stories attached to each item—is very painful, but also healing.

"Here, you keep this." Lori handed me my mother's Rolex. I had felt left out when my mother and sister each bought Rolex watches, but I never imagined getting mine like this.

"I'd really like to keep her diamond heart pendant, if that's okay?"

"Of course. Do you mind if I hang on to this cocktail ring?" Lori asked as she held up one of the last pieces of jewelry my dad had given to my mom right before my wedding.

"No, not at all." I smiled at my sister.

My sister and I conversed like this for three hours as we reminisced over my mother's jewelry, perfumes, scarves, and clothing. In some odd way, I felt closer to my mother as I touched, and sometimes smelled, all the items she once held close to herself. Lori and I cried and laughed. We were mourning as I struggled to create my new normal—again.

Six months later, while playing a normal game of triple solitaire with my sister and her husband, without any warning, Lori blurted out, "I have breast cancer."

I dropped my cards on the table and stared at her.

She and John had already chosen her doctors, treatment plan, and surgery date. Mom had needed a mastectomy, but my sister chose a lumpectomy. She needed chemo, too. "But I won't lose my hair, like Mom did."

Lori seemed most upset about needing daily radiation treatments for five weeks.

She continued to play her hand as if we were talking about the autumn weather. "I'm going to be fine, Wand. The doctors have told us there are so many new treatments since Mom's diagnosis, right Johnny?"

John agreed and swallowed a mouthful of wine. They seemed to have it all under control and I had no reason to believe otherwise.

In just six months, Lori had completed her treatments and, other than excessive fatigue, she felt great. My sister and I were golfing alone one Saturday afternoon when I told her I had felt a lump in my right breast. I had a history of fibrous cysts, but this one felt different. "It's not like the others I've had. This one is hard."

"Have you called the doctor?" We both had the same breast surgeon as Mom.

"Yeah, I'm going next week."

"I'll go with you. Don't worry about it."

The doctor indicated the lump had developed as a result of leftover scar tissue from all the cysts he had aspirated over the years.

"Either way, though, the lump does not belong there. It's benign, but it needs to be removed and analyzed to be sure."

The nurse scheduled the surgery for two weeks later.

Lori and I walked to her car. "I think that was all good news. He would have insisted the surgery be scheduled sooner if he was concerned."

"Right." But all I'd heard was the doctor's contradiction—"it's benign . . . analyze to be sure." So, the doctor really had no clue if the lump was benign or not.

I tried to inherit my sister's positive thoughts, especially when I broke the news to my husband.

"The doctor wants to remove the lump with simple outpatient surgery."

"Should I go with you?"

"No, Lori is taking me." At that moment, I preferred that my sister take me. After all, breast surgery is a girl thing, right? I waited one week after the surgery to hear the doctor confirm that the breast cyst really was benign. My sister and I both immediately sighed with relief. I had no idea I would wait an entire month to hear how my husband felt about my good news.

Dean returned from golfing sometime after five o'clock on a Saturday afternoon. He walked into our duplex apartment and saw me sitting at the kitchen table, paying our monthly bills.

"Hi," he grumbled under his breath as he plopped down in his oversized brown leather chair.

I rolled my eyes when he grabbed the remote control, turned on the TV, and immediately found the weekend's PGA golf tournament.

"Are we still going to dinner with your sister?" I asked.

"Yeah," Dean responded without looking at me.

"You taking a shower?"

"Yeah, of course," he replied, again without looking at me.

I stood up and walked to the bathroom to take a shower. Forty-five minutes later, my husband had not moved from his leather chair.

"I'm done. Your turn," I announced as I headed for the bedroom to get dressed. Staring at the clothes in my closet, I struggled with what to wear. Dean's sister always looked so put together. After choosing khaki cropped pants, a red T-shirt, and brown sandals I walked out of the bedroom and saw my husband sitting in the same position on his leather chair. I walked into the living room and sat on the matching brown leather couch across from him.

"Don't we need to leave soon?"

"I don't feel much like going out."

"Oh? I thought we were meeting your sister at seven for her birthday dinner?"

"Yeah, uh, I don't think we should go to dinner."

"Oh, what do you mean?" He had left the apartment early this morning and golfed all day in the hot sun. I figured he must be tired.

"I'm not happy, and I'm sick of you being mean to me. Linda, honestly, you're miserable and just not very nice to me."

I stared at him with my mouth open, not sure what to say.

"I want a separation. We should get divorced, try being friends again, and maybe get remarried later."

Dean had never criticized me or made any decisions on his own. I never expected to hear this from him. Ever. Stunned, I took a deep breath and wondered who put him up to this.

"What?" I squinted my eyes and pulled my head back.

Dean stared at the TV.

"Are you kidding me? You think I'm miserable? My mother died of breast cancer a year ago, my sister just finished treatment for breast cancer, and I just had my own scare a month ago. I've dealt with all of this by myself because all you ever do is go out and leave me home alone. And I'm not very nice to you?"

Dean still stared at the TV. I stood up from the couch and screamed at him, "You want to be my friend? Be my friend now."

I stomped toward the bedroom. "Call your sister and tell her we're not going to dinner."

"I already did." He laughed.

I turned around to face him again. "Already told her we're not meeting for dinner or already told her that you want a divorce?"

"Both."

I knew it! He never could have made this decision on his own.

"So, I must be the last to know?"

"You shouldn't be surprised."

Okay, so I knew we had a really bumpy start to our marriage, but he never appeared unhappy. Sure, he still went out with his friends without me. He had done this before we were married, too, but we always kept Saturday date nights. Why hadn't he told me how he felt before it had gotten to this point?

I walked back into the living room and stood beside his chair. "I don't understand. I'm meeting with a therapist next week to talk about my mother . . . and . . . my sister. . . . Can't you wait until I get some help?"

He never stopped staring at the television. "No. I don't think so. My mind is made up."

I wondered what had happened to make up his mind. I wondered if maybe he was really afraid when I found the lump in my breast. I remembered that, when my cyst turned out to be benign, I told my sister, "It's a good thing this is benign because Dean wouldn't know how to take care of me if I had cancer."

At the time Lori told me that Dean had called her the night before my surgery and said, "Lori, I know you're taking

Linda tomorrow, but I don't know . . . shouldn't I take her?" My sister's response to Dean is one that I will never forget: "You shouldn't have to ask."

I sat back on the couch and stared at my husband. "We could have talked about this together—before it got this far. This isn't fair." My voice cracked but I never felt like I would cry. "You could come with me to therapy. I mean, I made the appointment to talk through my mother's death, but we can ask her about couple's counseling."

"There's no point in a therapist telling me how to be a better husband when I'll always go back to just being me."

At the time, I thought his attitude was selfish and immature. But years later, during my first yoga class, I thanked Dean for his honesty and for setting me free to just be me.

Dean had always appeared jovial, so I had no way of knowing how unhappy he really was with me. I walked into our bedroom, sat on our bed, and called my sister. Without crying, I told her what had just happened and she simply told me to pack a bag and come to her house. Shortly after, I walked back into the living room with my suitcase. Dean was still sitting in the same position in his leather chair and never looked at me.

"I'll be at Lori's. I guess I'll be back when I run out of clothes."

As I drove to my sister's, I stressed over what others would think of me and my failed marriage. If Dean refused to change his mind within the next two weeks, everyone would surely hear the news at the Fourth of July parties.

I tried to keep a low profile at my sister's party, but my dad found me sitting on Lori's bedroom floor. He claimed he had to use the upstairs bathroom. He slid his back down the bedroom wall and met me on the floor.

"How are you doing?" he asked me in a soft voice.

"I guess I'm okay. I don't know, Dad." My head hung down as I stared at the rug.

"Listen to me, this is only his loss. Do you understand me?"

"Yeah." I looked into my dad's blue eyes.

"I always knew he was a man's man, Linda. He never struck me as someone who really wanted to be married."

"Yeah, I guess you're right. I mean, he still went out with his friends every Friday night and then when he started bartending for extra money at the Sons of Italy, I should have known something was up. How could I be so blind?" I never suspected a problem with our finances and I never even questioned Dean when he wanted to bartend a couple of nights a week. My sister thought he felt inferior because my salary was higher than his.

Only then I remembered the night—wait, the morning—he had come home from work after two AM without his wedding ring on. He claimed he stayed late to help clean up, but if the bar closed at midnight, I wondered what took him two hours to get home. When I asked about his ring, he insisted he took it off while he bartended because it slid off his wet hands while washing glasses.

"This isn't your fault. You will be fine. Trust me." My father held my hands and pulled me back to my feet. Then he walked me back to the party.

I stayed with Lori and John for a couple of weeks, even after I had emptied my first suitcase full of clothes. I finally asked myself why I had to move out when Dean wanted the divorce, so I pressured him to move out of our apartment.

My husband seemed very happy to move back in with his mother and I heard my own mother's voice echoing from heaven, "Linda, are you sure you want to marry him? He's so attached to his mother." I wondered if maybe my mother had actually meant that Dean's mother was so attached to him. So attached that she never gave him the space to learn how to take care of himself and my mother knew, therefore, he may never be able to take care of me.

I shook my head from side to side and remembered the wisdom my mother and sister had shared with me before I married Dean—the wisdom I ignored when I first heard it.

Now that I had actually encountered the evidence that proved them right, I deposited the lesson into my own wisdom bank.

One day after Dean had moved out, I called him and his mother answered the phone.

"Oh, hi, Linda. How are you doing?" she asked.

"I'm fine. Is Dean there?"

"I'm so sorry about all of this, Linda. I knew I should have taken you to grief counseling."

I remained silent and thought, you what? You think this is my fault? I'm sure it has nothing to do with the fact that your little boy has no idea how to be a husband through sickness and health, good times and bad. Maybe you should have taken him to husband training. Maybe you should have stopped making his lunch every day after we were married. Maybe you should have let him purchase his own socks and underwear after he married me. Who are you kidding? You're not sorry. You're ecstatic to have your little boy home with you again.

"Really?" I asked my mother-in-law. "I'm taking myself to counseling next week . . . but thanks."

After a few months of living apart from Dean, one of my single friends convinced me to go on a cruise to the Bahamas with her and three married couples. I had always wanted to go on a cruise and thought the timing was perfect. While I was on the phone with a friend talking about the trip, Dean came to the apartment unannounced and heard me.

"Where are you going?"

"I'm pretty sure that is none of your business."

"Who are you going on a trip with?"

I said good-bye to my friend on the phone, then said to Dean, "Again, none of your business and, by the way, you don't live here anymore. You can't just barge in whenever you want without calling."

"Oh really? I'm pretty sure this is still my home and I'll come here to shit and shower whenever I want."

By the time he left, he had apologized for showing up unannounced and agreed to call first next time. I was skeptical though, and the next day, before I left for work, I stuck a long piece of string in the door jam. When I returned home, I found the string on the floor and I knew someone had entered the apartment. I also hit redial on the phone and heard a woman's voice on the other end. The last phone call I had made that morning was to the automated bank system to transfer money to my checking account to pay my divorce lawyer.

The next day, I called my lawyer and told her I thought Dean entered the apartment when I went to work. She advised me to change the locks. I hesitated, but I trusted her legal advice so, without notifying Dean, I changed the locks.

Two days later, Dean called me at work. "Hey I'm trying to get some clothes at the house, but my key isn't working."

"Really? I thought you were going to call me before you tried to get in again."

He stumbled over his excuse so I reminded him of our agreement. "If you had called me ahead of time, I would have told you that I changed the locks."

"You did what!? I still own that house! You bitch," he screamed so loudly I pulled the phone from my ears and covered it so my coworkers couldn't hear his tantrum.

When his ranting ended, I pulled the phone back to my mouth, smiled, and asked, "Hey, can we still be friends?"

Chapter 8

I'm Melting

I walked into my first psychotherapy appointment just four days after my husband had asked me for a divorce. When I made the appointment two weeks earlier, I had only intended to focus on how I had been feeling since my mother died a year and a half earlier. My life felt hollow without my mother and I wondered if I would ever be happy again. I had received one week of paid bereavement leave and after that week it felt like everyone around me—at work and at home—expected me to go on with my life as if nothing had happened. It seemed easier to stay sad because I felt guilty when I laughed or smiled. I wanted happiness again, but just like when I had injured my back, I needed to know all my options before I could choose the best solution to get rid of the pain shooting down my leg. I hoped the therapist would give me some options to get rid of the pain of living my life without my mother, and now without my husband, too.

I guess my necessity to know all my options is what led me to become a business analyst and project manager. At work I met with clients to assess their business processes and I identified options to build solutions that best met their business requirements. I often used the same process to make decisions in my personal life—whether I was buying a home or a car, or choosing a doctor. I always needed to know all the possible options, analyze the pros and cons of each, and pick the best solution for me.

I sat and waited to meet my very first therapist while listening to the soothing hum of a clean air filter. I wanted to talk to someone other than my girlfriends and my sister—someone trained to get inside my head and fix me. A tall and thin woman, with dark eyes and dark wavy hair pulled back from her narrow face, opened a door and extended her hand. "Linda?" she asked.

I stood up and shook her hand. She was about my age or a couple of years older. I wondered if she had ever met anyone as screwed up as me and, more important, could she fix me?

"Yes," I answered and thought, of course I'm Linda. No other person had entered or exited the waiting area and I suspected she scheduled all the appointments far enough apart so patients wouldn't see one another.

"I'm Diane. It's very nice to meet you." I recognized the soft and energetic voice I heard on our brief telephone conversation. She waved her hand toward the door. "Please, come in. Make yourself comfortable. Sit wherever you like."

Located in a multifamily house, the office felt very inviting—like a cozy living room. The afternoon sun came through the brown mesh shades covering the windows and, along with the steady sound of another clean air filter, created a peaceful place for us to chat.

Diane gathered a folder, pad, and pen from her antique wooden desk and then sat with her legs crossed on a leather swivel chair in the sitting area. Hey, what if I wanted that chair? I examined my other seating choices—an upholstered chair and, just like on television, an upholstered couch. Should I sit or lie down on the couch? Surely, Diane would start to analyze me beginning with where I sat, right?

I sat on the couch, placed my pocketbook on the floor by my feet, and placed both hands on my lap. I wondered what my choices revealed about me.

"Are you comfortable there?"

I nodded. *Yeah, why, shouldn't I be? Should I have chosen the chair?*

"Great, so let's see if I can read my own handwriting here. Okay, I remember—you want to discuss how you've been feeling since your mother died, right?" She removed her reading glasses and looked at me.

"Well, sort of. When we originally spoke about a month ago, my intent was to talk about my mother's death over a year ago, but—since I made the appointment . . . something else has happened."

"Oh? Okay, well, we can talk about whatever you like, Linda."

"Well, my husband wants a divorce." I reported the news with a how-dare-he tone in my voice.

"Oh, Linda, I'm so sorry." She moved the box of tissues closer to me. Was I supposed to cry now? I had no urge to cry.

I stared at the flowery blue box for a few seconds and realized how awful I had treated Dean while I cared for my parents. When the reality hit me—I had failed at my marriage—I began to sob. I gasped as I tried to catch my breath and stop crying, but it felt good to let it out. "I'm sorry, I know, I'm pathetic. I should be able to handle these things on my own."

"Oh Linda, please, feel free to do and say what feels good to you. I'm not here to judge you."

"I don't want to be weak." I blew my nose.

"You suffered a traumatic event when your mother died, and now a divorce is another traumatic event."

"I never considered my mother's death to be a trauma. Car wrecks and other gruesome accidents are traumas. Does that make any sense?" I felt stupid or maybe naïve, but I had a bachelor's degree in computers and a master's degree in business, not psychology.

"It sure does make sense. From a physical perspective, those things are traumas. And from a psychological perspective, a trauma is anything that causes emotional pain," Diane explained.

"I think I may have had that." I sniffled and dropped my head as I twiddled my thumbs before I looked back up at Diane.

"I think so, too," she agreed.

"Can you tell me a little bit about what may have happened with your marriage?"

I leaned forward to grab a clean tissue from the box on the coffee table in front of me and then leaned back on the couch, crossed my legs under me, and shared the painful details of my life over the past four years. "My mother became terminally ill with breast cancer four weeks before our wedding, a little over three years ago, and ever since then much of my time had been spent taking care of her and my father—he has lymphoma—and he suffered a major stroke four months before my mother died."

"How is your dad now?" she asked as she took notes.

"He's much better. We had to feed him through a tube in his stomach, but he learned to walk, talk, and eat again. And now he's golfing again." I smiled.

I had never recapped this ongoing sequence of bad events out loud—or even in my own head. As each negative thing happened to my family, one right after the other, I just went through the motions, almost subconsciously, to get through the days.

"There's more, well, one more thing I guess." I wondered what she must be thinking about me. Was I just being a whiner? "My sister was diagnosed with breast cancer six months after my mother died."

"Linda, my goodness. How is your sister now?"

"Okay, I guess. I wasn't very involved with her doctor's appointments and treatments."

Diane repositioned herself in the leather chair. "Is your sister married? Does she have children?" she asked. She then stood up, placed her left leg on the chair, sat on that leg, and then bent her right leg off to her right side. It seemed as though she was trying to make herself comfortable for the rest of this entertaining, yet depressing Lifetime movie.

"Yes and no, well, yes, I guess. Lori is married to an older man and she has three step-children and five step-grandkids. Her husband takes good care of her. She finished her treatments a few months ago and she's fine now." I smiled.

"I'm happy to hear that."

She asked me about the relationship I have with my father and my sister.

"Well, I think my father and I became closer after my mom died. Lori and I have become closer, too. She is a sister and a mother for me now."

I noticed that I was staring at the ceiling instead of looking at Diane while I thought hard about how to answer her questions the right way.

I continued, "Lori was the first person I turned to when my husband sprung the divorce on me. Lori and I have dinner with Dad every Tuesday night."

"And tell me more about your siblings. You have just one sister?"

"No. Well, yes, I have one sister. She's nine years older than me. I also have two brothers. One is eleven years older and the other is fourteen years older than me. I always felt like an only child though." I must sound like such a complainer. Maybe Lori and my brothers were right—I'm just a brat who thinks life stays perfect forever.

"Uh huh, I see." Diane recorded all of this in her notes.

"My siblings teased me a lot as a kid, but I think they treat me more like an adult now. Well, Lori and Frankie do. I don't hear from my oldest brother, Arthur, as often."

"Oh, why is that, do you think?"

"I'm closer to his wife—I mean, his soon to be ex-wife, Cynthia. She's been a big part of my life since I was four. They have two children, twins, Faith and Andrew. Unfortunately, my brother and his wife are getting divorced, too. After being together for thirty years. Anyway, he's the one who teased me the most."

"How did he tease you, Linda?" After all I had just shared, Diane was focusing on how my oldest brother tormented me?

"He always played practical jokes on me—like hiding my favorite toys and stealing the last piece to a jigsaw puzzle so I could never finish it. He suffocated me with a pillow and constantly told me I was a mistake. Actually, my sister often told me I was adopted. They all called me Wanda."

"Wanda? How did that come about?"

I explained to Diane how my nickname started when I'd made a witch with my Lite-Brite toy.

"And how did the nickname make you feel, Linda?" I wondered if she really cared how I felt or if she asked the classic question as part of the common therapist checklist.

I never really thought about my nickname's origin being anything other than my Lite-Brite witch. Cynthia and my siblings hardly ever called me "Linda" and whenever they had I thought I might be in trouble.

I glanced at my watch and realized that in just forty-five minutes Diane had pushed me to discover that my twenty-three-year-old nickname may have played a huge part in molding my personality. She suggested that I most likely felt obligated to live up to being the witch called Wanda. She gave me permission and the courage to ask my siblings to stop calling me Wanda. I never had to explain why I wanted them to stop, but it took less time than I thought it would for all of them to break the habit and, within months, Wanda, the witch, melted away.

Diane asked me questions about my eating, sleeping, and social habits. I told her I had lost a little bit of weight, wanted to sleep all the time, and oftentimes I had not wanted to see or talk with any of my friends.

"We're almost out of time, Linda." She glanced at the small clock that I had only just noticed on the table between us. "How do you feel?"

"I feel better. A little lighter, actually."

"That's good. Let me tell you what I think is going on and then we can talk about next steps, okay?"

"Sure." I was anxious to hear what she had been writing down all this time.

She reviewed the details I had given her—the loss of my mother, my father's illness, my failed marriage, my sister's illness, my brother's divorce, my weight loss, increased fatigue, and decrease in social activities—and in a split second she diagnosed me with clinical depression, most likely triggered by the trauma of losing my mother. She assured me that depression was a common mental illness and treatable with continued therapy and sometimes medication.

"I can recommend some psychiatrists whom I have worked with in the past or you may have a primary care physician willing to prescribe medication as well."

Okay, so this is not what I expected from this therapist at all. Diagnose me? I never expected to get a diagnosis of anything at all. I just thought we were chatting. I mean, people who need a psychiatrist are crazy, right?

I asked Diane why I needed both a psychiatrist and a psychotherapist. She explained that psychiatrists were able to prescribe medication while she provided the verbal— or what I had considered "touchy-feely"—therapy. Of course, even after just one session with Diane it felt like my own head had become a Lite-Brite and, as hard as it had seemed to get in touch with my inner feelings, I finally understood the benefit of talking through them with a therapist.

"What do you think?" she asked me.

Are you kidding? Right now I think I'm doomed. My life is a mess.

"Um, I think I need some time to process this a little bit."

"That's fine—and normal, Linda. I will write down those recommendations and you can call me once you have had some time to think and let me know if you want to continue with me, okay?"

"Well, I actually already know I want to set up another session with you, Diane. I mean, we haven't even touched upon my mother's death—or my divorce yet."

I liked Diane. I walked into my first therapy session to talk to a complete stranger about my life without knowing what to expect from it, but I felt that Diane and I had connected. Maybe she had once experienced similar downturns. Maybe she understood my issues because of our common Italian heritage. I never felt intimidated by Diane and I trusted her with my innermost thoughts. We set up an appointment for the following week and I accepted her list of psychiatrists, but I had already decided I would call my primary care physician about the prescription.

I sat frozen in my car for a few minutes, thinking about what had just happened in the course of an hour. I mean, seriously, everyone is depressed, right? People cry. So what if I cry in private? And everyone wants to lose weight, what's the big deal with that? So, I like to sleep, who cares? Then I realized my diagnosis could be good news. I wasn't Wanda, the bratty complainer. Diane had validated the fact that I had dealt with some pretty serious and traumatic events—they weren't normal or expected events in everyone's lives. Aside from just being able to talk about these things with an objective person, she offered other options that could help me.

My primary care physician prescribed what I called my "happy pills" and I saw Diane weekly to talk openly about my life, thoughts, and feelings. After three or four sessions, I forgot that I actually had a mental illness and started to feel a bit proud to have a therapist. I felt like I had made a breakthrough—maybe I gained a piece of my own wisdom. I realized my life would never be perfect all the time; bad stuff had happened to me and more bad stuff would likely happen in the future—and the simple act of sharing that reality lifted a burden from my shoulders that I still believe today. I am never alone—other people deal with difficult situations, too—and most important, I really don't need to be perfect all the time.

Chapter 9

And Then It Hit Me

Maybe I could let go of wanting a perfect life all the time—I mean, over time . . . a lot of time—but I still wanted to have the perfect marriage. I thought I had gotten over the initial shock of Dean wanting to divorce me, but even after he moved out and I changed the locks, I still tried to plead with him to change his mind. I actually went into the basement and pulled out the notebook we studied during our marriage prep class.

I pouted. "Don't you remember what we talked about in the marriage prep class?"

"Yeah. I mean, no." I always wondered if he had ever taken that class seriously.

"Look, it's right here." I pointed to a page in the book and read from my own handwriting. "Two kids and a four-bedroom house on the water. I thought we wanted the same things?" I look back now and know the house was just a material thing, and I'm so grateful to have learned about what is actually critical to have in common with a partner. I'm even more grateful we never had kids together even though my mother had given us other guidance. I stared at Dean as he insisted he no longer wanted to be married and I realized I had to accept that our marriage was over. I wished my mother could tell me how to handle what I always assumed was a common situation between spouses. I mean, all married couples had disagreements—there were even times when one spouse no longer wanted to be married to the other, but they worked it out. I never anticipated my husband would just give up.

When Dean and I got married, I had no way of knowing how much my life would change after my mother died. But what I did expect was for him to change with me, in the same way. Therapy helped me realize I couldn't change Dean if he never wanted to change, and it gave me the permission to be myself—my authentic self.

Day by day (or therapy session by therapy session) I started to tame my emotions and accept that we would not reconcile. So maybe we could have an amicable divorce? Boy, was I wrong! In fact, I am convinced there is absolutely no such thing as an amicable divorce when splitting up marital assets is involved.

I had hired a high-powered female divorce lawyer, the president of the Rhode Island Bar Association at the time, and she had a reputation for being aggressive. Besides advising me to change the locks, she had given me the best, although disheartening, lesson when she told me that once I made it through the emotional part of the divorce, I'd be left with just the business of it all.

"It's just accounting," she said.

And there it was: that mind-blowing college course I had hoped I would never have to deal with again—the course I would have failed if my sister hadn't tutored me. Maybe the negative experience I had with accounting during college had been preparing me for this real-life accounting test.

"I won't touch your 401(k) if I can keep my house," Dean said.

"Your house?! Really? You mean my 401(k) that only I contributed to versus our house that you built with the money I gave you before we were actually married?"

Just five days before Christmas, when life should have been festive and jolly, we sat on opposite sides of a mahogany conference room table with our lawyers beside us. Dean had hired a male lawyer whom I had never heard of, but I knew enough to trust him as much as I trusted Dean. He actually looked like Dean—smiled a lot, with dark hair and eyes—but he was much taller. My lawyer distributed copies of the spreadsheet I had prepared for the meeting. The document listed every single item and financial account Dean and I owned together or separately and its estimated value.

Dean repeated his proposal, "I won't touch her 401(k) in exchange for the house."

I squirmed in my seat and grinded my teeth while my lawyer responded before I could add another sarcastic comment.

"The challenge is that the equity is a fixed amount in cash while the value of the 401(k) will continue to fluctuate over time based on the investment allocations," my lawyer explained.

Dean's jaw dropped when he saw the results of the real estate appraisal. He never expected the house to be worth that much since he had built it at cost. He demanded another appraisal. I agreed but insisted he pay for it, which made him squirm in his seat, shake his head, and groan.

My blood still boils when I think of the legal conversations that had started calmly but gradually turned into arguments over the business of our marriage. If I had not agreed to forfeit the house equity, Dean demanded his share of my 401(k), an employment bonus I would receive in six months, and a portion of the small inheritance my dad had given me after my mother passed away. I wished I had never used my inheritance to pay for Dean and me to join a golf club with Lori and John.

While Dean had never imagined the duplex would be worth its current value, I never imagined us getting divorced. While we argued about everything from money to kitchen utensils, I still thought about the love we once shared on our wedding day, the vows we had exchanged, and the plans we had made together. I wondered what had happened to make him turn his back on me.

Even today, when I think of all the negative things I have faced in my life, getting divorced still ranks number one as the most stressful event of my life. Losing my mother to breast cancer had been stressful, too, but mostly because the illness and her death were out of my control and I couldn't save her. I guess I felt out of control throughout the divorce, too, but the bulk of that stress stemmed from the fact that I finally realized how naive I had been to believe Dean loved me unconditionally, the way a parent loves a child.

A couple of days after the initial asset negotiation meeting with Dean, my dad surprised me when he pulled into my driveway. He seemed a little fragile as he recovered from the stroke and losing the love of his life, so I sugarcoated some of the divorce arguments for him, although Lori had probably spilled most of the dirt already. I opened the door and hugged him before he even entered the apartment.

"I was in the neighborhood," Dad claimed, even though I knew he lived more than fifteen miles away and had no friends in the area.

We sat at the kitchen table. My father placed his hand on top of mine and looked at me with his crystal blue eyes. "I just wanted to come by and see how you're doing."

"I'm okay, I guess. I'm starting to get used to it."

"I know you'll be fine. We knew it wouldn't work out."

Putting my elbow on the table, I rested my chin on the palm of my hand and asked, "Who knew?"

"Me and your mother."

"Really?"

I sat back in my chair, placed both hands in my lap, and said, "I had no idea. Neither of you ever said a negative thing about Dean to me before we were married. Okay, Mom once tried to warn me about the relationship he had with his mother, but only once. She still helped me plan every inch of the wedding."

"I know. We thought if we tried to talk you out of marrying him you may have married him anyway and then never talked to us again."

"I don't know what to say, Dad. Thank you? Thank you for letting me marry him even when you thought it was a mistake."

I thought I may still want children of my own someday, but as I stared at my father, I wondered if I had the patience to be a parent—I mean, a really great parent. Finding the right spouse with whom to share the parenting must be the key. I remembered when my father (not my mother) disciplined me for one thing or another—flinging my new eyeglasses across the floor or talking back—and, most times, I repeated the unwanted behavior one more time just to test his patience. Or those few times my parents said no when I begged for something—ice cream, a new toy, a sleepover—and I kept nagging until they finally gave in just to shut me up. Worst of all, I wondered if I could have the patience to watch my child get lost in a heartbreaking situation even after I gave her the best GPS and reviewed the directions several times before she drove away. Marriage seemed like a pretty big road trip to me, yet even when my parents knew Dean wouldn't be the best guy for me, they trusted me—no, wait, they trusted themselves and the values they had instilled in me—and knew exactly which battles were worth fighting.

"Live and learn." My parents repeated those three short words to me so many times that the words seemed trivial, not to mention annoying. I never predicted there would be a day when I finally knew what the words meant—a day when I could say, maybe this divorce happened for a reason and maybe that reason was simply to give me the wisdom to choose more carefully the next time.

Getting divorced was stressful, but it helped me learn how to put loss into perspective. Whether my parents knew it or not, letting me marry the wrong guy had allowed me to realize I had the potential to learn at least one new thing every single day and that my life will change in some way because of it. Today, I don't believe in mistakes. How can something be a mistake if I learn a positive lesson from it?

As my father stood up to leave, he stared at me again and pleaded, "And, please, please, please promise me you won't give up the golf membership." It was hard to think of golfing in December, but I nodded in agreement.

Chapter 10

Pinch Me

Throughout that winter, my sister and her husband kept me sane. We were inseparable. We lived about twenty minutes from each other, and I had an open dinner invitation with Lori and John every night, even when they dined out with their friends. We ran errands together on the weekends, and those days almost always included lunch at a local pub. Lori even became obsessed with finding me a new home; she loved checking out all the open houses.

As luck would have it, a condo twenty seconds away from Lori's became available to rent. And who wouldn't fall in love with a waterfront condo? I signed a lease that started the following month, in February.

Lori and my brother Frankie organized the entire moving process for me. They hired the trucks, brought me the boxes, and helped me pack in just one weekend. I asked Lori to take care of the liquor cabinet. The equitable divorce agreement stated that Dean, the part-time bartender, kept all the liquor, and I kept the hand-painted cabinet.

The divorce agreement also stated that I would keep the dining room furniture, living room furniture, and pretty much every single thing in the kitchen because I had received most of it as gifts from my bridal shower. Dean called me after he walked into his barely furnished apartment. He confirmed that everything looked as he expected, but there were more bottles of liquor missing than he thought should be and he had a specific question about a bottle of Pinch.

"A bottle of what?"

"It's scotch. My uncle left it to me after he died," Dean explained with a sense of urgency in his voice. "You can't miss it, for God's sake, it's in a triangle-shaped bottle."

Besides thinking, what a sentimental inheritance, I had never seen Dean drink scotch in the ten years I had known him.

"I'll have to ask Lori. She unpacked the bottles so the movers could take my cabinet."

I called my sister and asked her if she had seen the bottle of Pinch.

"Oh that, yeah, well, if I saw two or more of the same liquor, I left one for the jerk and took one for you."

"And what about the bottle of Pinch? Were there two of those?"

"No, but fuck him. You'll be dating real men, and real men drink scotch."

I had forgotten about the ridiculous bottle of booze, but Dean asked about it again and I told him Lori took the Pinch by accident and I'd drop it off the next time I was in the area.

"Great. Thanks."

Settling back into my new home, I shopped with Lori for new furniture, televisions, lamps, and curtains. But I was most excited about buying a stereo. For the first time, I realized I missed hearing music. My parents always played music—Frank Sinatra and Dean Martin—in their house, and I always blasted pop music in my car. I even had a portable AM/FM radio on my desk at work. But it occurred to me that I had never known what type of music Dean liked. We had never bought a stereo and most of the time he planted himself in front of the television and watched sports. So I bought myself a cherry wood entertainment center to match my new living room tables and used it to store my new television and stereo.

My landlord actually left me what became my favorite piece of furniture: a pub-style, glass-top outdoor table and chairs. The condo had an open alcove with floor-to-ceiling windows that jutted out from the living room, which was next to the deck and overlooked the rocky shore on one side and a pond on the other. Due to it being winter, I moved the outdoor table into that cozy alcove, and it became my favorite spot to sit and stare at the water and wildlife. I planned my future as a single woman living in a waterfront condo—everything from what I would make for dinner to my next vacation to my next relationship, which, by the way, I was in no rush to find.

Now that I think of it, I only helped to plan dinner back then because I never had to actually cook it. Lori covered the dinner menu during one of our four or five daily phone calls. She'd look at the ingredients she had in her kitchen and give me two or three choices for meals she could make, and I'd let her know what I might be in the mood for that night. Honestly, I hardly cared what we ate for dinner because everything Lori served tasted delicious and I had learned that it just plain sucked to cook dinner for one.

Before I knew it, spring had arrived and the divorce hearing was only a month or so away. Trying to keep my promise to Dad, I kept my membership at the golf course and tried to play with Lori as much as possible.

One Saturday afternoon, Lori stood behind me and watched as I drove the white golf ball with a prominent pink ribbon on it straight down the fairway of the sixth hole. The ball hadn't traveled far, but it landed with perfect placement for my second shot.

"Nice! This is why he is divorcing you, I swear," Lori declared.

"Thanks. What are you talking about?" I asked her as I retrieved my pink tee and stood behind her while she hit her drive.

"He couldn't stand that you were getting better, Wand—whoops, I'm sorry." She covered her mouth with her hand. "He saw you getting better. Sure, he had a monster drive—in length, Linda—but how many times had he used your drive in a best-ball tournament because his ball got lost in the woods?"

Lori reminded me that Dean and I had our worst fights on the golf course. He had been embarrassed to play with me because I was a beginner. He had been playing golf much longer than I had and he had no patience for coaching me. The few times we had played together, if he shot a bad round, he blamed it on me and all the time he'd spent helping me. "I can't play well when I play with you," he'd say.

My father liked to remind me that Dean was not the great golfer he proclaimed himself to be. I later figured out that, because Dean had no self-confidence in himself, he would build himself up by focusing on my bad shots and never praising me when I had done something right.

When May rolled around, it occurred to me that I had never returned the bottle of Pinch to Dean, even though he had asked for it every time we talked. The day before our divorce hearing, my lawyer faxed me a copy of the settlement agreement and then called me at work to review what seemed somewhat standard.

"So everything seems reasonable. Oh wait, I do have one question. What is going on with . . . is it a bottle of scotch?"

"What?!" I put my elbow on the desk and held up my head with my free hand.

Apparently, Dean's sneaky lawyer stated that all assets were divided as agreed by both parties except for a bottle of scotch that Dean had received from his late uncle. I told my lawyer the story and she just laughed. I promised to take it with me to court in the morning.

"Great. Just leave it in the car and you can hand it over after the hearing."

Lori and I met my lawyer in the lobby to review the agreement and I showed her the corrections I wanted, especially that the reference to the bottle of Pinch must be removed before I would sign the public document.

Before the hearing, Dean's lawyer returned with the updated agreement and I confirmed that the ridiculous mention of alcohol had been removed. Once the judge called our case, and I sat on the witness stand, I was able to confirm that Dean's lawyer was nothing but a piece of scum. Although he had removed the bottle of Pinch from the public settlement agreement, he made sure it would be included in the public court transcript.

"As you know, my client expects the bottle of Pinch returned to him. Did you bring it with you today as agreed?"

You son of a . . . I stared at my lawyer, squinted my eyes, and let out an elephant-size sigh as I turned to Dean's ruthless attorney and answered, "Yes, I brought it."

"Wonderful." He smiled and began to sit down.

But then he placed both hands on the table and lifted himself out of the chair again. "I'm sorry, Judge, I do have one more question for the defendant."

"Of course, counselor, proceed."

"That bottle of Pinch . . . it's not open, right?" His tone was that of a father scolding his sassy teenager.

Before I could answer, my lawyer stood up. "Your Honor, if I may," and as she looked at me, but cocked her head toward Dean's attorney she replied, "The bottle was unopened when my client brought it here, but it's been left outside, in a car, in Providence, so we can't be sure of its disposition now."

After the judge adjourned, I shook hands with my lawyer and thanked her for being so professional. She wished me luck. "I have the feeling you'll be fine, Linda. Good luck and take care of yourself." She turned to my sister and shook Lori's hand. "It was a pleasure to meet you."

I just wanted to get Dean and his scum-of-the-ocean lawyer out of my sight, but we still had one more piece of business to take care of. The two thugs followed me and Lori to the parking lot across the street from the courthouse to retrieve Dean's precious bottle of Pinch. I couldn't get away from them fast enough, but as Lori walked around to the driver's side of the car with Dean, his attorney sauntered up beside me, smiled, and had the audacity to whisper, "Maybe we can get a drink sometime?"

I opened the car door, glared back at him without acknowledging his question, and sat in the passenger seat just as Lori shoved the bottle of scotch into Dean's hands. She started the car and turned to look at me with a smile. "Well, little sis, it's time for you to celebrate and start living the life you were born to live."

Chapter 11

The Second Time Around

I continued to settle into my single life on the waterfront. Living there reminded me how much I loved summertime and being near the ocean. Most days, I felt satisfied just sitting and staring at the water for hours, analyzing my past, living in my present, and planning my future.

I had imagined getting divorced must be like getting fired or laid off from a long-term job I liked—something I hoped would never happen to me. Sometimes, we get too comfortable in our lives or our jobs. We go with the flow without asking ourselves if we are still getting what we want from the relationship or the experience. After ten years, I felt comfortable with Dean, his family, and his friends. Dean and I laughed a lot when we were together. We always had each other to hang out with on a Saturday night and a guaranteed date for parties and weddings. I never wanted people to think of me as a loser for being single when every other woman at the party arrived with a date. My family had tried to get me to expect more from a marriage, but I thought laughter and fun would be enough to keep us together. I never thought about what might happen if Dean and I ever stopped laughing.

But when things are going well and we feel happy, who the hell wants to think about what could go wrong? No one wants to be morbid. No one wants to be a pessimist. Surely neither of us could have prevented my mother from dying, but maybe we could have supported each other better afterward.

I remembered my father's words on the day he visited my apartment and helped me forgive myself for my failed marriage: "Live and learn." I realized his simple words were the basis for what I had learned about risk management at work and that maybe I should apply some of those ideas to my personal life. Sometimes, especially when we try something for the first time, we have no idea what could go wrong with our decisions. Instead, we need to live through them to learn what we need to change to achieve better results the next time. This realization made me think of another simple lesson my father had taught me on the golf course.

When we stood on the plush grass of a putting green and my putt left the ball short of the hole, he always offered the same advice, "Come on, Linda, you gotta hit it." He explained that, if I missed the hole, my goal should always be to have the golf ball land beyond the hole rather than not reach the hole at all.

His advice never made any sense to me when I clearly had the right line to the hole and could just tap it in the next time, allowing me to hear the clink of the ball falling into the tin cup. "Dad, that makes no sense to me," I whined like a bratty child.

"Coming at any target from a different angle the second time around will give you the perspective you may have needed the first time."

On a golf green there are tons of peaks and valleys, which is why, if you watch the professionals, they sometimes walk all the way around the green and get down on their knees to stare at the hole from every angle before they putt. Sure, even a professional will miss the target after lengthy preparation and setup, but my father wanted me to at least try to apply his advice. They say practice makes perfect, but what they cannot tell you is how much practice is needed to achieve perfection. And when it comes to people, was it even fair of me to think I'd ever find a perfect person for me?

So, instead of striving for perfection in a man, I thought about how I could avoid or minimize the risks of a failed relationship the second time around. For starters, I thought I should write a list of requirements the next guy must meet: polite, courteous, sensitive, funny, respectful, handsome, smart, and responsible. Next, I thought about my dating life and realized I never really had one. I never enjoyed the process of meeting a new man and starting a relationship from scratch. I never liked to deal with conflict and never mastered the best way to say "I'm not interested" or "this isn't working for me." Maybe that was why I stayed with Dean for seven years and eventually married him.

I had no problem being alone—and I learned there was a difference between being alone and being lonely. The therapy must have been working because I continued to become more comfortable with myself. I thought about the guidance one of my college roommates had once shared with me: "you won't be happy with someone else until you're happy with yourself." But it seemed society still thought I should have a companion because everyone I knew had someone they wanted me to meet.

My manager played matchmaker with Guy #1. He entered my driveway in his black Porsche and walked to my front door. He had dark hair and lots of it—everywhere. It wasn't only on his head; there were bushes of dark hair on his arms and popping out of from his shirt where he had one too many top buttons undone. I decided not to invite him inside so we headed right back to his car. He opened the passenger side door for me and suggested we head to Newport for dinner. We talked while we strolled down Thames Street before reaching our destination. He was an entrepreneur and had invented a contraption for scrubbing your back. Unlike the typical loofah on a stick, his product had a place to store the body wash behind the loofah. He seemed polite and smart, but I never felt any physical attraction to him. When he dropped me off at home, neither of us indicated we wanted a second date and I walked to my door alone. Inside I grabbed my list and added "sexy" to it.

My best friend's husband played matchmaker with Guy #2. He had been divorced from some debutante whose father had tons of money. He resembled a blond version of John F. Kennedy Jr. I have no memory of his car, but I do recall watching him saunter to my front door. I didn't invite him inside, and I am fairly certain he never opened the car door or any other door for me. He took me for drinks at Castle Hill, incidentally where Dean and I had had our first date, but I swear Guy #2 thought he owned it. Or maybe he thought I owned it because he never objected when I offered to pay for the drinks. I couldn't wait to get home and wished I had brought my own car because he had not been polite, courteous, sensitive, funny, or respectful. He had nothing comforting to say about my mother's death or my sister's illness. I walked into my condo, closed the door behind me, grabbed my list, and added "compassionate" and "empathetic" to the list of requirements.

Believe it or not, my father introduced me to Guy #3. My father had provided me with many life lessons and had never steered me in a wrong direction. Guy #3 would be perfect, right? He and my dad belonged to the same golf club and the two of them golfed together most weekends. He looked exactly like Michael Chiklis from the TV series *The Commish*. I had accepted "bald and beautiful" from a cancer perspective and now I had the chance to experience it with a healthy guy. David and I went to a local Irish pub in my hometown, sat at the bar, and drank beer. I stared at David and decided bald looked good on him, maybe because he also had a great smile and blue eyes. I listened to him tell stories of golfing with my dad, but the more he talked, the more I sensed nothing between his ears. He seemed shallow, a bit of a player—and I don't just mean a player of golf. One too many beers later, I accepted shallow because this guy knew how to kiss a girl.

I don't remember how many days passed before he called for a second date. We stayed local again and sat outside for a casual dinner at a pub on the water. At one point, when I felt chilly, he offered to get his jacket from the car. That night, we ended up on my couch, making out like teenagers. The next morning, we woke up in my bed and I felt like a complete slut. What would my father think? Nothing, I thought, he and no one else would know anything about this—well, that is, until now. Guy #3 left early that morning and I never heard from him again. Maybe Dad needed more practice in the matchmaker department.

If "playing the field" meant learning what I wanted to find in a man, then the casual dates that turned into nothing were worth it. I learned that my updated list of requirements had been reasonable, and I still had hope that the perfect guy existed. I also learned that being alone and lonely was far more acceptable than ever allowing myself to be lonely in a marriage again.

Chapter 12

A Better Person

I wondered if maybe my list of requirements for finding a better guy had been missing an important trait. I remembered a conversation with my sister-in-law, Cynthia, when we were in the midst of our respective divorces. Given that I had met Cynthia when I was just four years old, I had always felt close to her, even closer than I ever felt with my brother. She sometimes called me after putting Faith and Andrew to bed and we tried to cheer each other up. Cynthia had said something during one of those phone calls that made me think I needed to update my list of requirements even further.

One night, shortly after Dean had moved out, I lay on my bed, on my stomach with my knees bent and feet pointed toward the ceiling, holding the phone up to my ear. I listened to Cynthia's advice. "Your spouse should inspire you to be a better person."

"What do you mean?"

"Well, being with that person should make you want to excel in your own life."

"Oh." Did she mean that I should want to be a better person than my husband? Or maybe that if I'm with someone smarter or equally as smart as I am, it will always make me want to be smarter, more athletic, a better cook?

"I just remember when you got your master's degree and Dean didn't seem happy for you. He seemed . . . embarrassed maybe? Maybe because he only finished high school."

"Yeah, I know. My mom had told me she noticed the same thing at my graduation ceremony."

Cynthia helped me realize that I needed to find someone with the same ambition as my own. I never wanted to compete with someone, only to always do my best. And my partner should want the same for himself and for me.

Around the same time I had earned my master's degree, the movie *As Good as It Gets*, starring Jack Nicholson, had been released. I heard a line in that film that I will never forget. Melvin (Jack Nicholson), a cranky, reclusive, obsessive-compulsive writer, has his life turned upside down when Carol (Helen Hunt), the zesty yet insecure waitress at his favorite breakfast spot, takes a leave of absence to care for her sick child. Melvin's breakfast orders are just not the same without her. An unlikely relationship develops between Carol and Melvin, and at one point, Melvin proclaims, "You make me want to be a better man."

My sister had always pointed out that Dean never accepted nor congratulated me when one of my golf drives turned out better than his. He never encouraged me to work out at the gym with him either. I had never been much of an athlete—I could just about walk a mile in twenty minutes—but instead of encouraging me to play racquetball with him, he encouraged me to stay home.

A year after our divorce, at thirty-five years old, I didn't know if I needed to prove something to Dean or to myself, but when Lori's dear friend and neighbor, Bob, who had lost his first wife to breast cancer seven months before we lost Mom, asked me to join him and his daughter on a sixty-mile walk to raise money for breast cancer, I felt excited and more than a little apprehensive.

"But where do we sleep? What do we eat? Where do we shower? " I asked.

Bob visited my condo fully equipped with a color brochure—lots of pink—and blue tents.

"We find tent mates." He pointed to the brochure. "And I think these eighteen wheelers have state-of-the-art showers and bathrooms."

"Interesting." I replaced some of my doubt with excitement. "Could we stay at hotels along the route instead?"

"I don't think so, princess." Bob giggled. "But from what I have heard, it's quite a production. They provide plenty of rest stops and snacks along the three-day route, as well as hot meals and night-time entertainment."

I knew Bob would have preferred a hotel, too, but our comfort would not be the focus of this event.

"How bad can it be? Let's do this." He finally convinced me.

I wanted to walk in my mother's memory. I wanted to honor my sister for surviving her own breast cancer challenge with courage and bravery. And since I had faced my dating fears and learned something about myself, I felt like I wanted to push myself in other ways, too. Ironically, the physical exercise never scared me as much as sleeping in tents with bugs and dirt, but when I thought of what cancer patients had to endure, I asked myself again, how bad can it be?

Over the next four months, I trained my body to prepare for walking sixty miles over three days. Lori wanted to support me and loved walking with me when she felt good, but she had recently been complaining of a pain on the lower left side of her abdomen. Even though she had completed chemotherapy more than eighteen months before, she still tired easily and often felt out of breath—both complaints that her doctors assured us were normal long-term side effects of the chemo.

Every weekday, Bob and I walked at least five miles, and although we strived to reach twenty miles on the weekend days, the most we ever completed was twelve. We had to believe that would be enough to get us to the finish line. It turned out the physical exertion paled in comparison to the emotional exercise I experienced.

Surrounded by cancer survivors, their caregivers, friends, and family I realized how many of us were affected by breast cancer. Each time I shared my mother's fate from breast cancer and my sister's diagnosis, I listened to a fellow walker's story that seemed much worse than mine. I remembered what my mother had shared with me after a doctor's appointment or chemo treatment. "Just when I think I'm having a bad day, there's someone feeling worse than me." She felt better when given the opportunity to console someone else instead of focusing on her own troubles.

That Sunday, the final day of the walk, Bob's wife and Lori met us at the finish line with the biggest smiles. "You did it!" Lori yelled as she hugged me. I just wanted to melt—or maybe collapse—in her arms. We drove home after the closing ceremony and I shared many of the stories I had heard that weekend before I dozed off. When we arrived at my condo, Lori waited while I showered, gave me some pain relievers, and tucked me into bed.

I took Monday as a vacation day to recover, but still wanted to go for a short—two-mile—walk, believe it or not.

Lori called around eleven to check up on me. "Hey, how are you feeling?"

"Better than I thought I would. I'm sore, but I think I should go for a walk anyway. Wanna come, maybe just a short one?"

"I would, but I have an appointment for a chest X-ray at one. I thought we could go for lunch afterward."

"Oh shit, I'm sorry, I forgot. Okay, I'll pick you up at twelve thirty."

That Thursday, Lori and John went alone to get the results of the X-ray. She called me at work. "There are some spots on my lungs."

"You had spots before. They're scars from the radiation you had, remember?"

"These aren't scars, Linda. The doctor thinks my cancer may have spread to my lungs. I am going for an MRI of my liver right now."

I hung up the phone. This could not be happening again, I thought. I mean, really? My mother suffered with a breast cancer recurrence. Why did Lori have to deal with a recurrence, too?

I left work early and sat in my alcove, staring out the window and waiting for Lori to get home. As soon as I saw her and John pull into the entrance to our condo complex, I walked out of my kitchen door and headed to their condo.

Lori met me at her kitchen door looking tired and defeated. We sat on her ivory leather couch surrounded by floor-to-ceiling windows that gave a panoramic view of the sunlit harbor. I don't remember if her oncologist had requested the MRI results immediately following the test, but somehow Lori knew the results by the time she arrived home.

"There are spots on my liver, too, and they're doing a biopsy tomorrow." Lori frowned.

I sighed. I knew that the fact that her doctor had moved quickly with the biopsy would probably yield bad news, but I wanted to remain as positive as possible.

"Well, it's good that she is moving quickly. The faster we know, the faster we can deal with it, right?" I offered my sister a small smile to encourage her to be positive. But as I thought about Lori's recent symptoms and the preliminary test results we had received so far, it became harder for me to push away the negative thoughts invading my mind.

A few days later, the liver biopsy results confirmed our worst fears. Lori's breast cancer had metastasized to her liver and she needed to see a specialist to determine if the tumor could be removed with surgery. Whether the liver could be operated on or not, her lungs were inoperable and Lori needed to have chemotherapy that was more aggressive than she had received after her first diagnosis.

I forced myself to stop thinking of my mother's fate after her recurrence and only thought that for as long as Lori's oncologist had treatment options, if I pushed my sister to turn on her positive mental attitude, she would beat this breast cancer recurrence and feel better again.

Chapter 13

The Voice

After hearing Lori's cancer had returned, I tried to be the voice of positivity, but most days I just wanted to scream.

Lori's oncologist prescribed an aggressive chemotherapy cocktail and I wondered why she hadn't been prescribed this particular combination a year and half ago, but apparently Lori's breast cancer biopsy and staging hadn't warranted it back then. In fact, given her original prognosis, a recurrence made no sense. How could this have happened? Lori had seventeen lymph nodes removed from her left armpit and all of them were negative for cancer. She was left with painful swelling in her arm, but because cancer has to travel through our lymph nodes to enter the blood in order to spread, the fact that they were negative gave us hope that the cancer had not spread outside of her chest. She trusted her surgeon and oncologist and chose the treatments they'd recommended—lumpectomy, radiation, and chemotherapy. I never asked if she had other treatment choices and it's possible she never asked either. After her cancer returned, I wondered if she had made a mistake by choosing a lumpectomy instead of a mastectomy. Of course, my mother had a mastectomy and she died, so who really knew the best treatment choice when faced with a breast cancer diagnosis?

Lori and I never discussed it, but the only thing I thought could have fueled her recurrence was that her surgeon—the same surgeon who had performed my mother's mastectomy and the surgery to remove my benign cyst—never confirmed a clean margin, leaving one or more cancer cells in Lori's chest, and those cancer cells broke loose. I never heard Lori's oncologist offer an explanation for why or how Lori's cancer had spread.

I insisted on being by Lori's side to hear everything the doctors and nurses told her, everything she asked them, and everything she chose not to ask them. I always wished I had attended more of my mother's medical appointments. I wanted to be Lori's advocate in case she or John stopped listening. Certainly, patients never intend to stop listening, but I had no idea what it must feel like to be a cancer patient or the spouse of one. I mean, how much does anyone really hear after the words "it's cancer"?

Lori waited until our Tuesday night dinner to tell Dad her latest news. John joined us, so I sat on the same side of the booth as my dad, and Lori and John sat across from us. After we ordered drinks, I winked at her to give her the courage to repeat the familiar words Dad had heard just five years ago.

"So, Dad, I'm sick again. The cancer is back," Lori blurted out. I wished she had eased into telling him, but that had never been her style.

Dad was still getting chemotherapy himself and he looked so fragile when he looked at me as if to ask "is this true?"

Lori added, "I started chemo last week. I'm going to lose my hair, but I'll be fine."

I don't remember any of us talking or eating anything else after Lori's announcement.

My brothers and I alternated driving Dad to his chemotherapy, and John and I alternated taking Lori to her appointments. Regardless of which patient I accompanied on any given day, the conversation only included those topics that had the best chance of being positive—the weather, golf, and the young, healthy children in the family.

By July, it seemed we had a routine in place to care for my father and my sister, and each seemed to tolerate the side effects of their chemotherapy treatments. One Saturday morning I had some time to myself and felt anxious to get a little exercise and fresh air. I pulled back my blond hair, applied a little pink blush and lip gloss, and put on my black shorts, white tank top, and running sneakers. I ate a crisp and crunchy Granny Smith apple—not the mealy kind that I always threw away after the first bite—and drank a bottle of cold spring water. I was heading for the kitchen door when I heard the phone ring. I stepped back into the kitchen, glanced at the caller ID, and saw an unfamiliar number. Instead of ignoring an unknown caller, I raised the phone from its cradle, held it next to my right ear, and stared out the window at the boats moored in the harbor.

I heard a man's voice, "Hi, Linda?"

"Yes, who's this?" I asked.

"This is Marc. Barbara gave me your number."

I had hired Barbara as a consultant to help with one of my projects at work and she and I had become friendly. She reminded me of my mother—petite, impeccable clothes, hair, nails, jewelry, and well, she wanted to find a nice guy for me. Marc lived across the street from Barbara, just a few miles away from me. She had heard he had recently broken up with his girlfriend and she had moved out. When Barbara saw Marc puttering in his yard one day, she stopped to tell him about me. I had giggled when she told me how she had described me to him: "She's supersmart, funny, and she looks like Princess Diana."

She had told me he was cute, and when I asked her what he did for a living she claimed he maintained the grounds—that is, he mowed the lawn—at a private boarding school. Barbara and her husband left for a two-week sailing trip and she had planned to introduce Marc to me when she returned from her vacation, but apparently, after he heard her description of me, he preferred not to wait two weeks and asked for my phone number.

I never expected to hear from him so soon and felt caught off guard. Before I knew it, we had been on the phone for three hours and I had paced the hardwood floors around my kitchen and living room for what felt like at least a mile. I learned Marc had five younger siblings, had been divorced several years ago, had no kids, and rescued a cat. He'd taken in several cats in the past, but now he cared for just one stray named Sophia. He owned a house on the water, a boat, and a wave runner. He loved to hang out in Newport or watch Water Fire in Providence with his friends and their kids. His mom had died of breast cancer many years before and his oldest sister was being treated for it now. He had done most of the talking and I found myself falling in love with Marc's voice.

I sat on my leather couch, hugging a soft chenille pillow and looking out over the water through the sliding glass doors, but for some reason, I couldn't stay still while I talked to this guy. I paced the floor again. He apologized for being forward and asked if I had plans that night. Saturday was date night, right? Lately, Saturday night dates were rare for me, but that night, I actually did have a "date"—with a girlfriend who had recently separated from her husband and needed a girls' night out.

Had I still been in high school, I may have left the girlfriend high and dry to go out with a guy, but the new me still wondered if any guy was worth losing a girlfriend over.

I told Marc the truth. "I'm, sorry, I have plans with a friend of mine tonight." My girlfriend probably would have been fine with me saying yes to a date, so I wondered if I turned him down so I wouldn't seem desperate. Or maybe I turned him down because he caught me off guard and I hadn't planned to hear from him so soon. Or maybe it's because I had never dated two people at the same time—I had not broken things off with Carl yet.

Carl lived in Maine and was the brother of another coworker who lived on Cape Cod. When Carl was visiting his sister one weekend, the three of us golfed and ate dinner, but ever since then, Carl and I had only talked on the phone. He kept inviting me to Maine, wanting me to stay at his house, but something about him never seemed quite right. He called me two or three times a day after we learned about my sister's diagnosis. At first, I thought he seemed sweet and caring, but after I had repeatedly turned down his invitations he became more persistent in a stalker kind of way. I realized I still needed to work on dealing with conflict and the best way to say "I'm not interested" or "this isn't working for me."

When Marc persisted and asked if we could meet the following day, he never seemed as freaky as Carl.

"That would be nice, but I'm golfing with my father."

"We could meet for coffee in the morning."

Well, I thought to myself, I'm meeting my father at two and since I had never been on a coffee date before, maybe it's a sign of something positive. Just based on our three-hour conversation, Marc and I had a lot in common—we both loved the ocean and boating, and our mothers had died of breast cancer while our sisters were currently being treated for it. I wondered if maybe everything had happened for a reason. Even though I had just come to terms with the fact that I might be single and alone for a while, I thought that maybe the reason Dean and all the other guys had not worked out was so I could meet the real love of my life, Marc.

"Sure, that may work."

I called my sister immediately after I had accepted the date and she seemed really impressed with the morning date idea.

"That's perfect. Having coffee takes less time than dinner, and we're golfing with Dad so you have a reason to leave—you know, in case it isn't going so well," she explained.

"And I never told Marc our tee time, so at any point, if I'm really hating him, I can just say, 'Oh, look at the time, I have to go.'"

The next morning, I didn't feel nervous about meeting Marc. I remembered the sound of his voice—so sincere and soothing—and wanted to hear him talk some more. I never felt intimidated by him, which may have been the reason I stuck with the first outfit I put on rather than changing it three times.

I watched him pull into my driveway, but flowering bushes blocked my chance to check him out before greeting him at the door. Barbara had given me no clue what Marc looked like other than to say he was cute—and "cute" meant different things to different people, but since I loved Marc's voice I assumed he must be my kind of cute.

When I opened the door, a sense of relief came over me as I thought, so far, so good, he's dressed nicely and he looks clean. He looked different from the guys I had always been attracted to. Marc had light blond hair and a lot of it, a thick mustache the same color as the hair on his head, and crystal blue eyes that reminded me of my father's.

When he said, "Hello," my body melted at the sound of his voice.

"Hey, come on in." I waved him into the kitchen.

"Wow, this is a great spot. Look at the view." He stared at the boats in the harbor.

I gave him a quick tour of the first floor. "There are two bedrooms and two bathrooms upstairs."

"It's very nice. So, where's a good place for coffee and maybe some breakfast?"

I was never good at thinking of places to eat on the spot, so I had asked Lori for suggestions the day before. Marc drove while I navigated.

"Have you had breakfast?" Marc asked. "I'm starved."

"No, not yet." *Who can eat right before a date?*

"Great, let's order something."

I never liked eating in front of guys, especially on the first date. What if food got stuck between my teeth or I spilled something on my boobs?

I ordered chocolate chip banana pancakes, which I had never before ordered in my life, and I didn't think about the possibility of a rogue chocolate chip making me look like a witch with a missing front tooth. Marc ordered eggs over easy, a side of ham, and decaf coffee.

"Decaf? Really?" I asked. I always needed caffeine in the morning.

"Yeah, I get migraines if I have too much caffeine," he explained.

I thought it seemed odd for him to suggest going out for coffee when he ordered decaf, but coffee is coffee, right? Or maybe not—I am a bit of a coffee snob. The bolder, the better.

I offered Marc a bite of my pancakes and I had a piece of his ham. The conversation between us continued to flow. After breakfast, we drove back to my condo and walked into town, along the seaside, frequently brushing our hands against each other, and continued talking. Marc owned a power boat, like my father had during my high school years, but Marc also knew how to sail, like Arthur and John. Marc once worked as a "runner" for a boat dealer, driving boats from Boston to Fort Lauderdale. My dad still owned a condo in Fort Lauderdale. Marc told me his age and I quickly realized he and my sister were born in the same year. In fact, his birthday occurred just eleven days after Lori's. It dawned on me that I had no trouble talking to Marc because he reminded me of my siblings.

We stopped at a café, bought bottled water, and sat outside at a table on the sidewalk. He tried to persuade me to spend the rest of the day with him. "Come on, we could hang out in Newport, have dinner . . ." He smiled.

"Wow, that sounds really nice, but remember, I'm golfing with my father today. He wouldn't be able to find another partner on such short notice." I wanted to spend the entire day and night with Marc—and his voice.

We walked back to my condo and said our good-byes.

"Thanks very much. I had a really nice time."

"Me, too. I hope we can do it again soon. Maybe dinner next time?"

"Sure. I'd like that." He got in his car and drove away.

Marc called me the following Wednesday night. "I know this may seem a bit too soon, but my sister is getting married and her shower is this Friday night."

"Oh?" It would be very strange for me to attend his sister's shower alone and meet her for the first time.

"It's a double shower—Jack and Jill—guys and girls. My whole family will be there and many of my friends since they are close to my sister, too. Would you come with me?"

"Um." *What would my sister do?*

"Trust me. Everyone will love you."

After just two phone conversations and one date, I believed him. If his family and friends were anything like him, I probably would get along with them. I wondered if it may be too soon to meet his family and friends. I wondered if I should take some time to think it over before I answered him—so as to not seem desperate. "Sure, what's the worst that can happen, right?"

"Great. If you feel really uncomfortable, we can leave. It's not a problem." He must have offered that option to be polite because I would never leave my sister's shower or any family event early.

When Friday arrived, he called to give me directions to his house. He wanted to introduce me to his best friends, a couple married for more than twenty years. "I know you'll get along with these guys, and that way you'll know more people before we get to the yacht club." He impressed me each time he took my feelings or fears into consideration.

The bridal shower felt more like a wedding to me with well over a hundred people there. I met Marc's dad, who seemed like a very sweet man; a couple of his aunts and uncles; his three sisters and two brothers; their husbands, wives, girlfriends, boyfriends; his nieces and nephews; their boyfriends and girlfriends; and more of his friends who were also friends with his sister. I felt overwhelmed with all the names and faces, but never felt out of place.

When the yacht club party ended, Marc invited most of the crowd back to his house after the shower. I noticed that partying at Marc's house seemed like a normal event to everyone. The refrigerator and coolers were stocked, and the music seemed preselected and ready to go.

Marc and I gravitated to the front porch overlooking the street, but people filled the house and back porch, too. We hung out and talked with most of his friends, and we were able to sneak in a couple of kisses, too. At one point, I looked at my watch and saw that it was one in the morning. The crowd had thinned out, and the music sounded softer. The next time I looked at my watch, it read three in the morning and I was lying next to Marc on his couch. Everyone had gone home. We kissed some more and then he suggested we move into his bedroom and get more comfortable. The next time I looked at my watch, the sun was shining in through the big picture window in his bedroom, overlooking the river.

"Ouch. My head hurts," I announced.

"Mine, too." He laughed. "What a night," he said with a smile. "Hungry?" he added.

"A little, yes."

"I'll go see what I can find." He rolled out of bed and put on his jeans.

A little disoriented, I jumped up to find the bathroom and a mirror to assess the damage to my face and hair. I heard my cell phone ringing and walked back to the bed to find it. I saw my sister's home number and walked back to the bathroom. I wasn't quite ready to share the details of date number two.

Chapter 14

A Whole New World

The morning after our second date, Marc and I finished breakfast and I drove home to shower, change, and call my sister.

"Hi. I wondered when I might hear from you. How was the shower?"

"It was really nice—at the yacht club in Tiverton, beautiful place, great view."

"Yeah, I've been there for a wedding. It is very nice. How was his family?"

"I met Marc's dad, who is just a big teddy bear—a very sweet man—and a couple of Marc's aunts, who seemed nice. And then all his brothers and sisters—my God—three sisters and two brothers and all their kids. I don't think I've ever been to a bridal shower like that before."

"Me either. So you had fun? You like him?"

"Yeah, and then after the shower ended, most of Marc's family and friends drove back to his house to party until after three in the morning." I wondered whether I had admitted too much.

"Oh, that's late. Where are you now?"

"Home. Taking a shower and heading back to his house for a boat ride."

"Wow, well okay. I hope you're not taking this too fast."

"Um, you married John ten months after you met him and that's worked out fine."

I really had learned to appreciate my sister's advice about men and relationships. She tried to warn me about Dean, even if only that one time. She obviously knew what she required in a man, waited until she found him, and married right the first time.

"Just be careful."

Being with Marc seemed easy to me—maybe because he planned and took care of meals and social events, or maybe because he doted on me. Basically, he met all the requirements on my list.

"I think you'll like him . . . he's polite, courteous, sensitive, funny, respectful, handsome, smart . . . did I tell you what he really does at work?"

"No, not yet," Lori answered.

"He does not mow the lawn! He's the operations manager. He manages everything—the finances, the facilities, the security—everything but the academics."

"Wow, that's cool."

"Yeah, so he's responsible."

I skipped over the sexy details with Lori, but the truth was that I had a physical attraction to Marc, too, and I assumed he felt the same about me after our night together.

I hung up with Lori, finished getting dressed, and headed back to Marc's house. After the boat ride, he offered to cook dinner for me. I woke up beside him again on Sunday morning. I can't recall how we spent the day together, but I do remember he had thought of and planned all the activities that kept us and all his friends entertained and well fed. Monday morning, I awoke early enough to get showered and dressed at my own house before heading to work.

For the rest of that week, Marc and I alternated sleeping at each other's houses. As each week passed, our clothes and other belongings ended up in both places. For two people to live together, my condo was the better choice as it had much more space than Marc's house, but neither of us wanted to leave Sophia alone, so most nights we stayed at his place.

Much to my surprise, Sophia liked me. I had never had my own pet, but Arthur's dog lived at my parents' house for seven years so I just assumed, if I were ever to have a pet, it would be a dog. Our neighbors had four or more cats and my father always complained when he found them in his flower or vegetable gardens. Every time I tried to approach a cat it seemed to dash or scurry away from me.

And then I met Sophia—a beautiful cat (and she knew it) with patches of black, brown, tan, and orange fur. She had green eyes, and an extra toe on each paw. From our first meeting, she greeted me with a full body rub against my ankle and then she followed me through the house until I settled on the couch so she could perch herself behind or beside me. She became my little buddy—my shadow—and I realized why so many people named their pets Shadow. Meeting Sophia helped me realize how much I liked having someone greet me at the door and follow me around the house, even when I may have wanted some private time in the bathroom.

Several weeks after I had met Marc, I watched the movie *Meet the Parents* for the fourth or fifth time, but it was the first time since I had met Sophia. During a scene that included Greg (Ben Stiller) and his fiancé's father, Jack (Robert De Niro), I learned the difference between cat and dog owners. Jack found many reasons not to like his daughter's choice for a husband, but he felt most offended when he learned Greg did not like cats. Jack explained to Greg how a dog is very easy to break, but cats make you work for their affection.

Before I met Sophia, cats had intimidated me and I never worked to gain their affection. Marc felt differently. "You have a natural way with Sophia and she senses it."

I thought Sophia could be a good indication of Marc's character—he must have taken the conscious steps to earn her trust and affection. Sure, he had owned dogs in the past, too, but the time he invested in the relationship with his cat made me think he must be good at human relationships, too. In October, Marc and I made plans to spend Christmas and New Year's in Las Vegas. Since we had made plans to spend Christmas together, I loved knowing I would have a special person with whom to spend Thanksgiving, too. Lori and John hosted John's family and, for the first time in my life, and maybe because of Marc's willingness and ability to entertain, I felt like I wanted to host Thanksgiving for my family.

Marc agreed with no hesitation. He helped to plan the menu and handled what I had always thought must be the most challenging aspect, maybe the one part of Thanksgiving no one wanted to screw up: the turkey. Frankie and his family, my dad and two of his unmarried siblings, his brother Tony and my aunt Angie, joined us for dinner. That may have very well been the first time my dad shared a holiday dinner with his siblings in more than forty years.

My father had plans to leave for Florida a few days after Thanksgiving. And, that year, Dad followed through with what he had tried to do for many years with my mother: He spent Christmas in Florida and planned to stay there through the entire winter. My mother would have never agreed to spend a holiday away from her family; she had preferred no more than two or three weeks away at a time. Because of these short visits, Mom never wanted to build a new condo either, but Dad decided to tackle that project, too. Since his health had been stable over the past few months, none of us challenged his decision to head to Florida with a one-way ticket. Lori, Frankie, and Arthur made travel plans to visit—okay, check up on—Dad and maybe, if Marc and I survived travelling to Vegas together, we would visit Dad in Florida, too.

Chapter 15

The Day after Valentines' Day

Shortly after Thanksgiving, many of Marc's shirts and ties started living in one of my two bedroom closets after he admitted that my condo offered us more space for living together. Of course, we needed a certain someone's approval before we really took the plunge so Marc and I decided to take Sophia on a field trip to my condo. After she surveyed every room on both floors, she finally made herself comfortable on the wicker chair in the sunny alcove overlooking the water. With no fanfare or formal announcement, Marc and I—and Sophia—just sort of moved in together.

In February, Lori had a break before beginning her next round of chemotherapy, so she and John visited Dad and they all watched the Patriots win the Super Bowl. Dad only watched two sports on TV—golf and boxing—but he made an exception because Lori loved Tom Brady.

Lori returned home and confirmed Dad looked as good as he had in November. A week later, he sounded like his normal self on the phone when he ranted to me about the best round of golf he had ever played the day before. When I mentioned that Marc and I wanted to buy a boat, he insisted, "Whatever you do, Linda, don't give up the golf membership. Even if you become a social member. Don't stop golfing."

The next day, my father's best friend, Bob, called Frankie. Dad had been admitted to a hospital in Florida. When my father never showed up for golf, Bob went to check on him and found him sweating and barely conscious in his recliner.

Frankie and his family were already headed to Florida for the kids' school vacation. When they landed in Fort Lauderdale, Bob picked them up, dropped off Deb and the kids at Dad's condo, and drove Frankie to the hospital.

Lori and I felt better having Frankie in Florida, but the doctors gave him little to no information. The next day, right before I left for work, I answered the phone in my kitchen and heard Frankie's voice. "Lin, he's worse. They put him on a respirator."

"What? What happened?" I felt nauseous.

I had assumed this hospital visit would be just like all the other times Lori and I had brought Dad to the hospital in Rhode Island. The doctors would load him up with fluids and antibiotics and release him within two or three days. My father had never needed life support.

"Arthur's on his way here from a business trip in Arkansas. I think you and Lori should come, too."

"I can't believe this. I need to call Lori at work. I'll call you back."

Lori had just started another new series of aggressive chemotherapy treatments the day before.

"Hi, it's me. Frankie just called me. Dad's on life support," I blurted out without asking how she felt.

"What? What the fuck." I expected to hear those exact words, but louder. She probably had clients waiting to meet with John.

Lori had left her role as controller at the family jewelry business sometime after her first breast cancer diagnosis and she now worked part-time with John at his financial planning firm.

"John's with clients. Can you meet us here so we can figure out what to do?"

Instead of heading to work, I drove to Lori's office. I called Marc and left a message on his voice mail. Lori called

Frankie, who told her more about what had happened to Dad. My sister tried to reach Dad's primary doctor in Florida, but had no luck. When she asked his Rhode Island doctors to get involved they used some excuse about cross-state medical boundaries and other sickening red tape that prevented them from helping us.

Lori looked pale and tired when I arrived at her office. I followed her into a conference room where John already sat at a small round table near the window. Lori looked at me. "Linda, one of us needs to be there." She turned to John and then back to me. "And I just don't feel well enough to travel right now."

"I don't want her to travel again right now," John added.

"Can you go? I mean, I think this could be serious," her voice cracked.

I drove to my office and explained to my manager what had happened to my father. He and my whole team pitched in to help me. A coworker called his wife, who called her travel agent and six hundred bucks later I had myself a flight to Florida that night. I reassigned my work and started to pack up my briefcase when my office phone rang. The security guard told me I had a delivery. A friend offered to get the delivery and returned with a large vase of flowers.

"Wow, are we sure these are for me?" I asked.

"Your name's on the card."

I opened the card and read a simple message: "I love you, Marc." I had never received flowers at work. I hadn't connected with Marc after my first message so I called again and thanked him before I gave him the update on my father and my flight. He told me he'd meet me at home to help me pack.

When I arrived at home, Marc and Sophia were waiting for me in our bedroom. He had grabbed my suitcase from the garage and placed it on the bed for me. I sat on the bed, staring at the empty suitcase with no idea what to pack, or for how long, or for which activities. This was sort of how I felt when Dean asked for a divorce and I packed to go to Lori's, but different. I grabbed underwear, a bra, T-shirts, jeans, and whatever else made sense—although nothing made sense at that moment. Sophia thought taking her along made sense so she jumped into a corner of the suitcase on top of my underwear and pajamas. I wished I could take her to keep me calm with her soothing purr that sounded like the constant hum of a motor running.

Marc insisted on taking me to the airport. He walked me into the terminal and, because we had some time before I could check in, we decided to wait in the bar. Shocked, I saw a friend from work sitting on a stool drinking a beer. Beth had heard about my dad, asked one of our coworkers for my flight details, and drove to meet me before I left for Florida. We had known each other for ten years and socialized outside of work once in a while, but I still would not have expected her to go out of her way to meet me at the airport. I know for certain now that the saying is true: only when we go through rough times in our lives do we find out who our real friends are.

Beth and Marc walked me as far as they were allowed. And then I walked alone. Alone to see my dad, on life support, in a far-away hospital surrounded by unfamiliar doctors and nurses.

While I waited to board the plane, and then throughout the entire flight, I wrestled with so many questions. Had Dad missed a symptom before a fever got out of control? Maybe he just needed more antibiotics than usual? Why weren't the doctors giving us any information? Why hadn't I tried to discourage him from going to Florida for such a long time?

Bob and Frankie picked me up at the airport, and Bob drove directly to the hospital. He asked me how I had been— before this happened, of course—and he specifically asked about Marc and me. I told Bob that Marc and I were doing well and that we had moved into together. He wasn't surprised and confessed that he actually had known. I never officially told my

Dad that Marc had moved into my condo, but I had wondered if my father suspected we were living together when we hosted Thanksgiving dinner. Bob told me my father liked Marc very much and he felt relieved that I was happy again.

We arrived at the hospital, and when Frankie pointed in the direction of the intensive care unit, I looked at him and then at Bob. "Really? Intensive care?" Standing outside my father's room, Arthur looked exhausted with his arms crossed against his chest and his head hanging. I pushed past him to see my dad. Arthur grabbed my arm to stop me. "It's bad, Lin."

I entered the room and gasped at the sight of big machines surrounding my dad's bed and the sound of air being pumped through the tube stuck down his throat. I wondered how long he would need to get better this time—so he wouldn't need those machines to help him breathe. I approached his bed and his eyes were slightly opened, glossy, or maybe teary, and the tube prevented him from talking.

I stared at him with one of those smiles that meant this sucks, *I'm sorry you're in this scary hospital, daddy*. I thought about the last day we had golfed together, with Lori and John; it was the same day I had met Marc. Even after forty-eight years of golfing, a single-digit handicap, a Senior Club Championship, and a hole in one, my father always had the patience to teach me about the game he loved.

Dad and I had shared a golf cart that day and he drove to the first tee. After he picked his club, he helped me choose mine. I had trouble hitting the ball with my driver and grabbed my three wood, but he encouraged me to try the driver again. He wanted to analyze my swing and determine what I needed to change. I pulled the driver out of my bag, removed the cover, and grabbed a ball with a pink ribbon on it. I watched my dad hit, and his ball soared off the tee into the blue sky over the green trees, straight down the fairway. After John hit, the guys moved the carts to the women's tee as Lori and I walked up to take our shots. Lori hit first and, as usual, her ball traveled straight, not too far, and landed in the center of the fairway. As I approached the tee, my father stepped out of the golf cart and stood behind me. He could stand right beside me before any of my shots and never make me nervous. As I set up my shot, he adjusted my grip and stance and firmly whispered, "Keep your head down." Everyone remained quiet as I hit my ball and then, all at the same time, their heads followed the ball as their hands sheltered their eyes from the sun. My dad clapped, put his arm around my shoulder, and pointed to where the ball had landed. "Perfect."

And that described the rest of the day, too. I had more bad shots than good ones, but as always, my father only required I have one good shot to remind me "that's the shot that makes you come back!" I couldn't wait to get back on a golf course with my dad again.

I continued to stare at his lifeless body in the hospital bed and, although it reminded me of his condition after his stroke five years ago, something seemed different. His determination and perseverance were missing in action. He looked at me as I held his hand in mine. He looked behind me and I knew he wanted to see Lori. I explained that she had not felt well enough to travel and squeezed his hand. "I love you, Daddy."

He closed his crystal blue eyes.

My brothers came back into the hospital room and we stood and stared at our father and at each other for what felt like hours. I wanted my older brothers to tell me what to do next. A little after midnight, we decided to get some rest and headed to Dad's condo. I tossed and turned on the sleeper sofa in the living room on the first floor. Around five in the morning, I heard the phone ring and someone upstairs answered it. I sat up in the bed, pulled the covers up to my chin, and wondered if anyone ever received good news on the phone at that hour. Within minutes, Arthur walked down the stairs and into the living room. Frankie and his wife stood behind him.

"Dad died, Linda. He's gone." Never before had I wished for one of my brother's practical jokes. I stared at Arthur, hoping to hear him say "just kidding," but those words never came.

I looked at Frankie and then Deb. "Why didn't they call us before he died? He was alone?"

I wanted to scream. I would have never left my father alone if I thought for one second he could die. No one—not the doctors, not my brothers—told me he could die. I never thought my father could die. Sure, his determination and perseverance weren't in that hospital with him, but I assumed they were on a short vacation and would show up again when my father's strength returned. Lori and I never left our mother's side in the days before she died, but her doctors had the kindness and respect to tell us that her death was imminent.

I grabbed the phone beside the sofa, but I couldn't bear to tell my sister the worst had happened. Maybe Dad would still be alive if she had come to Florida with me. I sobbed into the phone, "I never even thought he could die." I sniffled. "I'm so sorry I left him alone." I bit at my thumb nail. "Why the hell did we let him come to Florida? This would have never happened at home."

I still don't remember Lori's exact words, but her encouragement stopped me from blaming myself. I'll never forget Marc's reaction when I gave him the sad news. "Crap. I got robbed." He had hoped to spend much more time with my father.

The next few days in Florida were a blur except for the time I spent swimming in the pool with my brothers, sister-in-law, and nephews while we all shared our favorite memories of my father. I just wanted to cherish all the good memories we were fortunate to have and not focus on the fact that my father had died the day after Valentine's Day.

I had thought nothing in my life would hurt me as much as losing my mother. I was wrong. Losing my father hurt me just as much. Having my father alive eased the pain of losing my mother—the woman who had given me life, nurtured and guided me, and loved me unconditionally. And having my sister alive eased the pain of losing my father—the man who I had counted on to give me a red, foil-covered, heart-shaped box of Russell Stover candy every year for Valentine's Day—the man who never stopped showing me life's blessings and teaching me life's lessons—the man I had sometimes called a royal pain in the ass and now hoped he knew he had always been the smartest pain in the ass a daughter could ever ask for.

Chapter 16

Don't Put Off Till Tomorrow What You Can Do Today

I must have inherited my love for jigsaw puzzles and really all puzzles solved with my hand, like the Rubik's cube, from my father, but I never asked if he liked Sudoku. In March, about a month after my dad passed away, with the dim light from the lamp on the nightstand, I sat on my bed working on my fifth Sudoku puzzle of the night—a ritual that helped me melt into the pillow and put me to sleep. There was a time when I loved to read before bedtime—mostly fiction books— but after my mom died, I would start reading one book, get bored, and then start reading another. I had two or three novels started at the same time and I never finished any of them. I guess I missed our mother-daughter book exchange and never liked to feel like a failure for not finishing a damn book, so I stopped reading all together. I achieved more satisfaction by completing a crossword or Sudoku puzzle, even if I peeked at the answers at the back of the book once in a while.

It also occurred to me that reading fiction seemed like a waste of my time. I wanted to read real-life true stories, maybe ones that mirrored my own life—a story of a girl who encountered one emotional trauma after another and seemed to never catch a break. I mean, after losing both of my parents to complications brought on by cancer and still having to watch my sister suffer with breast cancer, I needed to find hope. I needed to find the kind of hope I had received when I met Marc. After my divorce, just when I thought I may never find another man to love me, and I had accepted that I could survive without a male companion, *poof*, Marc entered my life.

Familiar with my nightly routine for falling asleep, Marc chose not to disturb me so he watched TV downstairs. Sophia stayed with me and slept on an edge of the chenille blanket that covered my feet. As I stared at the puzzle, I raised my right hand to my left breast and pressed my pointer and middle fingers on a spot right near my nipple. I felt the lump and then I turned my head toward the nightstand and the framed photo of my mother and me at my MBA graduation. I had first noticed the same lump a month ago and ignored it because my father had just died from cancer. At the time I thought, there's absolutely no way in hell this could be what I think it is. My annual mammogram was scheduled for July, and although my father always said, "Don't put off till tomorrow what can be done today," I never called my doctor to get me in sooner. I ignored the lump for another four months.

I finally had the mammogram and, as always, the technician asked me to wait while she confirmed the radiologist could read the film. The technician walked toward me with a blank stare. "Linda, will you come with me again?" I followed her back into the room where the dreaded mammography machine still stood.

"Linda, the lump you and I both felt is not showing up on the film," she explained.

Another woman wearing a white lab coat walked into the room. She reached out to shake my hand at the same time the technician introduced her as the radiologist.

"I'd like to perform a compressed mammography if that's okay with you," said the radiologist. It was more of a statement than a question.

"Sure," I agreed and thought, what the hell is a compressed version of a mammography? I always imagined that a regular mammogram mimicked what it felt like to close my boob in a refrigerator door. So I wondered what a compressed mammogram had in store for me. Before long, I learned that it felt like I had my boob run over by a delivery truck carrying my new refrigerator and a new refrigerator for every house in my neighborhood.

After the compressed test, I remained in the same room, staring at the stainless steel delivery truck and waiting for the results. The radiologist reported that she still saw nothing on the compressed films and referred me to a breast surgeon. I could have scheduled an appointment with the same surgeon who removed the benign cyst in my right breast three years ago, the same one who operated on my mother and my sister, but I chose to meet a new surgeon the radiologist had recommended.

I walked into the surgeon's office and checked in with the smiling receptionist. I handed her my mammography films and then sat in the waiting area. After a few short minutes, a nurse called my name and escorted me into the examining room. The surgeon looked like my high school guidance counselor: a petite guy with dark eyes and dark hair. He was soft spoken and kind. He examined me and indicated that he felt the lump. Afterward, he stepped outside the exam room to review the mammography. He returned with a nurse.

"I want to perform a biopsy."

I assumed I'd get dressed and make an appointment to come back for the biopsy at some time in the future. If he wanted me to come back sooner than later, I'd take that as a sign to worry.

"Johanna will assist me." I watched her put on latex gloves, open cabinets, and grab stainless steel instruments, gauze, and other medical supplies I preferred not to have near me.

"What? Now?"

The doctor told me the procedure would be done right there and then. I began to shiver and lay back on the table as they continued to prepare themselves and the tools. I preferred to know exactly what happened next, but the doctor inserted a needle into my left breast with no warning.

"Is that it?"

"Not quite. That was the needle to numb the area." He rested his hand on my left arm. I wished he had numbed my boob before he stuck a needle in it to numb the area. I cringed from the prick that seemed to last more than a few seconds.

Johanna stood beside me, ready for action. I turned my head toward her and asked, "Could you hold my hand?" She agreed with a smile that kind of screamed "pathetic," when I really needed sympathetic.

I focused on the doctor's hands as they approached my breast, this time with a stainless steel instrument that looked like a scissor. I wanted to know how this tool worked, but instead of asking for an explanation, I squeezed my eyes shut. I clenched Johanna's hand. "I'm sorry if I'm hurting you, Johanna."

"This will only take a few minutes," the doctor said. "You will hear a few clicks, like this." He demonstrated the sound with a few clicks of the scissor.

I felt a little pressure on my left boob and, as expected, heard the loud click of the scissors.

"That wasn't bad at all. Are we done?"

"Not just yet, I want to get five or six pieces."

"Oh, sure, five sounds reasonable." I thought about negotiating that number down even more but I trusted that the doctor knew his own job better than I ever would. I just knew from the sound of the scissor and the sick feeling in my stomach that the sooner this little procedure ended, the better, for all of us.

I closed my eyes tighter. *Click. Click. Click.* The doctor indicated one more and he'd be done. Poor Johanna. I offered her no more apologies. *Click.*

"That's it. We're all done. You did great. I'm sure this is benign." He removed his gloves and tossed them in the basket.

I only heard the word "benign" and wondered how he could know that from looking at the fleshy pieces of my boob. I had always figured cancer cells must be black so the doctor must have just removed a clump of white cells from me to know they were benign.

"We'll have the results for you tomorrow."

As I lay on the table, I watched the doctor plop pieces of my boob into glass vials and then the room started to spin.

"Are you okay?" They both stared at me.

I lifted my head up from the table and started to sit up. "Oh boy." ; placed one hand behind my back and my other hand on my stomach.

"Here, lie back down." The doctor reached for my hand and supported me as I leaned back.

But I just wanted to get up. I wanted to get out of there. I wanted to run away from what had just happened. I drove home with a numb feeling—and not only around my breast.

With my family's history of cancer, I expected a diagnosis of my own someday, but I never expected to be thirty-six years old when it happened. Aside from my mother and sister, two of my dad's sisters also had breast cancer. One of my aunts died several years ago, but my Auntie Angie had survived and recently turned eighty-three years old!

About a year ago, when Lori's cancer spread to her liver and lungs, I consulted a genetic counselor to assess my risk of getting breast cancer. Some may have called me a pessimist, but I needed to know everything about this disease that plagued my family. Having the knowledge would help me make the best decisions, and I'd never have any regrets about my own health. When I disclosed my family's history to the counselor and she informed me that the breast cancer gene tended to be more prominent on the father's side, I decided to have the gene test. I asked my sister to have it done, too, but she never saw the point after her recurrence.

The results of the gene test were negative for the BRCA1 and BRCA2 gene (the only two genes that had been discovered at the time), but my overall risk of getting breast cancer was still higher than the average woman's risk for one reason: My mother received her first diagnosis at age fifty-six and my sister received her first diagnosis at age forty-two, but the genetic counselor only raised her eyebrows at the mention of Auntie Angie's age at diagnosis—thirty-five.

Maybe if my profession hadn't involved project and risk management, I would have just stopped thinking about my risk of getting breast cancer and gone on my merry way. But I am a planner and a person who assesses the "what ifs" in life. So, after I learned my overall risk of getting breast cancer and that the gene test offered no guarantees—some women have the gene and never get diagnosed while others don't have the gene and do get diagnosed—I thought about what I might do if I ever received a breast cancer diagnosis in the future. My mother had removed one breast and the cancer returned to her bones ten years later, and my sister had just removed the lump and the cancer returned to her liver and lungs in less than two years. It seemed like a no-brainer to me: If I ever ended up getting diagnosed with this wretched disease, I wanted a double mastectomy. I had to do more than both my mother and sister had done to fight this disease.

After the biopsy I had endured and the anxiety I had to live with overnight, I thought about pursuing a double mastectomy regardless of the results.

Before I reached my condo, Lori called to ask about my doctor's appointment.

"He did a biopsy, and I need to return to his office tomorrow for the results."

"Oh . . . really?" I wondered if Lori was really that surprised to hear I had a biopsy or was she being the best big sister ever and trying to minimize my anxiety?

"Yeah, his office is right near where you get your chemo, so I figured we could swing by afterward, okay?"

"Of course. So, did he say anything else? I mean, like what he thought it could be? "

"No, he just said it would be benign. I guess it's good that he wanted to be thorough. It's probably another cyst."

I called Marc at work to give him an update on my appointment. He had made plans for us to see a movie with his brother and his girlfriend that night. I was happy to take my mind off the test, and we agreed not to mention anything to anyone until we had the results.

The next day, I drove my sister to the hospital for her chemo appointment and we chatted for two hours. My parents had been treated in the same hospital, but since then, the treatment area had been completely renovated. It had been one big room lined with windows and filled with recliners arranged in a circle. Everyone could see and hear each other's business. I thought about the time before Lori had a port implanted into her chest, when the nurses had the worst time inserting her IV so they pushed her recliner all the way back so her feet were above her head while they wrestled with her veins. It bothered me to watch my sister suffer. I thought the other patients shouldn't be haunted by the possibility of having to endure the same scenario themselves.

The new clinic design separated the patients by walls and curtains and, although it gave the patients more privacy, it also limited their interaction and the support they might give each other. I knew they had formal support groups for that, but for patients like Lori who never wanted to talk about her feelings, they would now miss out on what may have been their only means of emotional support.

While I sat with Lori, I tried not to think about our next destination or me sitting in one of those recliners with chemo and other drugs running through my veins. Despite Lori's challenges, she made the process of getting the chemo seem painless. When in public, she practiced what she preached: "You have to have a PMA." The acronym stood for Positive Mental Attitude. For the sake of the people around her, she had made the best of a bad situation by telling jokes, and she had even taught her oncologist and favorite nurses how to knit.

Each week, her body accepted more chemo and experienced more negative side effects, but Lori repeatedly bounced back, smiled, and kept living life.

We arrived at my doctor's office with a few minutes to spare and sat in the waiting room with two other patients. A woman entered the room and my sister and I both recognized her at the same time. She was the sister of Lori's high school friend. As they reminisced, the receptionist called me into the examining room. My sister stood up to come with me, but I insisted she stay with her friend and catch up.

"Stay and chat. This should be quick. I'll be right back."

I settled onto the exam table with the latest *People* magazine and heard the door knob turn as the surgeon entered the room. He held my hand and his eyes gave me the results of my breast biopsy. "It's cancer."

I held my breath and looked up toward the ceiling. I turned back to the doctor. I waited for him to reverse his words. I saw his mouth moving, but only heard bits and pieces of what he was saying. The scene seemed surreal because I had heard "it's cancer" so many times before that moment. But this was my moment.

"I know this must be difficult for you. I was certain it would be benign. But listen, cancer is not a life sentence anymore. It's not the Big C, like it used to be."

Who the hell are you kidding? I knew more than most newly diagnosed women about the journey ahead of me. I had witnessed all the ups and downs with my mother, sister, and father. I knew about the endless doctor's appointments, a ridiculous amount of blood tests, X-rays of everything, body scans, chemotherapy, radiation, needles, vomiting. On one hand, I felt fortunate because I knew what to expect. For me, less surprises meant less fear of the unknown. On the other hand, I was afraid to allow that poison into my body. Oh my God, I'm going to lose my hair!

I stared at nothing on the empty white wall behind the doctor, blinked, and begged to be granted multiple wishes.

When I opened my eyes, I hoped to see my mother standing beside me, promising to take care of everything, like she promised whenever I had a cold. I wanted to feel my father rub my knee and to hear him say "it's okay," just like he had assured me before my back surgery and after my divorce. But I had really outdone myself this time, hadn't I? This was bigger than a cold and back surgery, and part of me felt thankful that my parents would be spared from watching their second daughter—their bonus child—go through breast cancer. I hated to burden Marc with this. And I dreaded giving this news to my sister.

"I need to tell my sister." My voice cracked and I felt like I would vomit.

Johanna already knew to get Lori for me. My sister walked in the exam room, saw my mouth quiver and my eyes tear up, and exploded with her classic "What the fuck?"

The doctor recommended I have a lumpectomy and sentinel node biopsy. This was a new biopsy procedure since Lori's first diagnosis when they removed seventeen of her lymph nodes. With a sentinel node biopsy, the surgeon only removed the sentinel, or primary, lymph node between my breast and my arm. This procedure decreased my risk of having lymphedema, or painful swelling in my arm. Cancer had to travel through this central node in order to reach the bloodstream and spread throughout the body, so if the biopsy came back negative, the doctors could presume the cancer only existed in the breast. The results also helped the oncologist choose the right chemotherapy to prescribe.

Now I wondered if I still had the courage to follow through with the decision I made a year ago.

"I want a double mastectomy."

"You don't need to do that. Research has shown that a lumpectomy along with chemotherapy and radiation offers the same survival rate as a double mastectomy."

I thought about my mother's choice and her outcome and the result of my sister's choice and I only believed—with all my heart—that if I removed both breasts, the cancer could not return there and chemotherapy would kill any cancer in my bloodstream. I couldn't decrease my sister's hope for survival by defending my aggressive medical decisions in front of her. And, at that very moment, I only thought about the disgusting black stuff in my boob and wanted it removed immediately—like, where are those scissors now, doc?

"Fine, let's schedule the lumpectomy. I can decide if I want to pursue more surgery later, right?" I still wanted a double mastectomy and I needed time to find a surgeon willing to do it. At that moment though, I just wanted the cancer out of my body as quickly as possible.

"Of course. Once we have the pathology on the sentinel node and the lump itself, we can revisit any questions you or your family may have."

As I drove home, each time my cell phone rang I handed it to Lori to answer. I couldn't repeat the words out loud without crying.

I parked in Lori's driveway. She stared at me and shook her head from side to side. "I cannot believe this is happening to us—happening to you. But it's okay, we'll get through this just like everything else." She kissed my cheek and we hugged.

Marc's car was parked in our garage. He had left work right after he spoke to Lori. I walked upstairs to our bedroom and just wanted to lie down on the bed with my chenille blanket and Sophia. A few minutes later, I heard Marc climbing the stairs and Sophia's bell jingling close behind him. They both walked into the bedroom as I grabbed another tissue. He walked over to my side of the bed and handed me a bottle of water. I tried to stop crying. I wanted to be strong for him.

"They could be wrong," he said. "We should get another opinion."

Marc had built his own house and maintained all the buildings on the school campus as part of his job. He always wanted to fix or improve things around my condo—leaky faucets, broken appliances, loose railings and deck boards. A bit of a perfectionist, he only trusted himself to get these jobs done right.

Marc picked up Sophia as she squirmed in his hands. He insisted my doctor had been wrong about my biopsy so he performed his own test—holding Sophia over my body he waved her plump, furry body from my head to my toes and back again—performing his own CAT scan to get the results he trusted.

"See, they are wrong. Sophia's scan says you're fine."

The lumpectomy had been scheduled for August 15, two days after Marc's birthday. Apparently, life still happened after a breast cancer diagnosis and the two weeks flew by because Marc kept us busy. He drove me and our friends to the Newport Folk and Jazz Festivals by boat, set up dinner with friends at home and at my favorite restaurants, and decorated the deck with new furniture and flowers in preparation for my outdoor recovery on the water. Because my surgery would take place two days after his birthday, he postponed our boat trip to Block Island and planned a lobster dinner celebration at a restaurant nearby instead.

Sometimes, I felt better surrounded by friends, but I got tired of talking about breast cancer, answering questions, and acting positive and upbeat all the time. Other times, I preferred to just be alone. Surely, my friends meant well, but many never knew the right thing to say, opting for "you'll be fine" or "it'll be okay," when they had no clue how my life would turn out. And then my personal favorite: "I can't believe this is happening to you. Your family has been through so much." No kidding. Yet somehow, this sad fact alone is what gave me the strength to fight like hell. I had to beat this disease that had already taken my mother and so many other loved ones.

The day before my surgery, I searched the Yellow Pages for a cancer support group—an action that neither Lori nor my parents had ever taken. The first group I called actually told me they had no openings in their scheduled support groups, and today I know that is an unacceptable answer for any cancer patient. Sad and discouraged from being turned away, I called another group in the area and the founder talked to me for an hour or more. She had so much information to share: a list of oncologists, general and plastic surgeons, and various medical and alternative treatment options. She gave me the schedule for the support group focused on newly diagnosed patients and the name of a local survivor, Mickie, to call for a ride to the meeting. I mentioned my surgery in the morning and she invited me to the full-day retreat open to all survivors that was scheduled three days from then.

Instead of being discouraged, I felt blessed that the timing of this retreat coincided with my diagnosis and surgery date. I had breast cancer and I felt blessed!

The next morning, I woke up before the alarm went off, took a hot shower, shaved, and put on my favorite sweatpants and a white cotton shirt that zipped up the front. Marc drove to the hospital and stayed by my side wherever and whenever the nurses would let him. He held my hand and watched the nurse insert an IV. I laid on a gurney, almost naked (without putting up a fight) but covered with a thin white blanket, and he walked beside a petite female nurse (not a male Neanderthal) who wheeled me to nuclear medicine for the injection to light up my sentinel node. Marc even supported me when I asked the technician for the maximum anesthesia possible.

Right before the nurse transported me to the operating room she turned to Marc. "Give her a hug and a kiss." I must have fallen into la-la land right after he kissed my lips because the next time I opened my eyes I looked down to see bandages covering my chest. I felt tired, sore, and peaceful. The cancer had been removed. I had plans to attend a retreat for survivors, a list of oncologists to interview, and a task list that most definitely included finding a surgeon to perform the surgery I really wanted.

Chapter 17

My Way

Being unable to shower had been the most annoying part of having cancer removed from my boob. Okay, maybe having to wait a week for the results of the full pathology report sucked more, but I wanted to make a good impression on the fellow cancer survivors at the retreat. I settled for what my mother had called a "sponge bath"—I used a face cloth to wash my important parts, or those parts most prone to emit a foul odor, and Marc offered to wash my hair as I bent over the kitchen sink.

Lori shocked me when she agreed to attend the retreat with me. I couldn't imagine how I might react to a cancer recurrence, especially if the cancer had spread beyond my breasts, but I often wished my sister would seek support from other survivors dealing with a diagnosis similar to hers. In public, she always smiled and let others think she was feeling positive, but there had been times since the recurrence when the two of us were alone that she seemed less than positive to me.

One day, after she'd smiled and laughed with the nurses during her two-hour intravenous chemotherapy infusion, we were driving home and she put her hand over her mouth and mumbled, "I'm gonna be sick."

"Should I pull over?" And then I realized what a thoughtless question that was.

"Yeah, quick." Lori gagged.

I put my right turn signal on, looked over my right shoulder, and crossed over one lane of traffic to reach the breakdown lane of a busy highway. Even before I came to a complete stop, Lori opened her door, leaned outside, and vomited on the side of the road. I rummaged through my glove compartment for a napkin or anything my sister could use to wipe her mouth.

I handed her a tissue from my purse and she sobbed. "It must not be working."

"What's not working?"

"This chemo. If I'm getting sick, my body must be rejecting it."

"See, I think just the opposite. I think the chemo is working and what you're throwing up is all the bad stuff . . . you're throwing up the cancer." I rubbed my sister's back.

Whenever my sister shared a negative comment, I turned it into a positive one. Once in a while, Lori would ask, "Why me and not so-and-so?" and she'd fill in the "so-and-so" with someone on the short list of people she thought had wronged her in the past. I always answered with the only response I cared to speak out loud: "Because you're strong enough to handle it and so-and-so isn't." If she refused to attend a cancer support group, I wished she would consider therapy to eliminate any negative energy from her body.

An entire year had passed after our mom died before I considered going to a therapist and maybe even longer before I decided I wanted help. I saw Diane for at least a year while she helped me cope with the loss of my mother, my father's illness, my divorce, and my sister's first breast cancer diagnosis. I had stopped going to therapy prior to my sister's cancer recurrence and my father's death, but I started seeing Diane again after my own breast cancer diagnosis. Throughout those five years, I think I only asked, "Why me?" once—after the very first tragic event happened in my life: when my mother died. Okay, I may have asked the question, "Why did my mother have to die?"

more than once, but only because it took four years—and a few more tragedies—before I discovered my answer.

I finally understood that the sayings I used to think were silly and overused clichés were really insightful messages—pieces of wisdom—created by people who had survived one tragedy or another. These sayings appeared ridiculous until I had lived through enough of my own traumas to recognize the true meaning. We've all heard the same clichés. You don't know what you have until it's gone, and When life hands you lemons, make lemonade (or lemon meringue pie), and People come into your life for a reason, a season, or a lifetime.

By the time I had received my breast cancer diagnosis, I must have rolled my eyes at thousands of these bogus clichés. But then one of them finally resonated with me. *Everything happens for a reason.* For this cliché to really work for me, for it not to be annoying, I added my own wisdom to it, and now I like overusing the saying my way, "Everything happens for a reason, we're just not given the reason at the same time as the thing."

Maybe I never asked, "Why me and not someone else," but instead I wondered why I needed to deal with so much pain and sadness in such a short period of time. And what I discovered changed me—forever. I realized that I wouldn't have been prepared to handle each subsequent tragedy if I hadn't experienced and learned from one or more of the previous tragedies.

I needed to be present in my own life before I could look back to learn my own lessons and earn my own wisdom. I lived a full year after my mother had died before I reflected on the events leading up to her death. What I never realized then, but I have since learned time and time again, is that every moment of my life presents me with the opportunity to accumulate information and experiences that are valuable and necessary for me to make decisions for my future. Even the negative experiences—those that don't end up exactly as I may have planned—provide me with knowledge to increase the chances of a better outcome the next time.

When I thought about all the emotional pain I had dealt with over the past four years, I came to believe that maybe I lost my mother before my father so I would have the opportunity, as an adult, to spend time with my father and appreciate the priceless wisdom he shared with me. I will never know why my mother had to die of breast cancer, but I know that when I faced the same disease, the strength and dignity she exhibited every day, gave me the courage I needed for my own journey. Looking back even further, maybe I needed to experience my divorce to earn the wisdom my family tried to share with me before I could fully understand it myself and, maybe best of all, to know the difference when I met Marc, who continued to take care of me during my illness. I even had to admit that the nurses who tolerated me twenty years ago during my back surgery would be happy to know how much more civilized I behaved for the nurses who prepped me for my lumpectomy.

With or without a shower, I couldn't have been any more excited to meet other women living through breast cancer. I wanted to hear each woman's unique story. I wanted to know how each woman sifted through all the medical books, websites, and doctors' opinions to make their individual treatment decisions. For me to survive breast cancer, I had to know every single thing about the disease and analyze all my options before making an informed decision. For me, that was the only way to guarantee I would never regret my choices.

I had just finished getting dressed in our bedroom upstairs when I saw Lori's Jeep in our driveway. I walked downstairs and greeted her at the kitchen door. Sophia walked behind me with her tail straight up in the air except for that little curl at the very end. Like me, my sister never had pets—or kids—of her own, but unlike me, she walked by Sophia without even a small acknowledgment. Sophia sensed Lori's standoffishness and stayed close to me, rubbing up against my ankles.

"Hey, you look good. How are you feeling?" Lori asked.

"Okay. Still sore, but ready for a change of scenery. How are you feeling?"

"Eh, the same, tired, nauseous. I'm getting used to feeling this way."

"Are you sure you still want to go? Marc can drive me." Marc walked into the kitchen.

As much as I wanted my sister to join me I needed to fully enjoy the experience myself and not have to worry about whether or not she thought the group was helpful or just plain silly. Lori drove us to the retreat that day, and although I only remember a few of the activities (meditation, sharing personal stories, and journaling), I remember one thing for sure: I wanted to stay there, surrounded by courage and hope, forever. I realized I had two choices for how I wanted to travel on my breast cancer journey. I could travel alone and only focus on my fears of recurrence, death, and all the negative details of breast cancer. Or, I could recognize the enormous gift I had been given by meeting all these women warriors on the same journey with or before me—the enormous gift of sisters in survival. That day, I chose to never travel alone on my lifelong breast cancer journey.

A few days after the retreat, I had a follow-up appointment with the surgeon to review the results of my pathology report and hear my prognosis. The project and risk manager in me carried a list of questions to ask the doctor, but I couldn't go alone. I mean, after hearing the results, I might just think, oh my God, I have breast cancer, and then stop listening to everything the doctor had to say after that. I had acted as Lori's health-care advocate since her recurrence in case she stopped listening, and I knew she would want to do the same for me, but how could she? And although I trusted Marc to provide me with the best daily care, could he be objective enough to make the best health-care decisions for me? I never wanted to hurt Marc's or Lori's feelings and I still believed the more people who listened, the better, so I turned to a dear friend.

From the moment I had received my diagnosis, I knew I only needed one person with me to hear my prognosis: my best friend, Brenda. We hadn't attended the same high school, but we met because we had dated the same guy in high school. No, not at the same time. The guy had broken up with me to date Brenda and after they broke up, she and I happened to meet at the beach and we became instant friends. Maybe how we met isn't terribly unique, but the fact that we have remained friends for more than twenty-five years still amazes me. My definition of true friendship means we don't need to speak every day or every week—or even be mentioned on the first page or in the first half of my memoir—but when Brenda and I do speak, we fall right back into our last conversation, as if it had never ended. Brenda and I attended the same college for our master's degrees and when we could, we scheduled our classes together. I always thought I had exceptional study habits—that is, until I studied with Brenda. She took notes as if she were a tape recorder, and she had an uncanny talent for highlighting. It made perfect sense for Brenda to be the secretary and researcher on my breast cancer journey and I wouldn't have had it any other way.

Marc would be my security guard. He protected me and made me feel safe. And since he would be my primary caregiver—and emergency contact—it made sense for him to hear everything the surgeon had to say and also to have the opportunity to ask his own questions. I trusted Marc to confirm the doctor's ability as a surgeon, too, because Marc had the highest expectations of anyone who worked for him.

Of those on my three-person team, my sister put me in the most awkward position. After we lost our mother, Lori became my mother, the woman who loved me unconditionally. She guided me through my divorce. She helped me make financial decisions and sat beside me when I signed the papers that made me the sole owner of my first home. I had considered her my personal User Guide for Life; she was my life coach. I knew she wanted to act as my advocate and primary caregiver, but we agreed she had to focus on her own health. And as I confronted the biggest challenge of my life, I needed to reference a different User Guide than the one my life coach had followed when she was faced with the same challenge.

The receptionist escorted me and my team into what seemed like the office library. Medical journals and self-help books filled the bookshelves that lined the room. We sat in a semicircle on wooden armchairs with leather seats. I felt my palms sweating and heart racing as we waited for the surgeon to share the pathology results and, ultimately, my prognosis, which started with the breast cancer staging.

The definitions for the stages of breast cancer had not changed since my mother had been diagnosed seventeen years earlier. Breast cancer stages are based on the size of the tumor, whether the cancer is invasive or noninvasive, whether the cancer is in the lymph nodes, and whether the cancer has spread to parts of the body beyond the breast. Stage 0 indicates the best scenario: noninvasive cancer that has not broken out of its original location within the breast. Stage IV indicates the worst scenario: invasive cancer that has spread to other parts of the body, such as the lungs, bones, liver, and brain.

I sat beside my sister, who had been living with stage IV breast cancer for the past fifteen months. As I waited for the doctor to tell us about my tumor and my prognosis, I hoped for the best, but I knew more about this disease and the havoc it could wreak than most other newly diagnosed women. And with my sister beside me, I prepared myself to hear the worst.

"Linda, your tumor measures two centimeters." He looked up from his notes and at me.

I stared at Brenda and then watched her write it in her notebook.

"I was able to remove a one-centimeter clean margin around the tumor. We also found a second 'in situ,' or noninvasive, tumor and removed it."

"Was that within or outside of that one-centimeter clean margin?" I asked. Brenda nodded at me and then wrote in her notebook.

"The second tumor also had a clear margin and the sentinel lymph node showed no signs of cancer." I breathed a huge sigh of relief, knowing that the cancer had not traveled outside of my breast. I looked at Brenda and she smiled.

The surgeon classified my breast cancer as stage I. He explained other characteristics about the cancer that would help the oncologist choose the best treatment. My tumor tested hormone receptive positive, which meant I had more treatment options available to me.

"Have you chosen an oncologist yet?" he asked.

"No, not yet, but I have three appointments. I thought I needed the results of the lumpectomy to determine if I needed chemotherapy." I said.

"In my opinion, you should have chemotherapy, but an oncologist will know for sure."

"What are you—" Brenda and I asked a question at the same time.

"Go ahead, Lin." Brenda gestured with her hand for me to ask my question.

"What are you basing your opinion on?"

Brenda looked at me and mouthed, "That's what I wanted to know, too."

"The size of the tumor and your family history. What other questions do you all have?"

"Well, I still want a double mastectomy."

The doctor responded with the same answer he had given me when he first diagnosed me. "And the research still says that a lumpectomy followed by chemotherapy and radiation will provide the same survival rate as a double mastectomy and chemotherapy." I knew the research hadn't changed in two weeks, but I wanted him to know my decision hadn't changed either.

"I can't comprehend how these two vastly different surgeries can offer the same survival rate. If I have no breasts, the cancer cannot come back there." I stated this as a fact, not a question.

"Cancer travels in your bloodstream."

"That's what the chemo is for . . . to chase any cancer in the blood and kill it."

The doctor shrugged his shoulders. "Maybe that's a conversation you should have with your oncologist."

The doctor shook each of our hands. "Please, feel free to call the office if you think of any other questions. I know it's a lot to absorb all at once."

Maybe I had a lot to absorb and, although I heard it for the first time as it pertained to me, I had heard all of it too many times before this. And contrary to what this guy might have thought about me, I read the same research he read and my gut still told me to have a double mastectomy. I needed to find a surgeon who had the same gut feeling as mine.

"That's why I took my secretary." I giggled and put my arm around Brenda's shoulders.

Brenda and I walked out of the office and lagged behind Marc and Lori after I waved to them to walk ahead of us. I wanted to talk to Brenda privately. She looked at her notebook and recited her notes to me, correlating each point to the research she had found online before the appointment. She wholeheartedly agreed with my theory, understanding, and decision to choose the double mastectomy and chemo.

We caught up to Marc and Lori in the waiting area. I recall Marc being quiet, but my sister's comment will haunt me forever. "You're gonna do it your way . . . and you should. We all know what I did and . . ." Lori pointed to her chest.

I hated to think my sister had regrets about her medical decisions, and I felt guilty that I had the chance to make a different choice for myself because of the lessons I learned from her and my mother's choices. But in order to maintain a positive outlook toward my own survival, I had to believe they wanted me to learn from their experience. I thought about the time that I decided not to work for the family business and how my sister seemed relieved. I wondered then if she felt relieved because I never wanted her job or because she wanted me to do something better, bigger.

"I'll support whatever decision you make," said my life coach. And I believed her. Since we had survived that bumpy start as young siblings and entered adulthood, I knew my big sister always wanted the best for me.

Chapter 18

Is Anyone Ever Ready for Chemo?

It was hard to believe the black cloud still hovered over my family. In the last four years, we had lost Mom and Dad due to complications of having cancer, dealt with two divorces, and now Lori and I would be treated for cancer at the same time. Because many of our appointments conflicted with each other's, I enlisted my best friend.

During the last week of August, Brenda helped me develop my treatment plan in addition to getting her kids ready to go back to school. First and foremost, I had to find a medical oncologist—a main doctor who would oversee all aspects of my care and who specializes in treating cancer with chemotherapy and other drugs. Based on different recommendations, I had made appointments to interview two oncologists, both in the same week, but after my own online research, I was sure I had already made my choice even before the interviews.

Finding the doctor who would save my life seemed like it could be the most important decision I'd ever make. I knew the decision would ultimately be mine, but I wanted Brenda with me to take notes and be my sounding board. I don't remember if Marc wanted to be involved in this part of my journey or not, but I convinced him I had it covered. Also, I would rather he save his time off for my chemo appointments and the care I may need afterward.

I made the first appointment with the doctor I thought I wanted before I had even met him. A couple of women I had met at the cancer support retreat recommended Dr. Robert Legare, and aside from praising his brainpower and bedside manner, they'd added that he was "adorable."

Brenda, along with her notebook, pens, and highlighters, met me at the Breast Health Center, and I noted how much of a difference this was from when we were in our twenties and trying to look anything but nerdy at the dance club on a Friday night. We sat side-by-side in matching contemporary leather chairs while I filled out the patient questionnaire and we waited for someone to call my name. Between the mammography, the biopsy, the lumpectomy, and now this, I had provided the same personal information fifty times in the past month. It would be so much more efficient if my current medical history lived in a secure database where all my doctors could access it. I scanned the crowded waiting room and wondered what brought each patient to the office that day. Had she already received her cancer diagnosis? Is she having chemotherapy? Does she have children? Why is that woman alone? My curiosity about the lives of the other patients never stopped or distracted me from obsessing over my own situation.

After thirty or forty minutes, Brenda and I were escorted to an exam room. It may have been another ten or twenty minutes before the doctor arrived. Brenda and I winked at each other and I knew we agreed that this doctor had definitely inherited the handsome gene. He was probably in his early to midthirties, in great shape, with blond hair and blue eyes. But what we wanted to know was whether or not he was brilliant. After he reviewed my genetic risk assessment and pathology report he recommended a common protocol for my type of breast cancer: four cycles of chemotherapy, radiation, and five years of the drug Tamoxifen, which was an option for me because my tumor tested positive for hormone receptive cancer. This meant my cancer needed estrogen to grow, and

Tamoxifen worked by blocking the estrogen from feeding the tumor.

"That's what I thought you'd say, but of course I hoped you would say I didn't need any of those treatments."

The doctor smiled at me with serious eyes. "Of course, Linda. Given your type of cancer and what we know about it today, the data indicates this is the best course of treatment."

"I want a double mastectomy and reconstruction, so a plastic surgeon may prefer I don't have radiation to give me the best result."

"Okay." It seemed he agreed with my surgical decision. "I would start you on chemo right away, giving us at least twelve weeks to decide on radiation."

"I'm just not comfortable with Tamoxifen either. I mean my sister was rediagnosed while she was taking Tamoxifen, and my mother's cancer came back after she finished taking it. And the side effects, like blood clots and endometrial cancer, scare me." I bent my head down slightly, nibbled on my right thumbnail and stared at the doctor from the corner of my eye.

Dressed in a light pink unwrinkled shirt and a diagonally striped navy necktie that landed perfectly at his waist, Dr. Legare stood in front me. "I understand. We monitor your blood counts all the time, and we pay close attention to any symptoms that indicate the presence of those side effects." He seemed very confident.

"Okay." I slouched on the exam table, looked down at the hardwood floor and rubbed both of my palms back and forth on my thighs. *He has an answer for everything, doesn't he?* I probably sounded like a whiner, but I had hoped I could get away without one of the three treatments. Then I reminded myself that I wanted to take the most aggressive approach as possible to decrease the chances of my cancer returning and I wanted a doctor who knew everything.

"And with regard to the experiences of your sister and your mother, I'm certainly sorry to hear that, but their results cannot predict yours," he added.

That sentence alone may have been the only thing I needed to hear to confirm who I wanted for my oncologist. With all the negative experiences my family had endured from breast cancer, I needed to remain positive. I wanted to believe I could be like my Aunt Angie—diagnosed at thirty-five years old and still surviving at eighty-three.

I wanted to be perfectly honest with Dr. Legare, "I want to start the chemo as soon as possible, but we have an appointment for a second opinion."

"We can set up the appointment and it can always be canceled if you decide to go somewhere else. It's wise to get a second opinion. And, if you like, you can have a tour of the treatment facility upstairs."

Brenda and I both nodded. "Yes, we'd like that. Thank you."

The reception area for the treatment facility reminded me of a typical hospital triage desk, but when a nurse guided us to the area behind the double doors, memories of my grandmother's house, minus the aroma of pasta and meatballs, overwhelmed me. Each patient sat in a separate room that contained an upholstered recliner, a wooden side table with a lamp that provided dim lighting, and one or two other chairs that I assumed were for a nurse and the patient's caregiver. I never pictured a chemotherapy facility as cozy and intimate as this one, and I liked it much more than where my parents and Lori had been treated.

I was also fond of Dr. Legare. Besides the fact that he was cute, I liked that he never dictated my care nor spoke with a condescending tone. He spoke softly, but firmly. He spoke with confidence, but he wasn't overconfident. I mean, I knew he couldn't promise me I'd survive as long as Aunt Angie, but he never made me believe I would die because of cancer either. He just seemed real. He seemed sincere.

I admit, I knew the reality of being faced with cancer, a life-threatening disease, but I prayed for a miracle, like all cancer patients probably do. As I listened to Dr. Legare's neutral tone and demeanor, I accepted that doctors are only human, and I knew this man would try his best to extend my life.

The second opinion came from an oncologist in Boston, who had been recommended to me by a coworker whom he'd treated for breast cancer a few years earlier. Some people believe they need to go to Boston for the best medical care, especially when it comes to cancer. I respect that opinion, but even now, I'm not sure I believe it or not. But who could pass up a day trip to Boston with her best friend? Okay, so we wouldn't have a day filled with spa treatments, shopping, and eating, but neither of us cared. Brenda and I both needed to tackle my health challenge together.

I don't remember if we managed to get lost on the way there or on the way home or both, but I do remember how close I came to peeing my pants in the front seat of Brenda's Mercedes. With each wrong turn, we laughed harder. We laughed instead of worrying about being late because neurotic (me) and more neurotic (Brenda) left Rhode Island two and half hours earlier for an appointment that should have taken us one hour, max. Navigating the hospital parking garage and patient registration took longer than expected. "See, it's a good thing we left home yesterday to get here," she said, and we both giggled.

Brenda and I were escorted into a room with two chairs facing a large wooden desk. When Dr. Clark entered the room, Brenda and I turned toward each other with wide eyes. A tall man with curly, disheveled black hair, he looked like a mad scientist who belonged in Frankenstein's laboratory. He reviewed my chart and recommended the same treatment as Dr. Legare had, so I wondered why I might choose to drive to Boston—and probably get lost every time—to see a mad scientist, when I could get the same medical treatment in Providence with bonus eye candy?

After I confirmed my original choice for an oncologist, I was able to spend some time preparing my emotions for chemotherapy and all its side effects. The support group for newly diagnosed patients had been scheduled before my first chemo treatment (just three weeks away), and I hoped the women would share some new ideas for coping with the many reactions I might experience. If Lori decided to attend a meeting, she would not be turned away from this group but would likely be assigned to the metastatic group for patients who were living through a recurrence of cancer—and that group met on a different day.

Lori had not wanted to attend either of the support groups and the facilitator reminded me to call Mickie, a woman who lived in the same town as Marc and me. I called Mickie on a Saturday. Her voice sounded sweet and caring. She seemed thrilled that I had contacted her and, without me asking, she told me what time she wanted to pick me up for the meeting that Monday evening.

I felt both anxious and excited about attending the meeting, and I left work early to avoid traffic as I drove through Providence. I wanted time to change my outfit and have a snack before Mickie arrived. Sophia sat with me while I stared out the window, waiting to see the car Mickie had described to me when we'd spoken. When she pulled into my driveway, I grabbed my purse and a sweater and met her outside. As soon as I saw Mickie up close, I confirmed that her eyes matched the voice I had heard on the phone—sweet and caring. Her face looked just like flawless white porcelain. As she drove us to the meeting, we found we were never at a loss for words.

Mickie had been diagnosed with breast cancer a year and half earlier and, although she hadn't needed chemotherapy, she knew several women in the group who would help me through it.

"So, tell me about you, Linda."

"Well, over the past four years my mother died of breast cancer, my sister was diagnosed with and treated for stage I breast cancer, my husband divorced me, my sister's cancer returned as stage IV, my father died, and now me."

Mickie gasped, patted my left knee with her right hand, and stared at me for a second. "My dear, I'm certain we're headed to the perfect place for you to find some peace."

Mickie and I were the first two participants to arrive for the meeting and, after the facilitator welcomed us, she poured each of us a cup of hot chamomile tea. I sat on the oversize couch, surrounded by fluffy pillows, colorful blankets, and more peace than I felt at the retreat. Soon, other women joined us—none of whom I had met before—and the facilitator opened the meeting by reminding us that we were in a safe and confidential place to share our innermost thoughts. I listened to each woman's story and became sad and angry to learn that so many of us were suffering, but at the same time I no longer felt isolated. When my turn arrived to introduce myself, I recited the same saga I had shared with Mickie earlier except this time my throat constricted before I spoke the words about my dad dying. As I shared each subsequent tragedy in my life, I relived the emotional pain as if it all had happened yesterday. And as I watched the eyes of my new friends widen while they listened to me, I saw their sadness, and I realized I had never intended to burden them with my troubles. I mean, they had their own pain and didn't need mine too, right?

I thought about how I had handled my emotions over the past four years. In the year and a half after my mother died, I struggled between being happy and sad. I had shared some of my feelings with my family and friends, but never fully opened up to any of them, not even Brenda. I guarded my own sadness to prevent everyone from worrying about me. And I never wanted anyone to see me happy and think that I wasn't grieving the loss of my mother or father, or that I wasn't sad that my sister was sick. I never knew it then, but now I realize I found it easier to keep my feelings to myself and withdraw from social situations.

Once I realized I wanted help and met my therapist, it seemed I had finally found an objective listener. I spoke, she listened—never showing judgment or emotions, like my friends and family sometimes had. I felt a little lighter each time I met Diane because I felt free to release my entire mental state with her. But I always felt our sessions were one-sided because although I benefited from seeing Diane, I felt guilty for not providing some sense of relief back to her.

During the support group, sitting among more than one objective listener, something inside me shifted. I shared my sad story and the full range of my emotions with complete strangers, and each time I described my emotional pain, the reality that those awful things had happened became a little bit clearer. With each point of clarity, I healed another piece of the hole in my heart. And then, for the first time, and unlike my sessions with Diane, every person described their own troubles—not only related to cancer, but about life, in general. As I listened and sensed my new friends were healing, too, the guilt I had felt with Diane subsided.

Mickie dropped me off at home. Though most newly diagnosed patients might feel discouraged, I only felt fortunate. The retreat had perfectly coincided with my lumpectomy, allowing much of my anxiety about the surgery to subside. That night my new friends and I created a space to talk openly about the fear and uncertainty that surrounded all of us, but more important, to share the strength and courage we all needed to survive.

Just two weeks before my first chemotherapy appointment my doctor ordered several blood tests, X-rays, a bone scan, and a MUGA, or a multigated acquisition, scan of my heart.

I had always hated needles and especially detested having my veins punctured for the purpose of drawing my blood. The sight of seeing my blood travel through a tube and collect in a glass vial made me nauseous and light-headed. But I needed to find a way to get over it because over the next twelve weeks my blood would be drawn constantly to monitor the level of side effects such as fatigue, bruising, and vulnerability to infections. If ever my blood counts fell below normal, my treatments would be postponed until my body healed, and that meant I had to wait longer to schedule my mastectomy.

After the blood tests, I had the MUGA scan. My mother and Lori had had this scan, but I never asked why until I needed one for myself. I found out that one of the chemotherapy drugs prescribed to me could be toxic to the heart muscle and could lead to heart failure. The MUGA scan measured the strength of my heart muscle before chemotherapy and then again after I finished my last treatment. I could drive myself home after the test, so I went alone.

When I arrived at the hospital, the woman at the information desk told me to follow the signs to nuclear medicine. I felt the same sick feeling as I did when I had to go to nuclear medicine before my lumpectomy. The technicians needed to inject me with radioactive chemicals to light up my sentinel node for the camera during surgery, but I had been sedated the last time. I wouldn't be sedated for this scan and suddenly I wished I had someone with me.

After I changed into a johnny, I sat in the waiting room with other patients wearing the same garb, although some johnnies were too small. A male technician called my name and asked me to follow him. He brought me into a room and asked me a bunch of questions about my heart and other medical conditions.

"No. No. No. Right, just breast cancer," I answered. That's right—no heart murmur, diabetes, or high blood pressure. Just breast cancer.

"How is this test done?" I asked.

"I'll inject you with a small amount of radioactive material. We call it a tracer because it binds to your red blood cells so the camera can see how oxygen travels through your heart." He took his time to explain.

My right leg began to twitch and maybe he recognized my blank stare as fear so he added, "Other than the small pinch while the IV is inserted, you won't feel a thing."

"Okay, I had no idea what to expect, and I really don't like needles."

"I understand. Me neither. I'll do my best. I promise." He smiled.

So, not only would needles be inserted to take blood out of me over the next twelve weeks, but I'd get needles for injections, too. My sister had to have a port inserted into her chest because the nurses frequently had issues accessing her veins after they'd collapsed from too much wear and tear. I could never accept that for myself. Having a port implanted into my chest only meant "Cancer is here to stay!" and I never wanted cancer as a welcomed guest in my body.

A week after the MUGA, and just one week before my first chemo treatment, my oncologist scheduled my first bone scan to confirm my stage I diagnosis and that the cancer had not spread to my bones, a fear I would always have because it had happened to my mother. The baseline bone scan would be reviewed throughout my ongoing breast cancer journey if we ever suspected the cancer had invaded my bones. This time, I wanted to know what to expect when I arrived at the hospital. Lori told me I would get injected with more radioactive chemicals, which explained why I needed to wait a week between the two scans. The tech would inject the chemicals and then I had to wait an hour for it to attach to my red blood cells before having the scan. Lori offered to come with me and we went out for lunch between the radioactive injection and the actual bone scan. I imagined people could see me glowing from the inside out.

The last two tests before starting chemo were the chest X-ray and a CAT scan of my liver. Besides bone and brain, liver and lung were the two other cozy places breast cancer liked to spread, another fear I would always have because that's where Lori's cancer had spread.

On the Monday before my first chemotherapy treatment, I learned the name of the primary nurse assigned to me. Having the same nurse take care of me each time added to the intimacy and it was another reason I liked the medical practice I had chosen. Jane asked me to come into the hospital before my first appointment for a chemotherapy orientation session. I thought, what is this, college or a new job? Then I thought, I always tried to be a good student and employee, and I certainly wanted to pass the chemotherapy test. So, I participated in the orientation even though I thought I knew everything I needed to know about chemotherapy from the experiences of my parents and Lori. Every three weeks—for me it would land on a Thursday—I needed to show up at the hospital, smile, sit in an oversize recliner, smile, get stuck with needles, smile, watch the medicine fill my veins, smile, and wait for the side effects to hit me. As long as my blood counts stayed at an acceptable level, I would endure this routine four times.

After completing all the medical tests and the chemotherapy orientation, and learning as much about what to expect during and after each treatment, I felt as ready as I could be for the next twelve weeks of life with chemotherapy.

Chapter 19

Go Get the Monsters

On the next to the last Thursday afternoon in September, less than two weeks before my thirty-seventh birthday, the day of my first chemotherapy appointment arrived. Marc had gone to work in the morning and returned home in time to encourage me to eat before we left for the hospital. Jane had recommended I have a light lunch before each treatment so I chose a crisp red apple and crackers with hummus. Marc opened the kitchen door to call Sophia inside, and she showed up at the kitchen door with a dead or maybe roughly beaten mouse. Maybe that was her way of saying, "Go get 'em, Mom," but I hadn't even started chemo and I already wanted to vomit.

Marc and I met Jane at the front desk. We followed her into our personal and cozy treatment room. We settled in for what we were told could be between two or three hours, depending on how I reacted to the chemotherapy and other drugs. Jane repeated some of the important reminders from the chemo orientation: "Remember, it may feel cold at first and then you might feel a burning sensation, but only briefly. You need to tell me if the burning persists, and I'll be watching the injection site for any signs of irritation, too."

"Okay." I bit my lower lip and obsessed about what could go wrong with the injection and which side effects I could encounter and when. I watched Jane put on her latex gloves, took a few deep breaths, and stared at Marc. "I just want to get this over with."

"I know. I'm here. You'll be done before you know it. You're a trooper."

Before I realized it, Jane had inserted the catheter into a vein on the back of my right hand and had already started to give me the anti-nausea drug. After that first dose of Compazine had finished she asked, "Okay, are we ready for the Adriamycin?"

"Yes, I actually do think I'm ready." I had done everything in my control to prepare for this moment. I still had a long road ahead of me, but felt fortunate to have Marc taking care of me and a team of friends and family sending positive and healing thoughts my way.

Adriamycin is thick and red. Adriamycin would make me pee pink. Adriamycin could make my skin burn and damage my heart. Adriamycin would make my hair fall out before my next birthday. Jane held a large plastic syringe filled with this bright red medicine and she would manually "push" it into my vein for five or so minutes. The next type of chemo contained in a plastic bag that hung from the metal pole behind me would slowly drip into the plastic tubing and flow into my body for one or two hours.

Marc sat in a chair to my right and the three of us counted down from three. "Three, two, one," and then Jane started to "push" the Adriamycin out of the syringe and into my body. Marc and I stared at the injection site as the thick red fluid left the syringe and flowed into my veins. I felt the urge to say, "Go get the monsters," and then Marc joined in, "Go get the monsters." Hearing this mantra filled me with excitement as I visualized the medicine flowing throughout my entire body and killing any cancer that it encountered.

Within a few minutes, my eyelids became very heavy and I just wanted to sleep. I'm not sure how long I napped, but when I woke up, I had to pee really badly.

"Well, hello there," Jane said. "How are you feeling?"

"Sleepy, but I really have to pee."

"No problem, you're almost done. Let me help you." Jane gathered all the tubes and wheeled the pole holding the bags of intravenous medicine behind me as she guided me to the bathroom.

When I returned, a woman was standing in my treatment room. She asked if I wanted a foot massage.

"Are you kidding?"

She shook her head. "No, I'm serious. It'll take ten or fifteen minutes."

"Absolutely. Thank you." I sat back down in my recliner to let a stranger rub my feet. I closed my eyes and dozed off again.

Thirty minutes later, Marc looked at the bag behind me and whispered, "It's done. You did it." I had completed my first chemotherapy treatment—and I had happy feet.

When Marc and I returned home, Sophia followed us into our bedroom and Marc tucked me into bed. Sophia jumped up on the bed and pranced over to my face and sniffed my hair. She walked around in circles by my feet before she plopped down and the two of us fell asleep.

I drove to work the following day, and for the next two weeks, I couldn't take my mind off all the side effects from the chemo and when each would rear its ugly head. After that first treatment, I obsessed over exactly when my hair would fall out. I examined my pillow when I woke up each morning. Because everyone loses hair every single day, I waited for the clumps. Sure enough, just like the nurses promised, on the fourteenth day following my first treatment, the clumps showed up while I showered before work. After catching the first wet chunk of my own hair with my fingertips, I stared at it and cried. I had tried to defy this side effect by using special shampoo I'd found online, but I knew I would lose my hair even despite my attempts, and yet, when the first blob fell out, I sobbed like a baby needing a diaper change.

My hairdresser recommended we cut my shoulder-length hair really short—like Halle Berry in *Monster's Ball*—to lessen the size of the clumps and minimize the sobbing. That haircut worked for a day or two, but I knew it wouldn't stop the inevitable from happening. Just like I wanted to decide my own medical decisions, I wanted to decide when my hair would fall out so I opted to shave it all off before it had the audacity to fall out on its own.

One Sunday, before Marc and I met some friends to watch Patriots football, I asked him to help me. "It's time to just shave it off."

"Are you sure?" he asked.

"Positive. It's going to fall out anyway, and I can't stand finding it everywhere. Let's do it." I bounced on my tippy toes like a little kid on Christmas morning.

We stood in front of the mirror in the guest bathroom and Marc used his electric razor to shave my hair off completely—not to a buzz cut, but bald. We both rubbed my naked head with our open palms and were surprised by the softness of my hairless head.

"Wow, your head is perfectly shaped. You're beautiful."

Even before my first chemo treatment, I had purchased a dozen bandanas in all different colors and designs to honor the upcoming holidays. I chose the red-white-and-blue one to wear that Sunday in honor of Tom Brady, and then Marc and I headed to our friends' house to watch the football game. Even though we all knew I'd lose my hair, none of us—including myself—were really prepared to see my bald head. I thought the best way for people to accept it and for me to feel like they were okay with it, they had to touch it. "Do you want to see it, touch it?" I asked. They both nodded.

Losing my hair had been the most emotional side effect of chemotherapy. I knew it would grow back, but it still sucked because I couldn't hide the fact that I had no hair. One Saturday after my first treatment, Lori and Brenda planned an excursion—which meant they included time for lunch—to a wig shop in nearby Massachusetts. I modeled several wigs, which actually helped me laugh through it instead of cry, and although I considered becoming a redhead, we found a wig similar to my previous hairstyle that matched my natural—I mean, my highlighted—okay, fine, my dyed blond hair color. I think we named it Hannah. I took Hannah with me to Nancy, my hairdresser, and much like she had done for my mother on the day of my wedding, she worked her magic on my new head of hair. I wore Hannah to work and when Marc and I went out to dinner, but I couldn't deal with the constant itch. When I realized I only wore Hannah to make everyone else feel comfortable with my appearance, I tossed her back into her cardboard box and shoved the box to the back of my closet.

Then, after my third chemo treatment, around Halloween, I went to my second retreat with the support group. A woman arrived to provide henna tattoos for the survivors. Most of the women asked for a tattoo on their ankle or shoulder, but I had a different request.

"Would you tattoo my head?"

"Wow. Sure. Of course."

I sat still while the artist tickled my scalp as she tattooed a vine of ivy leaves around my bald head. When she finished, I walked into the bathroom to look at myself in the mirror and saw a princess again. Okay, maybe not a princess, and more like Demi Moore in *G.I. Jane* after she had shaved her head before becoming the first woman to enter military training for the U.S. Navy Seals.

At home, I loved the freedom of being bald, but whenever I went out in public, I covered my head with a festive bandana. Because I anticipated being bald through the winter, I bought pretty fleece hats with matching scarves and gloves. My emotions were always challenged when I saw the reactions from strangers who looked at me with sad eyes. I wanted to shout, "I'm bald, I'm not dying," but I just bowed my head and kept my mouth closed. And even today, when I see a bald person whom I suspect may have cancer, I only offer a smile and hope they see courage on my face.

Losing my hair was emotional, but the most painful side effect—the one that people would never actually see—was the forest of nasty ulcers inside my mouth and down my throat. If you've ever had a canker, multiply the pain by one thousand. I swear the smaller the sore, the more pain it produced. The doctor prescribed a thick pink Pepto-Bismol–like liquid called Magic Mouthwash, which performed absolutely no magic on me whatsoever. It numbed the pain for a short period of time, but it never eliminated the sores. I desperately needed relief so I searched online and found something called ORA5, a brown syrupy liquid that came in a set of three small dark brown glass vials. I applied a small amount directly on the sore using a Q-tip and the ulcer disappeared within hours. Now that's magic!

And the most unpredictable side effect after chemotherapy?—drumroll, please—the nausea. Like most—okay, all—people, I'm not fond of nausea or vomiting. My sister vomited after every one of her intravenous chemotherapy treatments and I convinced her that vomiting meant the chemo must be doing its job. And as much as I wanted to believe that theory for myself, after just a few days with constant nausea I turned to acupuncture to prevent nausea and vomiting. After one treatment with the acupuncturist, the nausea stopped and I never had the urge to vomit.

Most days I had my physical side effects under control, but I struggled to maintain a positive mental attitude. Every three weeks, after chemotherapy, I watched my favorite funny movie of all time, *Ferris Bueller's Day Off*, because it always made me laugh. And I laid with Sophia because she epitomized peace and calmness as she purred and slept in a curled-up ball. When I craved my mother's touch and voice as she rubbed my back while singing "You Are the Sunshine of My Life," I felt better knowing that she never had to witness my breast cancer journey. If I caught myself asking why I had to get sick at all, I reminded myself that we hardly ever get the reason with the thing. No matter how sad I felt, I always pulled myself back into happy land at the sight of Marc, who continued to protect and care for me like no other man I had ever known.

Before I knew it, twelve weeks had passed. With Thanksgiving the following week, I had so much to be thankful for this year. Because I had never missed a treatment, I headed into my oncologist's office eager to grab my chemotherapy diploma.

"You've done so well, Linda. You've tolerated the chemo every three weeks as scheduled. Your blood work looks great. So, if you're up to it . . . I'd like you to have two more treatments."

I stared at him, and at first I pouted with disappointment and defeat because I wanted the chemo to end. I mean, really? I tolerated all the side effects and measured my progress toward completing the chemo treatments based on there being only four cycles and now he wanted to move the target. Did he want me to have more chemo because I hadn't vomited yet? I realized that two additional treatments would provide me with extra insurance that the cancer would not return. And I still needed to find a willing and able breast surgeon to perform my mastectomy as well as a plastic surgeon to reconstruct my boobs. If I could continue to control my emotions from losing my hair, the mouth ulcers, the nausea, *and* maintain a positive mental attitude, I saw no harm in having two more treatments.

"If you're willing to proceed, I'd like to reevaluate your heart function with another MUGA scan before we make a final decision."

"Okay, if my heart is up for it, so is my head . . . I guess."

Chapter 20

Never Give Up

Not knowing my heart could stand more chemo, Marc had purchased concert tickets to celebrate my last treatment.

"It's okay. Thank you! Honestly, every day is a celebration now," I said.

Marc had been so thoughtful to surprise me. As excited as I was to see John Mayer live, the bigger surprise may have been that I finally puked—and not from the four cycles of chemotherapy, but from drinking too much beer.

Two weeks after Thanksgiving, I endured my fifth chemotherapy treatment and Marc and I looked forward to ringing in the New Year knowing I had just one more treatment to go. As the chemo continued to build up in my system, so did the two most uncontrollable side effects: fatigue and the risk of getting an infection. I always had chemo on a Thursday and up until the third treatment I had been able to return to my office the next day. After the fourth treatment, I needed Friday and the weekend to rest before I could return to work. The weaker I felt, the more risk I had of catching a cold, flu, or other illness. By the fifth treatment, my boss understood the need for me to work at home and he approved my request for remote access. This allowed me to work from home when I felt up to it. Instead of beating myself up about being so tired, I thought about what my mother had always told me in high school. On the weekend mornings when I stayed in bed until after noon, instead of my mother nagging me about my laziness, she always supported me. "Your body must need the rest," she would say.

Now more than ever, my body needed the rest to recover after each treatment so I could finish the search for my breast and plastic surgeons. A friend whom I had met through Brenda had an obsession—or maybe we should call it a hobby—of researching the top doctors in the area and finding the best in every field. She highly recommended I meet Dr. Maureen Chung, a very petite woman, about my age, with dark, straight shoulder-length hair and dark, kind eyes. In the past, when I met someone who talked as fast as she had, I stopped listening. But when I heard Dr. Chung's quick and articulate style of speaking, I only sensed her excitement and passion toward her profession.

For whatever reason, I went alone to the appointment. I sat on the exam table and Dr. Chung stared at me with concern after she glanced at the pathology report I had sent ahead of time. "Linda, tell me about your history."

"You mean aside from my own diagnosis, right?"

She smiled and rolled her stool closer to the exam table as she continued to stare at me.

"Okay, are you ready for this?" I asked as I raised my eyebrows.

"Yes, of course."

I took a deep breath and sighed. "My mom died four years ago from breast cancer that had spread to her bones. She was sixty-nine."

"I'm sorry."

"Thank you. My dad died six months ago from lymphoma. Two of my dad's sisters had breast cancer. One died many years ago and one is still living. She's eighty-three years old."

"That's what I like to hear." She made a note on a blank piece of paper she held in place on top of my pathology report.

I took another deep breath and continued, but my eyes filled up with tears. "My sister, she's nine years older than me, was rediagnosed with metastatic breast cancer in her liver and lungs a little over a year ago."

"How is she doing, Linda?"

"She's been on a different form of chemo ever since the recurrence, but she's a trooper."

"That's good to hear. Okay, any other history?"

"I don't think so. I have two brothers, but as far as I know, they are fine." I noticed my slouched back and sat up straighter. "I want a double mastectomy and the surgeon who did my lumpectomy was not enthusiastic about that so I'm here for a second opinion. . . ." I paused for a few seconds and realized I only wanted to know one thing. "What would you do, Dr. Chung, if you were me?"

She stood up from her seat. While I still sat on the exam table, her eyes were at the same level as mine. She moved her face closer to mine and with no hesitation she answered, "We're doing a double mastectomy. End of story."

I smiled and covered my mouth with the palm of my right hand. I wanted to sob with relief because I had finally found a professional and kind breast surgeon who agreed to do what I wanted to do. "Thank you. You have no idea how relieved I am."

Brenda and I had done some research online, and I guess I had suspected my decision to have a mastectomy would be a little bit more complicated than just "hey, I want to have a mastectomy," but I never anticipated all the options the doctor presented to me. She explained the different types of surgeries—simple or total, modified, radical, modified radical—and all the techniques that could be used with each—skin sparing, nipple sparing, total skin sparing—and my head started to spin. Who knew that trading in and buying new boobs could be as complicated as buying a car? My mother had chosen not to have reconstruction at the same time as her mastectomy and I knew for sure that I wanted my breast reconstruction (new car) the same day as my mastectomy (trade-in).

"You want reconstruction, yes, and at the same time?" she asked.

"Yes and yes."

"Like the mastectomy, there are many options to consider for the reconstruction, too. It's critical that we work with your plastic surgeon to agree on the best approach."

"I'm still searching for a plastic surgeon to perform the reconstruction. Can you recommend any you have worked with previously?" I told her the name of the doctor with whom I had already made an appointment and my propensity toward a second, and maybe a third opinion, before I made a decision.

"Let me think about it and I'll call you with a couple more names."

The following week, Brenda came with me to meet the first plastic surgeon. A few of the women in my support group had recommended him. "He's the best. He creates breasts beautiful enough for naked models." We sat in the waiting room for two hours without ever being approached by the receptionist. Neither of us minded being ignored because we were chatting and filling out mountains of paperwork, but when Brenda checked her watch she gasped. "Lin, we've been sitting here for two hours. I'm so sorry, but I have to go pick up Matt."

"That's fine. I'm ready to leave myself. This is ridiculous." Just then a nurse opened the door and called me in. Brenda couldn't stay so I met the surgeon alone.

I hugged Brenda. "I'll call you tonight." I followed the nurse into an exam room. I don't remember if the nurse weighed me or checked my blood pressure, but she handed me a johnny to change into and only said, "Opening in the front." The vibe that I had received over the past two hours coupled with this nurse's poor attitude indicated this appointment would be a royal waste of my time, but I decided to wait for the best breast plastic surgeon in Rhode Island to enter the room.

I had barely closed my johnny when the doctor walked in without knocking. "I'm sorry if I smell like an Italian grinder. I needed to finish my dinner," he blurted out as I caught a whiff of raw onions and provolone cheese.

He asked me to open my johnny and then, without asking, took a picture of my chest. "The before shot. Your face will not be in it." He winked at me.

Although crude and rude, I thought the photo must be part of the process for plastic surgery. We discussed my family history and I told him I wanted bilateral reconstruction.

"Cancer on the left side only, right?" he asked as he read my chart.

"Yes, but my mother died after a single mastectomy and my sister has been rediagnosed after only having a . . ."

"You know breasts are important to men, don't you?" he interrupted.

I blinked several times and took a deep breath. "What good are my breasts if I'm dead?" I closed the johnny and jumped off the exam table.

He started to describe the surgery he would perform if I were his wife. I turned my back to him and gathered my clothes that lay on the chair where Brenda should have been sitting had this guy honored his patients as much as his food.

"I'm not interested." I glared at him over my right shoulder, which pretty much gave him the sign to leave the room so I could get dressed.

I walked toward my car in the hospital parking garage and fumbled with my keys. I sat on my seat, closed my eyes, and let my head fall back on the headrest while I clenched the steering wheel. I growled and then sobbed. I struggled with being disgusted and scared. Did the best breast plastic surgeon just insult and scare me to death? How completely insensitive could one person be? Maybe I misunderstood the recommendations. Maybe he specialized in breast augmentation for perfect models, not breast reconstruction for women who have had breast cancer. Big difference.

While I waited for my change from the parking garage attendant, I dialed Marc at work. "How'd it go, honey?" he asked.

I drove out of the garage and cried, "We waited over two hours. Brenda had to leave so I saw him alone. He told me breasts are important to men!"

"Really? Are you kidding me? I would have gone with you had I known you'd be alone. What a jerk."

"I know. We didn't know we'd wait two hours for the jerk. How am I going to find another plastic surgeon that will help me?"

"Don't worry, you'll find another surgeon. Trust me." He had no way of knowing I would find a plastic surgeon I trusted to perform my breast reconstruction, but he turned out to be right.

Never believe anyone who tells you that all surgeons, especially plastic surgeons, are arrogant. After my diagnosis, when it came to searching for my team of doctors, the most important lesson I learned, or rather confirmed because I hadn't settled for the first surgeon I'd met when I needed back surgery either, is that there are absolutely no limits to the number of medical opinions a patient should seek. Keep searching and interviewing until you find the one doctor you "click" with—for me, the doctor must be brilliant, competent, full of compassion, and completely lacking a superiority complex.

Shortly after my appointment with Dr. Chung, she called me to recommend Dr. Paul Liu. Although she hadn't worked with him directly, she had heard nothing but good things about him.

Lori sat next to me in Dr. Liu's waiting room as I filled out yet another set of patient information forms. She scanned the room and pointed out the various ailments that had brought the diverse patients to see this one plastic surgeon. I worried he may not be the best breast surgeon if he performed other types of surgery, but I had so much respect for Dr. Chung and I valued her recommendation.

Lori and I followed a nurse into an exam room where she checked my weight and blood pressure. She handed me a johnny. "You only need to remove your clothes from the waist up and put on this johnny, opening goes in the front, and the doctor will be here in a few minutes, okay?" Already a completely different experience from the previous jerk.

The nurse left the room and I jumped off the exam table.

"So far, so good." I removed my clothes and handed them to Lori. "Not exactly the same as trying on clothes during one of our shopping sprees, huh?"

"We need one of those soon."

Dr. Liu knocked on the door just as I sat back on the exam table.

"Linda? Hi, I'm Dr. Liu." He was a jovial man with a huge smile.

"Hi, it's nice to meet you. This is my sister, Lori." I pointed to Lori and he shook her hand.

He held my records in his hand. "So, Dr. Chung gave me a little background and has agreed to perform your double mastectomy. And I know we're here to talk about reconstruction, but tell me what's going on."

I saw the anguish on his face when I recited my family history and then I told him my own course of treatment. "I had a lumpectomy in August, and I'm currently having chemo. I want to have this surgery as soon as possible after I finish my last two treatments."

"Man, you both have had a lot happen to you. I agree with Dr. Chung's surgery recommendation, and I'm happy to talk about your options for reconstruction."

The doctor examined my chest and abdomen while he explained the reconstruction options available to me. With traditional saline implants, he would implant and partially fill the tissue expanders on the same day as the mastectomy. After my incisions healed, he would continue to add saline to the expanders to form the pocket the permanent implant would ultimately occupy. This weekly expansion would occur over several months until the pocket could accommodate his recommended C-cup-size implants, at which point he would swap the expander for the permanent implant and create nipples.

"Is a C cup enough to ensure my stomach is never bigger than my boobs?"

I wanted a separation between my boobs and my stomach when I sat down. But part of me wanted to go bigger just because. Hey, I had breast cancer and removed my breasts so why not go for the Dolly Partons? But just like when I had thought I wanted red hair and ended up with a blond wig, I realized I only wanted to be me again.

Then he explained the tram flap procedure. He would use skin, fat, and muscle from the top of my back or my stomach (because even though I had lost weight since my diagnosis, my abdomen still had enough extra fat for him to use) to tunnel it to my chest to create a breast. He confirmed what I had heard about the long-term complications from this procedure, which included abdominal hernias and hardening of the tissue due to poor blood supply. Some women I had spoken to had confirmed the painful recovery they experienced from the flap procedure and, after confirming the possible side effects, I decided I wanted the traditional implants. And Lori and I agreed: I wanted Dr. Liu to reconstruct my breasts.

"I prefer the traditional implants, and honestly, I don't care about nipples right now."

"I think that's the best choice for you, Linda. We usually wait two months after a patient's last chemotherapy before undergoing surgery. I'll speak to Dr. Chung again to coordinate our schedules. And, since she is considered the primary surgeon and the surgery will be done at her hospital, I will need to apply for surgical privileges there."

"Oh, is that a problem? I mean, could your application be rejected?"

"No, it's really just a formality with paperwork, and I'm happy to do it."

Once again, just like when I had found my oncologist and breast surgeon, finding Dr. Liu provided me with a another life-saving sigh of relief. I thought back to the moment I first heard my own "it's cancer," and the unbalanced mixture of anger and fear I struggled with ever since. As we headed into the crazy Christmas season of last-minute shopping and dinner preparations, I only felt more blessed because I had discovered the final member of my medical trifecta. Finding the surgeons to perform what I considered as the most significant body transformation of my life gave me the clarity I never thought I'd find after being diagnosed with breast cancer.

I remembered Christmas Eve five years ago, the day I knew I had met the bravest woman I had ever known—my mother—when she stopped chemotherapy so she could live before she died. I didn't know it then, but I had survived through my anger and my fear because my mother had taught me to be courageous.

With my mother's strength, I pushed away any thoughts of defeat, jumped into my project manager role, and tried my best to ensure the optimal solution. I planned. I assembled a team. I assessed risk. I analyzed options. With chemotherapy coming to an end in just a few weeks, I had no time to wallow in self-pity if I wanted to be prepared for the next phase: Tamoxifen and new, healthy boobs.

Chapter 21

Bye Bye Boobies, Bye Bye

Marc and I saw Jane for my last chemotherapy treatment two days after New Year's Day. I watched the chemo drip from the hanging plastic bag for the very last time and thought, Bye-bye, thanks for killing all my cancer. I waited for the anti-nausea meds and saline fluid to finish before I claimed my personal victory. I had finished eighteen weeks of chemotherapy, blood tests, and oncology appointments, and I believed all the monsters had died. Jane removed the catheter. "Don't take this the wrong way, Jane, but I hope I never see you again." I smiled.

"I understand, but I do hope you will visit—I mean, just visit—whenever you're here to see Dr. Legare."

"Of course." I hugged her and never wanted to let go. "I can't thank you enough for being the best nurse on the planet."

A week later, I sat on the exam table waiting for Dr. Legare to arrive for my post-chemotherapy follow-up appointment. He walked in the room and shook my hand. "How are you feeling?" he asked.

"Other than being tired, I feel fine."

He reviewed my recent blood tests and congratulated me for finishing the extra chemotherapy. "You did great, Linda. Your blood counts look great, and I'm certain your body will continue to recover from the fatigue."

He agreed with my surgeons' plan to schedule my mastectomy and reconstruction in March so my white blood cell counts had sufficient time to return to normal. Both of my surgeons recommended I not have radiation. But I still had to make a decision about Tamoxifen.

"Have you made a decision about taking the Tamoxifen? I'd like to start that right away."

Of all my treatment decisions, I struggled with Tamoxifen the most. I mean, I felt lucky that it was an option for my type of cancer, but I still found it difficult to accept that I needed to swallow a pill to prevent cancer from growing in my body again. I feared the possibility of my cancer returning while taking the drug, like it had for Lori. And I thought about how my mother's cancer had grown again within months of her finishing her prescription. But most of all, I feared the side effects I may encounter. I had stopped menstruating less than a month after my first chemotherapy treatment and I had experienced a few mild hot flashes, but Tamoxifen could present more menopausal side effects, like mood swings and weight gain, especially in my stomach. Although five years seemed like an eternity, I thought about my mother's strength again—and that she had taken Tamoxifen for ten years—and I knew what I had to do. I just couldn't be sure how Marc would react to me in full-blown menopause.

Since I had been diagnosed, Marc and I had become less sexually intimate. He claimed he was afraid of hurting me after the lumpectomy. And then the chemotherapy left me exhausted and uninterested in sex. Despite both of our excuses, we always kissed, hugged, and told each other "I love you." I never noticed it at the time, but as I look back at it now I realize that once Marc heard a mastectomy offered no increased chance of survival, he never fully jumped on the mastectomy bandwagon with me. I don't think he ever understood or appreciated my choice of aggressive treatments. However, he still gave me all the attention and care I needed throughout the chemotherapy so I assumed our relationship had the foundation it needed to endure the full impact of my illness.

"Yes, I decided to take Tamoxifen, although I'm still not sure why. I'm really worried about all the side effects."

"I understand, Linda. We'll monitor all of your symptoms and work to limit or alleviate them if they occur."

I picked up the prescription on my way home. The bottle stayed untouched on my nightstand for at least a week before I fully accepted my own decision to take the drug. I persuaded myself to swallow the tiny white pill by believing that it would protect me from cancer returning for at least the next five years and then rationalizing that the sooner I started, the sooner I'd finish. But really, I thought, January 2008 cannot come soon enough.

Just as I had feared, my hot flashes increased after just a week of taking the drug and within a month the number on the bathroom scale had increased, too. I was still taking the happy pill, prescribed by my primary care physician to combat my depression, but when my oncologist suggested I switch to a different antidepressant that could also decrease the hot flashes, I agreed to try it. Within a month after taking the new antidepressant, the hot flashes seemed less intense and less frequent and my moods seemed to stabilize.

But my weight stayed up. Since I had started the Tamoxifen my stomach felt like a bottomless pit. I tended to overeat and I had been retaining more water than usual. It had been more than a year since I had completed the sixty-mile breast cancer walk and although I tried to walk several times a week since then, regular exercise had not become a habit for me. The more I complained about my weight, the more my friends and family told me I looked great, especially after everything that had happened to me. With all of these negatives against me, plus the lingering fatigue from chemotherapy, I had no idea how to stop gaining weight. And although other women in my support group had experienced similar weight gain, they convinced me not to worry about it.

Instead, we focused on the challenges within our control. One of the women had scheduled her double mastectomy around the same time as mine. During one of our meetings, the facilitator posed a question to both of us: "Would you be interested in having a breast cast?"

I looked at my friend and shrugged my shoulders. "I don't know, what is it?" I asked the facilitator.

"It's an amazing physical and spiritual experience and, in the end, you have a permanent cast of your breasts before you undergo your surgery." She stood up from the couch. "Let me get mine so I can show you."

She returned with a colorful cast of her own torso. "The best part is being able to decorate it afterward. It can be very healing for you and for those who see how proudly you display it."

"Wow, I'd love to do that." I remembered how the henna tattoo around my bald head helped me embrace and heal the emotional pain of losing my hair. I thought the breast cast could help me accept my decision to have a double mastectomy. And I would never lose touch with the shape of my natural breasts.

I shared my plan with Marc.

"That seems weird. What will you do with it?"

"I don't know. I want to decorate it and then maybe we could hang it in our bathroom. . . . Other people rarely use that bathroom so we'd be the only ones to see it."

One night the following week, my friend and I had a private session to create our breast casts. I felt peaceful surrounded by dim lighting, the smell of incense, and the sound of soft instrumental music. First, we applied a layer of petroleum jelly all over our own breasts and torso to protect our skin. After the wet, messy plaster of Paris had dried, I brought my artwork home.

Marc lay on the couch and ignored my return, but Sophia met me at the door. "Hey, Sophia." I blew her several kisses. She followed me into the living room where I carried my breast cast and stood on the side of the couch, near Marc's feet. I held the cast up over Marc's body while he stared at the TV.

"Look, here it is."

"Eeoww, is it dry?"

"Of course, touch it." I walked in front of the couch and attempted to sit but he never moved his feet to make room for me.

"I'd rather not, thanks, it's weird." To this day, no one has ever hurt my feelings as much as Marc did at that moment. I had been trying to come to terms with losing my breasts the best way I knew how and he had no compassion at all.

"Maybe because it's not decorated?"

"Yeah, maybe." He called for Sophia and turned his attention back to the TV.

I walked upstairs and placed the undecorated cast on the carpet in a corner of the spare bedroom. I sat across from it on a chair and stared at my sculpture—the natural shape of my breasts and abdomen—and felt the tears filling my eyes as I envisioned what my new body would look like in less than two weeks.

The night before my surgery, I sat up in my bed with Sophia curled up in her signature ball and sleeping by my feet. Marc watched TV in the living room downstairs. As I rubbed the soft peach fuzz that had grown on my head within the past month, I wrote in my journal. I had started writing in this journal the day I had endured the agonizing breast biopsy in my surgeon's office. After I jotted down the date, the way I began every journal entry, I wrote the first word: "peaceful." I believed I had no control over being diagnosed with breast cancer, but I always had control of my treatment options. After having my mother rediagnosed four weeks before my wedding, seeing her whittle away and die within two years, and then watching my sister endure chemo for most of the past four years, I had to do everything I could to prevent my cancer from returning. I had my mother's strength, my father's courage, and my sister's support to pull me through a surgery that many medical professionals and critics still considered a radical choice. I turned off my bedside lamp, fluffed up my pillow without disturbing Sophia, and curled up in the fetal position. As I shut my eyes the night before I would have both my breasts removed, at the age of thirty-six, I felt sure I had made the right decision.

In the shower the next morning I shampooed and rinsed my hair three times, knowing I wouldn't be able to wash it again for at least three days. And, unlike after my lumpectomy, Marc wouldn't be home to wash my hair in the sink or tend to my every need. Shortly after I had received my surgery date, Marc received an invitation from his primary vendor to tour its manufacturing plant in Germany. He scheduled his flight for one week after my mastectomy. Marc had been working tons of overtime to meet the construction deadlines for the school's new "green" certified dormitory, and this vendor provided the high-efficiency boilers and the solar heating panels. Although I had hoped Marc would choose to stay home and take care of me, I encouraged him to take the trip because I felt proud of him and his accomplishments. Between the visiting nurse, my sister, and Mickie, I knew there would be plenty of caregivers at my side.

Marc and I arrived at the hospital and were almost immediately escorted into a pre-op room. I removed my favorite velour sweat suit and changed into a thin white johnny with faded blue flowers and an opening in the back. Marc sat beside me as the nurse inserted a catheter and started the saline fluids. The operating room nurse came in to introduce herself, and the anesthesiologist visited to confirm any allergies I had and explain the procedure for putting me "under." I tried not to get annoyed as each of these hospital workers separately reviewed the same exact details of my medical history. Better to be safe than sorry.

And then the real woman and man of the next few hours arrived: Dr. Chung and Dr. Liu. To see them both in front of me, smiling and energetic, set my mind at ease and reminded me why I had chosen them in the first place. Marc met them both for the first time and I worried whether he liked them or not. Dr. Chung briefly explained the mastectomy procedure to me again, using a black pen to mark her targets, and then Dr. Liu used a red pen to explain how he intended to reconstruct my breasts.

"Just to confirm, we're not reconstructing your nipples today, right, Linda?" Dr. Liu asked.

"That's right. You said I can always decide to have nipples later, right?"

"That's right. Okay, then, we'll see you after the surgery." Dr. Liu and Dr. Chung headed to the operating room, or the bathroom, or maybe the cafeteria to have breakfast before my surgery.

"Do you like them, honey?"

"Yeah, they seem nice. You're in good hands." As I look back now, it felt like Marc was brushing his hands of me—giving me over to the surgeons and leaving the country.

And so there we had it. Before the nurse wheeled me away to the operating room I looked down at my chest one last time, ran my fingers over the black and red pen marks, pictured the sculpture of my breasts I had waiting for me at home, and thought, Bye-bye, boobies, bye-bye, Marc.

Chapter 22

A Chilly Celebration

I opened my eyes and saw my sister sitting in a chair reading a book by the window. "How are you feeling?" she asked.

"Cold." I scanned the rest of the room, looking for Marc.

"He just went to get some water. He'll be right back. The surgery went really well." My sister walked to the side of my bed and touched my right hand.

"What about the drains? How many are there?"

"You don't have any at all. He didn't use them." Lori smiled.

One of my friends had compared the postsurgery pain to having a burning hot and heavy grate from a barbeque on my chest, yet all I worried about was having to empty surgical drains filled with blood and other fluid after surgery.

"Yay," I whispered.

I looked down at my chest and saw a small bump from postsurgery swelling and bandages where my natural C-cup breasts should have been, but I felt nothing. Marc walked in the room, followed by a nurse.

"I think I'm going to be sick," I said.

The nurse grabbed a pink plastic bedpan just in time for me to vomit into it. Marc walked to the window and looked outside while Lori sat back down in the chair as the nurse rubbed my back. "It's okay. This is normal from the anesthesia."

But it didn't feel normal to be sick for the next two hours. Finally, the nurse asked my doctor if she could try a different pain medication. "I think you could be allergic to morphine."

I looked at Marc and Lori. "I'm really tired." I thought it would be rude if I fell asleep while they visited.

"I know. Close your eyes and rest. I'll come back in the morning," Lori said.

Marc kissed my forehead. "Rest. I'll see you tomorrow."

The next morning, I was feeling so much better when Dr. Chung came to visit. "You look great. The surgery went really well. I think you'll be very happy with the results."

I smiled and I looked at my chest. "When will I be able to see for myself?"

"Probably not until next week, but I just received the pathology on the tissue I removed from both breasts, Linda. Completely negative. Clean. There was no other cancer on either side." She smiled.

For a split second I thought, so I never had to remove them? But then I answered my own silly question. Of course I had to remove my breasts so cancer could never return. And the fact that the tissue in both breasts tested "clean" like my lymph nodes only reassured me that the extra cycles of chemotherapy had completely destroyed any cancer in my body.

That afternoon, I received bouquets of flowers from Marc, Frankie, Lori, Cynthia, Brenda, and Arthur. Part of me wished they had all pitched in for one bouquet instead of six, but the little spoiled brat I still had in me loved the attention.

When Marc returned to my room, the nurse handed me a gift card that had a stork on the envelope. "Seriously, this can't be for me. There must be a mistake." I knew most women came to this hospital to have their babies delivered and assumed the card must be for another patient.

"No, it's yours, Linda. It's just a standard envelope at the hospital," the nurse said.

My friend, Bob —whom I had walked with in the sixty-mile breast cancer walk more than a year ago—and his wife, Susan, had ordered a "Stork Dinner" for Marc and I to enjoy because they were away and couldn't visit me in the hospital. I giggled when I shared the card with Marc, but didn't feel much like eating steak or drinking wine just yet.

"You can order it for lunch, too. I think you'll still be here tomorrow afternoon, at least."

I looked at Marc and shrugged. "What do you think? Can you be here for lunch tomorrow?"

"Sure. That sounds great."

The next day, Marc and I ate filet mignon for lunch by candlelight. My pain medication prevented me from drinking the red wine, but Marc enjoyed it. About four hours later, he drove me—and all my flowers—home.

I smiled as Sophia greeted us at the door, followed me upstairs to our bedroom, and jumped on top of the bed. I pulled back the covers and slowly climbed into bed while Marc propped four pillows behind my back, neck, and head. Although a terribly uncomfortable position for sleeping, sitting up a little helped lessen the weight of the heavy barbeque grate on my chest. I just loved my own bed and loved my purring kitty cat even more.

About a week after my surgery, with Marc in Germany, Lori stood beside me in front of the mirror in the guest bathroom—the same mirror that revealed my shaved head just five months earlier. "Here goes." I removed the bandages covering my new breasts for the first time. Having the mastectomy caused me to lose all feeling in my breasts, and although I still sensed some pressure, Lori twitched more than I did while the tape came off. And then, there they were—two small mounds of skin, like the buds that formed on my chest when I was nine years old, except this time, instead of nipples, each perfectly round bud sported a three-inch straight incision in its center.

"Wow, other than being tiny and, well, having no nipples, they look pretty good, I guess." I looked at Lori.

"Wow, is right. The incisions are smaller than I expected. I mean the scars will fade in no time." Lori agreed.

My sister came with me every week and watched as Dr. Liu injected a large syringe full of saline into each of my temporary boobs. The tissue expanders would expand the skin and chest wall muscles in order to make room for my permanent breast implants. I think the procedure looked worse to Lori than it felt to me; I sensed the pressure on my chest and sometimes experienced shortness of breath, but never experienced any pain.

After three months of expanding my skin to create new breasts and, of course, a lumpectomy, chemotherapy, and a double mastectomy, I could finally see light at the end of the tunnel. After Dr. Liu had finished expanding my skin to accommodate the size of my new boobs (I agreed a C cup would make me happy), he wanted my breasts to rest before he swapped the expanders for the permanent implants. He gave me the okay to travel and I knew I wanted to book the trip of a lifetime to celebrate my survival.

Besides Vegas, Marc and I had taken a tropical trip to the Dominican Republic, but my body craved crisp and refreshing air after absorbing so much anesthesia and chemotherapy, so we decided to take a cruise to Alaska. My body also craved physical affection which, aside from a quick kiss and an occasional hug, Marc had still not given me since I had been diagnosed. I thought being on vacation might encourage, well, vacation sex.

In mid-June, while most people were anticipating the arrival of summer by switching their closets and drawers from winter to summer clothes, we packed two suitcases full of jeans, sweaters, boots, and long johns. Although my hair had grown to a length that just barely covered my head, I packed my colorful fleece hats and matching scarves. And since my body—mostly my midsection and butt—had grown, too, I packed jeans that were two sizes bigger than the ones I had worn last year.

We left Rhode Island and traveled an entire day before reaching Seattle and setting our eyes on the new ship, the Star Princess, for the first time. Marc had researched the enormous ship online and learned it measured 900 feet long, 200 feet high, and 160 feet wide. It held almost 2,600 passengers and 1,200 crew members. My jaw dropped open at the site of the ship's ornate interior. The main and central lobby had a three-story spiral staircase, mirrors everywhere, marble floors, gold and glass fixtures, and sparkling chandeliers.

I knew our cabin would be small and we wouldn't spend too much time in it, but I couldn't wait to check out our view from the balcony, unpack, and, well, see if I might get more than a kiss or a hug. "Let's go see the cabin." I smiled.

"Let's get a cocktail first." Marc took off to search for the best bar onboard. He found a table on an outdoor deck, overlooking one of the many pools. "Wait here, I'll go get us a drink. What do you want? Oh, never mind, I'll get us frozen mudslides."

Marc and I disagreed with each other from the moment we boarded the ship. He had always struggled with relaxing and he only stayed still if he watched a movie with lots of action. I admired his sense of adventure and willingness to travel, especially because my ex-husband, Dean, had neither. And although I appreciated that Marc always had to be first in line to find the best spot to snap a photograph or the best table at a restaurant or the best seat at an outdoor concert, I never appreciated being left alone when he walked ten steps ahead of me. I knew the photos he captured from this trip would be worth the rush to the railing on the top deck or front seat of the theater, but since being diagnosed with breast cancer, I only wanted to live in the moment and savor all the sites together.

After we finished our mudslides, we found our luggage outside the door to our cabin. Marc unlocked the door, grabbed both suitcases, and I followed him inside. We both walked past the closets and the bed to stare at the view from the sliding glass door. He opened the door and we stepped onto our balcony. I leaned against the railing, looked from left to right. "Wow, this is amazing." Granted, we overlooked the port of Seattle, but I imagined the view of open ocean and glaciers when we reached Alaska.

I walked back inside to unpack and shower before dinner while Marc remained on the balcony with his camera. It took me no time to get dressed and ready these days since I only needed to apply hair gel and I didn't need a blow dryer. I waited on the balcony while Marc unpacked, showered, and dressed for dinner. "Ready?" he asked.

We had chosen the later seating time for dinner, so we enjoyed a cocktail on the top deck as we watched the ship set sail before we headed to the main dining room. After dinner, I stared at one slot machine or another while Marc played blackjack in the casino into the early morning. When we finally headed back to the cabin, we both fell asleep as soon as our heads hit the pillows.

We spent the first full day of our vacation at sea as we headed to the first port of call, Ketchikan, where we had planned a group kayaking excursion. The weather had been warmer than either of us had expected so we bought T-shirts in the small town and stuffed our coats and sweaters into Marc's backpack. I had only kayaked once before in a double kayak, but Marc convinced the guides I could kayak on my own. I felt safe enough on my own since we all stayed pretty close to each other, but I never anticipated how tired I would feel. After three hours of paddling, spotting several bald eagles and searching for but not seeing any bears, I looked forward to reboarding the ship. After hot showers, we relaxed before dinner, and I became more excited for the excursion we had planned for the third day.

The next morning, Marc and I disembarked from the ship in Juneau, boarded a bus with twenty or so other passengers, and within an hour we had arrived at a small heliport. We all marched into one room of a small rustic cabin-like structure and listened to a brief safety overview before being fitted with our glacier boots and headsets. Our assigned pilot walked us to our very own helicopter. My first ever helicopter ride. It seemed like we were sitting in a small bubble, a bit hunched over, and surrounded entirely by windows. I sat up front with the pilot and Marc sat behind me. We each wore a headset in order to communicate while flying in the very noisy chopper. The sound of the helicopter propellers reminded me of the prominent sound I had heard many times while watching *M*A*S*H*.

While the pilot flew over the Mendenhall glacier, I listened to its history. I stared out the right side of the chopper in amazement as we flew over and in between the snow-covered mountains that surrounded us.

"Are you scared, honey?" Marc touched my shoulder after snapping several photographs from the left side of the helicopter.

"Not at all. This is nothing compared to what I've been through."

To me, fear was the feeling I had when I heard "it's cancer," and when the nurse wheeled me away from Marc and into the operating room for a lumpectomy, and every time the nurse inserted an IV into my wrist to inject me with chemotherapy and, most recently, when I woke up after a double mastectomy afraid to see myself naked again.

The helicopter could have smashed into the side of a mountain at that moment and I would have crashed into heaven. A chill covered my body from head to toe, but it had nothing to do with the temperature of the air and everything to do with my excitement. Even before the pilot pointed in its direction, I spotted our destination by the rows of mini igloo-like structures, sleds, and hundreds of dogs. We landed on

Norris glacier, home of more than one hundred dogs owned by Linwood Fiedler, an Iditarod racer. My eyes welled up with tears when I saw and heard so many husky dogs up close. I remembered Solo, my brother's purebred Siberian husky puppy who lived with us from the time I was seven years old until Arthur moved out when I was sixteen. I treated Solo as if she were my dog for as long as we lived together. She had fluffy black and white fur, strong bones and stance, and even prettier blue eyes than my dad's or Marc's. Solo's death at age fifteen left me sad for years and I loved watching my dad bring her back to life in his very first oil painting. I blinked my eyes and couldn't believe where I stood, surrounded by hundreds of these stunning husky dogs—on a glacier—in Alaska.

All the tourists were organized into groups and after a brief walk Marc and I were assigned to our personal musher. Her name was Brooke and she'd been born and raised in New Hampshire. She gave us an introduction to the sixteen husky dogs tied up and ready to pull our sled and then recited instructions on how to operate the sled itself. At first, Marc and I sat back in the sled and inhaled the fresh air and stunning scenery. When Brooke asked if either of us wanted to try mushing, Marc quickly answered, "Absolutely," as he jumped out of the sled.

Marc figured out how to navigate the sled with little direction and when he stopped, Brooke asked me, "Linda, how about you?"

I hesitated to stand up and steer the dog sled on my own and then I realized I might never have this chance again. Marc sat in the sled while I stood behind him and Brooke taught me to direct the dogs with the central gang-line.

"You're doing great," she said.

Once I relaxed, I found my balance and could have mushed forever. But just like when I used to ski in high school, as soon as I felt like I had mastered the sport, it was time to go home.

When I finally handed the reins back to Brooke, she brought us into the camp to visit and play with more of the adult dogs and puppies. Marc captured many priceless pictures on camera and then we thanked Brooke before heading back to our helicopter.

The bus took us back into the town of Juneau where we shopped before we stepped into the famous Red Dog Saloon. We bellied up to the bar where we looked up and saw the pistol that belonged to the notorious gunman Wyatt Earp. Probably best known for his involvement in the gunfight at the O.K. Corral, he allegedly checked this pistol into the U.S marshal's office in 1900 and never claimed it. Besides the gun, taxidermic bears hung from every wooden post and nailed to the wall above the bar were hundreds or thousands of dollar bills with names on them. Marc reached into his pocket and slammed a five-dollar bill on the bar. "Here, write our names on it." After I handed the bill to the bartender and watched him hang it with all the others, I briefly thought about the next time I might return to this bar and see that marked bill again.

Daylight lasted until after ten o'clock at night in Alaska so Marc and I never realized we were about to miss the ship. We threw back our fourth or fifth Duck Fart shot, which was concocted of Kahlua, Bailey's Irish Cream, and Crown Royal, grabbed our bags of souvenirs, and ran outside to catch a cab. We panicked when there were no cabs lined up outside the saloon. Marc was running up and down the sidewalk with a frantic look on his face when a guy in a Jeep Cherokee approached the curb and rolled down his window. I walked closer to the car and saw a little girl sitting in the backseat. The man offered to give us a ride to the ship and, with the child in the backseat, we felt safe. Marc thought we were rock stars for being the last passengers to check back onto the ship. After a long and exciting day, I passed out in our cabin while Marc explored the ship on his own, staying out until after one in the morning.

We ordered room service for breakfast the next day and ate at the small table on the balcony overlooking the port of Skagway. Marc ordered a bloody mary to cure the hangover he was suffering from after hanging out in the casino bar the night before. We were scheduled for a sport fishing excursion on a chartered boat that day and I wondered if Marc still wanted to go after his night of partying, "Are you sure you're up for this?" I asked him. Had it been me, I'd probably vomit over the side of the boat after the first whiff of fish guts.

"Of course, I can't wait," he said as if I was crazy for asking him.

We boarded a van with two other couples who had booked the same excursion. Marc spoke to his new friends more than he spoke to me, and I wondered if I embarrassed him with my short hair and chunky body. I also wondered if these couples were getting any vacation sex on this trip of a lifetime. On his own, Marc caught two salmon, one weighing around twenty pounds and the other more than forty pounds. The captain helped me reel in a small salmon that I had to throw back. Then the captain caught a baby king salmon, but kept it on the hook. He waved the fishing pole in the air at the stern of the boat and my jaw dropped as I watched a bald eagle stretch out its wings as it hovered over the pole to prey on the baby salmon. Marc caught the entire scene with his video camera.

When we arrived back at the dock, Marc and I posed with his twenty-pound catch and had to decide if we wanted to take either of his catches back to the ship where the ship's chef would likely cook it for our dinner. The other option was paying to send it home to Rhode Island. "We could have a party, serve the fish, and watch all these videos with our friends." Then we found out it would probably cost about four hundred bucks to cure the fish and ship it so we gave Marc's catch to the captain.

On the last night of our vacation, after a gourmet dinner, we walked outside to the top deck and sat on individual lounge chairs, staring at the mountains and glaciers. Marc brought me a cozy blanket from a pile that would have been pool towels had we chosen to sail to the Caribbean. And instead of a frozen mudslide, I warmed my hands around a steaming mug of hot chocolate with whipped cream. As I stared upward toward the stars I thought that my body's craving for crisp and chilly air may have been exceeded on this trip, but I'd have to wait longer to satisfy my craving for affection.

Chapter 23

Summers Suddenly Suck

Like most kids in Rhode Island, I'd always had fond memories of summer. Since the age of nine or ten—when my siblings were eighteen and older—my brothers and sister were allowed to stay home while my parents and I packed for two weeks at the beach. We spent most of our time swimming in the ocean, sitting with our feet in the sand, visiting local art festivals, and attending family cookouts.

When I was in high school, my father bought a powerboat and, although my brothers and sister were already living on their own, my parents loved having all of us together for a day on the ocean.

I liked to sit next to my dad on the long white leather seat in front of the steering wheel as I waited for him to say, "Okay, take the wheel and give it a try." Then he pointed to a target way in the distance. "That's it, head toward that piece of land way over there," he'd say as he guided me across the open ocean toward that day's destination. As much as I loved to drive the boat with my dad sitting next to me, I would much rather be working on my tan. As soon as Dad anchored the boat, I would grab my towel, sprawl out on the bow of the boat, and pretend to apply sunscreen. My brothers helped Dad dig for quahogs to eat raw, and Lori helped Mom serve Italian rolls with her homemade meatballs, sausage and peppers, and eggplant parmesan.

Shortly after Marc and I returned from Alaska, we gave into our craving for a bigger boat. We only added four feet compared to the boat Marc already owned, but I smiled when I realized that our new boat looked much more like my dad's boat. The new boat slept six, had a galley with a small kitchen, and a "head"—the nautical term for a toilet and shower enclosed by a real door with a lock. Sure, I had to duck my head and suck in my stomach to move around the galley and the head, but the upgrade made me happy since it reminded me how much I had loved spending time on the ocean.

Marc and I enjoyed day trips to many of the same places I had visited with my family, and we even stayed on the boat overnight on Block Island several times with friends. Unlike my dad, Marc insisted I take a boating safety class, especially for the times when he and I sailed alone. I must have just memorized the handbook to pass the test because I never remembered any of the rules in the middle of the ocean. As time went on, we rarely sailed alone; Marc always had a friend on board. He claimed friends could help in case of an emergency, but I started to feel like he just preferred to not be alone with me. I started to resent Marc's rejection of my need for affection—a little hug or a kiss, so I just focused on provisioning the boat with everything from toilet paper to food and being the hostess my mother had been for so many years.

But our first season with the boat had been cut short in September when Dr. Liu scheduled the surgery to swap my tissue expanders for the permanent saline breast implants. Although it was minor outpatient surgery and entailed a much easier recovery than the mastectomy, the thought of bumpy boat rides scared me so Marc decided to take the boat out of the water and store it for the winter.

The following spring, about a year after my original mastectomy, I decided to indulge in nipples and Marc decided he wanted something new, too: a brand-new Harley Davidson. I despised motorcycles and he knew it. As a young child, each time my brother Frankie had left the house on his motorcycle,

I waited by the window for hours, fearing the worst, until he pulled into the driveway.

Marc picked up his new bike a couple of weeks before Memorial Day weekend and although he had owned a motorcycle many years earlier, he needed to reapply for his license. On Memorial Day, he decided to run a quick errand to return a movie to Blockbuster about two miles from our condo.

"Should I grab another movie?" he asked.

"Nah, after watching *The Aviator* for three hours, I'm done with movies for a while, you?"

"Yeah, I agree."

About an hour later, around the same time it finally occurred to me that Marc had not returned home from his quick errand, the phone rang and his number appeared on the caller ID. "Hey, I just started to wonder what was taking you so long."

"I need you to come pick me up."

"Why? What happened? What's wrong with your car?"

"I didn't take my car. I took the bike and, it's no big deal, but . . ."

"You what? You don't even have your license yet. Did you get pulled over?"

"No, I got in an accident, but it looks a lot worse than it is."

"Are you okay? Where are you?" I jumped off the bed.

Still holding the phone to my ear, I stepped into a pair of shoes and grabbed a light jacket while I listened to Marc rant about what had happened. He told me the jerk driving the van behind him had looked down to pick up her coffee cup and never saw everyone stopping for the red light in front of her. Marc saw the van in his side-view mirror and somehow lifted himself off the bike and onto the trunk of the car in front of him before impact. He walked away without even a little scratch, but his brand-new toy was totaled.

I clenched my steering wheel as I drove toward the accident, imagining the chaos and maybe the blood I would see as I approached the scene. A police officer had blocked the road and put up his hand to stop me. I rolled down my window. "I need to get through, officer." I pointed to the wreckage. "My boyfriend was on that motorcycle." I drove past the ambulance, the fire truck, and several people blocking what appeared to be the bike.

Marc stood on the side of the road staring at his broken toy, but physically unaffected by what had just happened. "My poor bike. Look at it." I could not have cared less about the bike. I scanned up and down from Marc's head to his shoes and saw nothing—no rips, no scratches, and no blood—to indicate he had just been in a motorcycle accident. I despised motorcycles and feared deathly accidents so I had ignored the annoying piece of metal since the first day he had parked it in the garage. Other than seeing the rogue kickstand in the middle of the road, I had no clue what other damage it had sustained.

Although the summer started out with a different type of bang than I would have liked, we made up for it by enjoying several boat excursions with our families and friends. My brother Frankie, and his family joined us for a day of eating and swimming in Newport harbor while listening to the Jazz Festival from the water. At least twice, Marc and I took a few friends to Block Island and slept on the boat for a couple of nights. My sister only felt well enough for one trip to a local waterfront restaurant known for its lobster rolls—where we had eaten every week, just a couple of years ago, after our golf league—but after we arrived by boat that day, she couldn't even look at a French fry without gagging.

Considering she'd been enduring one chemotherapy drug after another, it was a wonder how she had received any nutrition at all over the past three years. Her life had been a roller coaster that would have made anyone vomit. Each new chemotherapy only worked for a few months and then routine testing would show the cancer had grown again. Each time,

Lori waited for her doctor to provide the next treatment option.

At the beginning of July, she started yet another new chemotherapy and for two weeks straight she vomited several times a day. Her oncologist finally ordered a CAT scan of her head. The technician never fully completed the scan because Lori had the urge to vomit throughout the entire test. A couple of days later, Lori asked me to go with her and John to get the results of the CAT scan. The doctor was still reading Lori's chart when she walked in the room. She looked up and stared blankly. "There are lesions on your brain."

"Is this related to the vomiting?" I asked.

"The lesions are pressing on the part of your brain that triggers vomiting," she stated, looking only at Lori.

Okay, lesions are not tumors; there must be a way to get rid of them and stop my sister from vomiting.

"Can we try another chemo?" I asked.

I stared at the doctor and wondered if all oncologists attended a required class in med school to practice how to deliver diagnoses and prognoses without showing any emotion. I realized it took a special, or maybe an emotionless, person to become a compassionate yet effective oncologist.

Some nights I tossed and turned for hours, worried about how to tell my manager that we needed more money or resources to complete a project on time. I knew my insignificant projects would never save any lives, but I always delivered these kinds of messages with some level of remorse or sense of responsibility. I wondered if any oncologist tossed and turned all night thinking about how to tell someone, "The cancer has spread to your brain, and there's nothing more we can do for you, but keep you comfortable."

Lori's oncologist never spoke those words to my sister. Instead she offered radiation treatments targeted at Lori's entire head because the lesions were not localized. Lori glanced at her husband and then stared right at me. "You know this may not work."

"Of course it will. It worked for Lance Armstrong." Lori knew I had just finished reading his first memoir, *It's Not about the Bike: My Journey Back to Life,* because I insisted she read it, too. I wanted my sister to catch Lance's contagious spirit and determination to survive.

Lori slouched in her chair. Her face wore a frown and she shrugged at her doctor. "Okay. I guess we'll try it."

The following day, I drove Lori to the first of several radiation treatments she would have on her head. Even with my car's beige interior, the strength of the July sun heated up the inside of the car. I turned up the A/C—or is it turned down the A/C?—regardless, I pressed the buttons on my dashboard to make the inside temperature colder. My sister's skin looked gray and ashen as opposed to her normal peachy complexion. She wore a frown instead of her infectious smile that lit up any room she entered. "Mom and Dad aren't praying for me." She sniffled and then began to sob.

"Of course they are. This treatment will work." I held my sister's hand.

Images of my parents began to float inside my head. I remembered the exact Christmas Eve when my mother had made the decision to stop her chemotherapy after three years of being tired and bald. I thought about how my father had never stopped his doctor's efforts to treat his chronic leukemia with chemotherapy as long as he could also have his carrot juice concoction. He eventually contracted an infection that was too advanced for his immune system to fight. Even though I wasn't at my dad's side when he took his last breath, I still believe he never just decided to quit living. Like my father, Lori had never quit anything in her life. Well, maybe her job at the bakery down the street from our childhood home, but only because she was headed to a better job working for Dad.

I gripped the steering wheel, glanced at Lori's pale face, and saw no twinkle in her eyes and no smile on her face. Never known for being quiet, Lori seemed different that day. She didn't ask what was new with our niece and nephews, talk about her weekend plans, or say that she looked forward to our next Nordstrom shopping spree. She didn't ask me about my job, how things were going with Marc, or Sophia—okay, she never warmed up to Sophia, but she always asked, "How's Sophia, the rat?"

That day, she didn't smile, laugh, or giggle, and I thought, it's okay for her to be tired today because tomorrow will be better.

Over the following two weeks, Lori struggled to finish the cycle of radiation treatments, but we knew it had worked because she stopped vomiting and agreed to go out for dinner to celebrate her forty-ninth birthday. That afternoon, I treated her to a manicure and pedicure. I sat on the sidelines and just watched her smile and listened to her giggle while she chatted with strangers and the owner of the salon, who was also a breast cancer survivor and a member of my support group.

I drove my sister home to have a nap before our dinner reservation, and it turned out I needed a nap, too. Around seven o'clock that night, Marc and I met Lori and John at a nearby waterfront restaurant. We were joined by Susan, Bob, Lydia, and Donald—the two couples Lori had recently traveled with on a Mediterranean cruise. My sister and I sat at opposite ends and sides of the table and I kept my eyes glued on her the entire night. She engaged in conversation but stuttered or stumbled on most of her words. The waitress asked Lori if she wanted her usual meal, grilled salmon with dill sauce and my sister nodded and said, "Yes, please."

And then my sister opened the gift that Lydia had designed especially for Lori. It was from all of us—a gold bracelet with a birthstone charm representing every person seated at the table. There were four charms for August—one for Lori, one for Lydia, one for Marc, and one for John, whose birthday fell on the same day he married my sister, almost fourteen years earlier. Lori's face brightened when she realized the significance of the bracelet and then she asked Susan to help her put it on.

Shortly after we all finished dinner, Lori pointed to the door and signaled to me that she wanted to go home. I helped her with her light denim jacket and colorful cotton scarf and walked with her to the restaurant door.

"I'm just tired, Lin. Thank you for a great day. Go back to the table. I'll be fine."

"I know. It's been a long day." I frowned and hugged her. "Happy birthday. I love you." I watched John open Lori's car door and help her into the car before I rejoined the others at the table.

Lori knew Marc and I had planned an early morning trip to Block Island for the next day, and although I wondered if she felt any better after a good night's sleep, I decided I'd wait to call and check on her. Sophia guarded the suitcases as I finished packing. Then she followed me downstairs and jumped on the kitchen counter, glaring at me while I filled the coolers with the food I had prepared. I disliked leaving her alone, but knew Marc's sister would check on her a few times during the week, which is all any cat really wants, right? Marc's friend was visiting from Las Vegas and had been staying with us for a few weeks, so after the guys carried all the gear to the boat, the three of us headed to Block Island to celebrate Marc's birthday week.

We enjoyed our coffee and muffins on the calm ride from Bristol to Newport and, as always, right after we passed Castle Hill, the swells became higher and the water turned much rougher. I couldn't hear the music Marc played so I leaned back into the white leather seat and became mesmerized by the growling of the outboard motor while I inhaled the fresh air. About an hour and a half later, just as we had reached our destination, we heard a call for us over the radio.

"Chillin' . . . Chillin' . . . Chillin' come in, this is the Coast Guard."

Marc slowed the boat to a crawl and responded to the call. They asked him to switch to a private channel. I couldn't make out the entire conversation, but heard "sister," and when I asked Marc for more details he used his hand as a stop sign for me to be quiet. At that moment, Marc's cell phone rang.

"What?" he asked frantically. "When?" And then he stared at me. He hung up his phone and looked around to ensure the boat had not drifted into traffic.

"Your sister . . . You need to call John." He handed me his phone, but I searched for my own cell phone, which I had stored in the galley of the boat. I became dizzy and could not stop shaking. I dialed my sister's house phone and hoped she would answer. John sobbed into the phone and I couldn't understand him. Then I heard one of his son's voices tell me my sister had died in her sleep.

By the time I had hung up the phone, Marc had turned the boat around toward home.

I called my brothers, Brenda, Mickie, my sister-in-law Cynthia, and Lori's best friend. Not one of them believed me. I slouched on the white leather seat opposite Marc the entire way home. I stared at the horizon in front of us and silently repeated what I had repeated to everyone on the phone, "Lori died . . . last night . . . in her sleep," and I couldn't believe me either. Without moving any other part of my body, I turned my head to the left and stared at the white caps as Marc tried his best to get us home quickly. My breathing turned shallow and my eyes felt heavy as I realized I may never have a happy summertime again.

I started sobbing. Marc signaled for his friend to sit with me, but I waved him away. I wished I could be alone. I wished I had stayed home. I knew my sister had struggled through her radiation treatments. I should have stayed with her. After what had happened to my father, I just couldn't believe I had left my sister alone and she had died, too.

Marc left the boat at our condo's dock instead of taking the extra time to moor it that day. I carried some of our bags from the boat and dropped them in the garage. I didn't go upstairs to see Sophia. Instead, Marc drove us to Lori's condo on the other side of town.

The paramedics and police were still parked outside my sister's condo when we arrived. I walked through the garage and opened the door to the kitchen. The sun filled the room through the big picture window. John sat at the glass-top table where my sister had served us so many home-cooked meals. John cried harder when he saw me. "She's gone," he babbled. Bob, Susan, and Lori's priest stood in front of the kitchen sink on the other side of the counter.

I walked toward Bob and we both began to cry. As he wrapped his arms around me, I rested my head on his shoulder. "How could this have happened? We were just all together last night." And when I said this out loud, I convinced myself that since we were together last night, the reality couldn't be true. I withdrew from Bob's arms and stood tall. "I need to see her."

"The funeral director just left, Linda. Lori's not here."

I wanted to stomp my feet and scream. I wondered if they had already cremated her and if I still had time to see her. I needed to see my sister one last time.

My brother-in-law had called Lori's oncologist to tell her Lori had passed away, and the doctor concluded my sister most likely suffered from a ruptured brain aneurysm caused by the radiation she'd endured over her entire head.

I held my right hand up to my throbbing head and wondered if I had asked my sister's doctor about the side effects of the radiation before Lori agreed to have the treatment. Marc followed me as I walked into the living room where I plopped my body onto the green microfiber couch, which was shaped like a half moon and faced the fireplace. My eyes scanned each object in the room—every piece of furniture, framed picture, porcelain bird, soy candle—and filled with tears as I remembered how my sister had spent the last couple of years decorating every inch of this two-level condo. She had impeccable taste, from the color and texture of the walls to the style and color of the blinds, to each rug and piece of furniture she had chosen.

I smelled her perfume. I heard her laughing.

I watched everyone's lips moving up and down, but I heard nothing. I struggled to participate in every conversation—every decision—and suddenly I realized I couldn't remember the last decision I had made by myself, without my sister.

John asked me and Bob to assist with writing Lori's death notice. I offered the words that included how she loved to travel with her husband, taught several friends and doctors how to knit, inherited her father's green thumb for raising orchids, shared many authentic home-cooked Italian meals with her family and friends, and loved to golf. When John insisted we preface my name with "loving sister," I stared at him and sobbed.

By the following day, my home had filled up with close friends, family, food, and flowers. I had never seen so many flowers outside of a florist's shop and only wished Lori was there to enjoy all the flowers she loved and appreciated so much more than I ever had.

That night, as I slept, Lori stood in front of me. We both sat down on pastel-colored swivel chairs in the living room of a beach house surrounded by floor-to-ceiling windows. We watched a man walk to the front door carrying a blue vase filled with white lilies, blue irises, and green ferns. Lori stood up from her chair and scurried into the next room, away from the windows, so the delivery man could not see her. She whispered, "I'll hide over here. He'll think I'm dead and then leave the flowers so you can enjoy them." When I woke up the next morning, I felt I had received permission from Lori to relax and enjoy the flowers that continued to be delivered to me.

I lived in a fog for the next few days. Bob and Susan helped John and me plan Lori's memorial mass, choose the urn to hold her ashes, and arrange her burial. They confirmed every decision I made, just like Lori would have. Friends and family brought me photos of Lori and, along with those I had already gathered, Marc created a collage that included photos of my sister as a baby right up until three nights earlier at her last birthday party. We also created a printed program for the memorial mass in which we listed readings, hymns, and names of those who had asked to read a reflection, or a eulogy, of Lori.

While writing my own eulogy, I checked my email and saw a new entry in my inbox from a friend in my support group. She had heard of Lori's death from Mickie and then wrote to share a story of her trip to a farmers' market to buy a bunch of sunflowers—the unique flower that reminded her of Lori's beauty and love of life. When she bent down to choose the perfect bunch, she had caught a glimpse of Lori in the flower's brown center, surrounded by bright yellow petals.

The following day, I became overwhelmed by the number of people in attendance at my sister's memorial mass, especially when I noticed my ex-husband, whom I had not seen in more than two years. I later found out that he had heard about my sister's death after asking a friend of ours at the golf course why the flag outside the clubhouse had been flying at half-mast.

Lori's priest delivered the most deeply moving homily I had ever heard. I had met him for the first time in my sister's kitchen the day she died, and he had told me that Lori had met with him several times during her illness. He never gave me the details of their private conversations, but he assured me that, with his guidance, my sister had accepted her impending death. Lori died in her sleep wearing her new charm bracelet and holding a prayer card of Saint Anthony—the saint of miracles—close to her heart. I believed my sister had asked for a miracle before she fell asleep. She knew her disease wouldn't stop spreading and she knew her treatment options were diminishing. She had supported finding a cure for cancer but she knew a cure would not be an option for her. I believed

Saint Anthony granted her the miracle of falling into a peaceful sleep. A peaceful sleep after she had celebrated her birthday with close friends and family. A peaceful sleep so she never had to gasp for her last breath. A peaceful sleep that delivered her directly back into the arms of our parents.

Surrounded by a church full of people, I only ached for Lori. Since she had died, I reached for the phone at least once a day to call her. Each time I picked up the phone, the reminder of her death burned even hotter than the last time. After our parents had died, Lori and I joked that our heads were going to fall off from shaking them so much from side to side in disbelief. I had no doubt I'd be headless after Lori died.

Four days after my sister's funeral mass, her ashes and headstone were ready, and I needed to find the strength to deal with the agony of burying her. We had invited only dear friends and immediate family to the memorial garden across from the church where my sister would be laid to rest. As I stood in the garden, between the steeple and Lori's plot, I covered my mouth and giggled after being startled by the clanging church bells right above my head. At first, I thought, how much rest would my sister actually get with those bells? But then I knew my sister would have loved this exact spot. She always loved to look out the many windows of her condo and watch all the traffic from the neighbors in the condo complex. No one could get out of the driveway without passing Lori's unit. Every Fourth of July, when the wind blew in the direction of her condo, she loved to hear the bands from the oldest parade in the country. I smiled when I realized that Lori's resting place, located directly on the parade route, would allow her to hear all the bands up close, loud and clear.

About an hour before my sister's burial service, Lori's best friend and I stopped at a local florist and asked for a simple basket of sunflowers. I probably should have ordered them earlier but when I explained to the florist why I wanted them, she asked us to wait. She went to the fridge and retrieved a bucket of bright, medium-size sunflowers. She placed it on the large metal worktable behind the counter. She grabbed a dark brown wicker basket with a handle, some green floral foam, and fern leaves before starting to create our bouquet. Within half an hour, the florist handed me the basket. I had never seen a brighter bunch of flowers.

When Lori's burial service concluded, I picked up the basket of sunflowers I had placed on a small table in front of us and handed a flower to every female guest. There were more flowers in the basket, although I had no idea how many, so I handed one to each male guest, too. I took one flower for myself and just one flower remained so I knelt down and gently placed it on Lori's headstone as I wiped a fresh tear from my cheek.

I continued to receive condolences for many weeks after my sister's passing and many times people offered the same expression of their sympathy: "You were so lucky to have a sister like Lori." I always smiled and said, "Thank you," because I knew they meant well, but hearing their words made me sad and angry. I couldn't stop thinking, I really was lucky to have the best sister on Earth and I want her back—now. My sister had never believed in receiving signs from the "other side," but I only hoped she changed her mind and would find a way to communicate with me forever.

Chapter 24

Writes to Survive

I always thought I had suffered the worst loss, the worst grief, of my life when my mother passed away. But when Lori died, I realized I had never thoroughly mourned the loss of my mother. How could I have? Within six months of her dying, I focused on my father's emotional and physical health, Arthur's divorce, and Lori's first breast cancer diagnosis. Then my own marriage ended, my sister's cancer returned with a vengeance, my father died, and I received my own breast cancer diagnosis. In the four short years following my mother's death, my life had been turned upside down and all around with one tragedy after another, and I had never been given any time to recover. And through all the constant turmoil that invaded our lives, I only survived because my sister had compelled me to move forward and never allowed me to surrender to the negative events that surrounded us.

When Lori died, I thought I would die, too. How could I move forward in my life without her guidance and wisdom? I turned to therapy again and confirmed that all the feelings I had—shock, sadness, anger, numbness, anxiety— were normal but confirming these emotions only increased my heartache. Maybe I had made a mistake by rehashing the previous seven years of emotional pain and trauma because I suddenly became keenly aware of and overwhelmed by guilt—survivor's guilt.

204 | Linda Carvelli

I had not yet been diagnosed with breast cancer when my mother died of the disease, and I felt guilty that I had to lose her just to grasp the full meaning of the concept "life is short." This simple life lesson helped me survive through my divorce and allowed me to appreciate my father and all the reasons why he loved life. I still had not been diagnosed when my dad died and I thought I had already learned the "life is short" lesson so I struggled to understand any meaning behind his death. I felt guilty when I realized I had to lose my father before I could learn not to take anything for granted. I found myself either craving, or just more aware of, the beauty in everything he loved—boating, golfing, gardening, art, wine.

When I received my own breast cancer diagnosis, although I felt guilty for being able to choose aggressive treatments based on my relatives' choices, I learned another lesson. My diagnosis allowed me to put my own life in perspective, and, along with the two big lessons I had already learned, I thought I had all the wisdom I needed to survive through the rest of my life.

When my sister died, I felt defeated by my own convictions. Lori's death was the most negative event that could ever happen in my entire life from that point forward. Only after Lori was gone did I start believing I was meant to survive for a reason. Since it had taken me four years to discover some purpose behind losing my mother, I realized it may take just as long—or longer—before I uncovered some meaning from my sister's death. I believed a lesson would be revealed to me and that fueled the passion I had for my own survival. I knew that my parents and sister wanted me to be a happy and functioning human being—they wanted me to be a survivor—and to beat the disease that had taken all their lives.

About a week after Lori had died, I returned to work. For me that meant I walked across the hall from the master bedroom into the spare bedroom, turned on my laptop, and fired up my email. Since my breast cancer diagnosis three years ago, my employer had allowed me to work from home for as long as I needed. Although I woke up at the same time as Marc, showered, and got dressed, often I waited until after he left for work to climb back into bed and pull the down comforter over my head. Sophia sensed my sadness, jumped on the bed with me, and while I curled up on my side she cuddled into the space between my belly and my heart. When I found it hard to breathe, I removed the covers from my head and stared at the designer accent pillows my sister had helped me choose just two months earlier. I listened to the steady sound of Sophia's purr and we fell back to sleep together.

I would have been happy staying in bed all day, eating chocolate, and watching Lifetime movies, but images of my heavenly angels cheered me on (or out of bed) while an image of my boss glared at me. I heard my mother's voice. "You're going to live, doll, so get up and do something with your life." And then I heard my boss's voice. "Come on, Linda, I need you to steer these very complex projects that only you know how to lead." So, the demands of my job (and my angels) dragged me from my bed to my computer to lead my project teams and check on the status of the tasks I had assigned to them.

At the same time, I struggled with the fact that the entire world around me continued moving forward after I had suffered the most devastating loss of my life. I felt completely incapable of making a decision—paralyzed and helpless—without my sister. One day, it took me four outfit changes before I even left the house just to go grocery shopping. And when I had finally reached the meat department, I had an internal temper tantrum while I stood staring at the chicken and then the beef, trying to decide what to make for dinner as if it would be my last meal.

When I felt helpless at work and had the urge to call my sister for advice, I leaned on many of my coworkers, who were also my friends, and they guided me with patience. Having that strong bond with my work friends caused me to realize something had been missing at home. Not only had I lost my sister, but instead of her death bringing me closer to

Marc, I watched the emotional space widen between us. I still believed he loved me because he had consoled me during the roughest periods of my life. But, I wondered: How much longer could I ignore that we had zero intimacy—no signs of physical affection—since my mastectomy two and half years ago? Each time I told him that I needed more of an emotional connection or touched his bare body, he pushed me away. "You're just being silly," he would say. I wondered if Marc could be right. I mean ever, since I had endured chemotherapy, I experienced bouts of foggy thinking or forgetfulness and blamed it on chemo brain. And taking antidepressants and Tamoxifen had messed with my hormones, so maybe I was more emotional than before I had cancer.

It may have been around this time when Marc called me "stupid" instead of "silly," although I cannot remember what I may have done to trigger this nickname from him. I never knew it then, but it's so easy to see now that this marked the moment he had lost all respect for me. Right after the word left his mouth, he followed up with "'tupid, I mean, don't be 'tupid," as if removing the "s" made it less of an insult and more of a pet name.

When I refused to believe my desires for an intimate relationship were neither silly nor stupid, I briefly thought about leaving Marc—or kicking him out—but I yearned to talk with my sister before I made such an important decision, and since that could never happen, I just stayed with Marc. Maybe sex and intimacy were not as important as having a trustworthy guy care for me while my life fell apart. Maybe over time I would admit that I stayed with Marc longer than I should have just like I had stayed with Dean. Or maybe I would realize that everything happened for a reason and, in time, the reason would be revealed.

Because I felt fully supported by my friends at work, I worked later every night and most weekends, and I welcomed any opportunity to travel during the week. But the more effort

I put into my work, the more work I received. I repeatedly asked my boss to lessen my workload, and although he empathized, his budgets were constrained. So I felt forced to accept the common theme around the office and just "be thankful you have a job." Because my job and coworkers were my only saving grace from grief, I made the best of it, but I wondered if there could be something better for me out there.

Just two months after Lori had died, I reached a major milestone in my life—my fortieth birthday—and I had no desire to celebrate it without her. A few days before my birthday, my brother-in-law found a gift certificate to a home décor store, a Christmas present I had given to Lori, and he gave it to me.

"Buy something for yourself, for your birthday, from your sister," John said with tears in his eyes.

Brenda and I had planned to meet for breakfast and the home décor store was right next door to the restaurant. After we were seated, I told her about the gift certificate.

"Are you kidding me, Lin? It's a gift from your sister."

Brenda's eyes filled up with tears. Both of us rushed through breakfast partly because we loved to shop, but mostly because we wanted to see what my sister had picked out for my birthday. Within a few minutes of entering the store, Brenda followed me as I walked toward a long, heavy wooden dining room table and pointed to the centerpiece—a long wrought iron stand that held six glass candle holders, each containing orange-colored votive candles, "That's it. That's my gift."

"Had you seen that before? You walked to it immediately."

"No, but I had a picture of it in my mind. I thought it would look nice on Lori's dining room table." I started to cry.

"She wants you to light up your own dining room table with it, Lin."

That night, Marc and John had planned to take me out to dinner, but instead "surprised" me with a private party. With help from Mickie and Brenda, they had invited all of my closest friends and family. For the past two months, they had compiled the guest list, chosen the buffet menu, and arranged all the decorations. They later told me that they weren't sure if I would have wanted a party or preferred to just let the milestone pass without Lori to celebrate with me. And then Mickie presented me with a gift she had commissioned with a mutual friend of ours—a painting of a sunflower, except in its brown center the artist painted my sister's beautiful face, copied from a photograph Marc had secretly provided to her. At that moment, I believed my sister may have found a new way to communicate with me and I realized my friends had made the right choice to throw the party. I still wasn't a fan of surprises, so I told them that next time I wanted to help with the planning. And when any of my friends complained about getting older, I promised myself that I would welcome each birthday and celebrate another year of my survival.

My friends and the happy memories of my life with Lori are what helped me survive my first major birthday and a year's worth of holidays without my sister.

And then, about a month before my forty-first birthday, Marc and I noticed changes in Sophia's personality and eating habits. She often vomited or had the dry heaves soon after eating, and her playfulness diminished on a daily basis. Despite many trips to the vet, medication, and even surgery, she showed no signs of improvement and often hid from us so she could be alone. Finally, Marc told me that he may have to put her to sleep.

"She's telling us it's time." He turned to call the vet.

The following morning, as she lay sleeping on the floor of the brightly lit sunroom, he picked her up with her favorite yellow fleece blanket and held her in his arms. She didn't squirm at all as I followed them down the stairs to the garage and opened the passenger side door of Marc's car.

"Do you mind holding her? I can't put her alone in her crate."

"Of course." I settled into the front seat and put my arms out to receive the bundle of black and brown calico fur.

We entered the waiting room at the vet and the receptionist greeted us with a shy smile. She led us to a room and Marc held Sophia in his arms until the doctor arrived. I had never been in this situation before, but the doctor explained the procedure. I looked at Marc and sighed. He placed Sophia on the metal table, on top of her favorite yellow blanket, and gently rubbed her soft little head. The doctor asked us if we were ready and we both nodded. He injected her with the medicine and left us alone for a few minutes.

"It's okay, Sophia. It's okay for you to sleep. I love you. It's okay. Go to sleep." I watched her eyes getting heavier. I kissed the top of her head as tears streamed down my face. Marc alternated between rubbing Sophia's back and mine. When the doctor returned, he listened to her heart.

"She's gone. I'm so sorry."

I never anticipated how I would feel when Marc and I returned home without Sophia. She didn't greet us at the door, her dishes of food and water were still in the kitchen, and her litter box remained clean in the upstairs bathroom. I lay on our bed and she didn't jump on the bed next to me. I fell asleep with tears in my eyes while Marc gathered all her things and stored them in the basement. I assumed Marc wanted another pet as soon as possible, but he insisted he needed a break.

He never indicated just how long of a break he needed. For my forty-first birthday, he gave me an eight-week-old kitten. She looked very much like a mini-Sophia—brown, black, beige, and dark orange fur with just a little spot of white on each double paw, just like Sophia.

I struggled to find the perfect name for my very first pet. Marc hated whatever name I suggested and vice versa. Marc agreed when I decided I wanted to name her Mitzi because of her double paws (or mitts), but within a month, he renamed my kitten to Chalupa. I couldn't deny that she reminded me of a Mexican jumping bean when she lifted herself straight up in the air with excitement, and Marc completely overruled my original decision.

Since I worked from home, Mitzi—Chalupa, that is—became my newest best buddy. Every morning, she followed me into the office and lay on a blue fleece blanket on the desk beside my laptop while I worked, and whenever I stood up to walk around she followed me. At night I liked to sleep on my side with one leg bent and one leg straight. When I climbed into bed, Mitzi always jumped on the bed with me and claimed her spot on top of the comforter, right up against my butt, in the little triangle that formed between my legs. Whether working or sleeping, I felt more relaxed with her around me. The sound of her motor running—her purr—assured me of what pure contentment must feel like and I decided I always wanted to purr just like she did.

Everyone grieves and handles survivor's guilt differently, but I believe the first year after losing a loved one is especially challenging for all of us. I felt sad at each annual event—holiday or birthday—and spontaneous family gatherings without the presence of my mother, and then more so after I lost my father. But whatever level of grief I had experienced then, my sister's laughter and wisdom always managed to get me out of my funks. The first year after losing Lori had been even more torturous than both years following my parents' deaths because I had to find ways to manage my funks alone.

One cold winter night, wearing nothing but a strapless, ivory terry cloth cover-up, I lay under a warm blanket, melting into the massage table. The spa owner, Alayne, was a friend of mine and she said to me, "You know, you should write about this shit, write your story. Maybe try journaling. I know a great teacher who has workshops, you could call her."

"Uh huh." I inhaled the scent of the spa products she used to cleanse and exfoliate my face, neck, and upper chest.

"I'm serious. She's fabulous." She massaged my head with hot oil.

"I know you are. Okay, give me her number. Now be quiet would you, I like this song." I giggled as I tried to relax under the touch of her hands and the sound of David Gray's voice.

I may have waited a month before I finally dialed the writing instructor's phone number. Maybe my job consumed me or maybe I doubted my ability or desire to write anything other than a grocery list. But then I remembered my birthday six years earlier—the year that my divorce had become final—when Lori handed me a wrapped present that contained a beautiful, brown leather-bound journal with pages edged with gold. "You've always told me you wanted to write a book," Lori had said.

Lori never forgot the time ten years earlier when I had first admitted I wanted to write a book and I declared it, out loud, in a work-sponsored training class on how to use the Franklin Planner. You know, those large and cumbersome leather bound books filled with calendars and lined pages where we are supposed to plan our lives, by month, week, and day?

At the end of the training class, the instructor asked us to think about our short- and long-term life goals. What did we want to accomplish in one year, five years, and ten years? I still have no recollection of the goals I wrote down for one and five years, but I distinctly remember—and now wish I had preserved the historic piece of lined paper I had written on—the goal I wanted to achieve in ten years: "Write a book."

Now seemed like the time to pursue that goal. As I stared at the journal my sister had given me just for this very purpose, Hannah, the writing instructor, answered the phone. I explained that we had a mutual friend who had encouraged me to call and believed I would benefit from journaling.

"That's great. So tell me a little about yourself. Do you journal now?"

"Well, I have a journal, but I don't write regularly. I'm a project manager at a bank that keeps gobbling up other banks. I have no spare time for anything else."

"Of course." Hannah explained a little about the types of workshops she held, and her energy excited me.

I enrolled in my first writing class. I loved being surrounded by other writers who had a passion for the craft of writing—that is, after I had actually learned that writing had a craft associated to it. If I ever had a fear of sharing my intimate thoughts with others, this class freed me of that fear. Hannah provided the safe and confidential space for us to share and provide constructive feedback.

About a year after I had started taking classes (and about two years after my sister had died), Hannah still recognized the pain in my eyes and the helplessness I continued to carry. I had been seeing a psychotherapist on and off since my sister died, but I wondered if I could be holding back some feelings in those sessions. So when Hannah offered private sessions, I agreed to try writing through my pain.

When I showed up for my very first private writing session, I walked behind Hannah as we entered her cozy office in the basement. There I met her two very furry cats, one of whom sensed my cat-loving nature, like Sophia first had, and rubbed up against my shins. Hannah shooed Lester out of her office. "We'll never get anything done with him in here." She welcomed me to sit in the oversize chair covered with a color-blocked afghan that looked exactly like one my grandmother had crocheted. Hannah sat in a traditional leather desk chair and rolled it away from her desk and closer to me. We both folded our legs in front of ourselves and held a pen and a notebook. Just like in her writing classes, Hannah opened our session with a "warm-up" during which she used guided meditation to set our intention. We both wrote for five or ten minutes and then shared what we had written.

I have no idea what I wrote during that warm-up, but it must have been something about my own breast cancer and my own breasts because I only remember saying, "Do you want to see them?"

Hannah shrugged one shoulder. "Sure," and that was the only syllable I needed to hear before I quickly lifted my shirt. "I don't wear a bra!"

"Wow, I see that. Wow, they look great."

With my shirt still lifted, I bent my head down to glance at my boobs. "Yeah, they aren't bad, are they?"

From that moment on, Hannah and I bonded. If you were to ask her, she'd say it was that very action that proved my willingness and ability to be raw with myself—and others. I don't remember how many private writing sessions I took with Hannah, but I will never forget the moment she helped me to realize the most important lesson of my life: "You most definitely can go on without Lori, Linda, because she's not gone. She's in you."

After I released the writer—and the pool of tears—I had hidden inside me, Hannah convinced me that my parents and my sister had left me with an enormous amount of their wisdom. My newfound passion for writing (and lack of passion for anything at home) drove me to enroll in all of Hannah's workshops. And with every journal entry and homework assignment, I felt a burning desire to find the reason why my life had led me in this direction.

So, maybe all my friends had been right all along. It may have taken me a while to accept, but every day I am reminded how truly blessed I am to have had Lori in my life—as my sister, as my mother, as my father, as my life coach. Our time together was cut much too short, but I now realize that some people live an entire lifetime without ever experiencing a sibling relationship as loving as ours.

Chapter 25

Make It Stop

My journal had become my new best friend. Whether within or outside of a formal writing workshop, I wrote through the pain of losing my parents and my sister and realized that although I had lost them physically and missed hearing each of their voices and their laughs, I could never lose them spiritually. When my sister had given me my first grown-up journal—brown leather as opposed to my previous fluffy pink one, not that there's anything wrong with that—I never imagined that writing might be a way for me to channel my sister's voice. No, I didn't write in her voice, but sometimes when writing through a challenge—for instance, how my boyfriend had become my roommate and how I had allowed my job to overtake my life—I arrived at a solution by talking to my sister and reading her advice in my writing.

About a year after Lori died, I started to experience a severe stiff neck, frequent headaches, and a dull pain that traveled down my entire left arm. I had difficulty sleeping at night and although I knew the stress from work and my declining relationship with Marc could be causing the pain that kept me awake, my mind jumped to only one conclusion. Facing a cancer recurrence always weighed on my mind and breast cancer had a tendency to spread to the bones, so I called my oncologist. Dr. Legare's postchemotherapy medical care included routine tests to ensure my blood counts remained within acceptable limits, but never an alarmist, he only ordered diagnostic scans or tests if I complained of relevant symptoms.

I hadn't been sleeping well and Marc knew I was suffering, but he never offered to attend the doctor's appointment—and I never indicated that I wanted him to come with me. Dr. Legare listened as I complained about all the stress at work and the pain in my neck, shoulder, and arm. He reviewed my four-year-old medical records and examined me. "It makes sense to have a blood test . . . and a bone scan," he said.

He never needed to add "to rule out cancer" because I already knew we needed the bone scan to see if any changes had occurred since the baseline scan I had after my original diagnosis four years earlier. He asked his assistant to schedule the bone scan for the same day and requested he have the results for the next day. His urgency made me panic.

The next day, I returned to my oncologist's office alone and, with sweaty palms, received the test results of the bone scan. I heard the door knob turn and held my breath as the doctor entered the room. He shook my hand. "Well, everything looks the same as four years ago."

I exhaled. "Now what?"

"I'm not sure, but I think you should consult with an orthopedic specialist." He gave me the name of the doctor he recommended.

I waited a couple of weeks for an appointment with the orthopedic surgeon, but I was already impressed by his proactive approach. He ordered X-rays ahead of time so he would have something to tell me at that first visit. I waited alone in the reception area and thought about how much I despised filling out the repetitive patient information forms. And it was the first time I realized that, at the age of forty-two, I already needed a second page to document my medical history.

A nurse escorted me to an exam room, took my blood pressure (which measured normal) and my weight (which was still embarrassing), and then had me dress into a johnny. The doctor entered the room with my X-rays in a large manila folder and shook my hand. He reviewed my medical history on the forms and I thought, at least they do read them. "Wow, you've been through a lot, haven't you?" he said.

"Yeah, but I've never had this kind of pain." I mean, maybe I had suffered with that same excruciating pain before my back surgery nine years ago, but I had no memory of it. I guess that's why women have more than one child.

He examined my neck and spine and then asked me to walk in a straight line across the linoleum floor before helping me step up and sit on the exam table. He turned to the X-rays and then looked at me. "Well, you have degenerative discs in your neck."

"Oh. I think both of my brothers have that, but I don't really know what it means."

He explained that the discs in my neck, those that surround and protect my spine, had started to erode. However, given my symptoms and the results of the X-ray, in his opinion surgery wasn't warranted. He knew I spent close to 100 percent of my work day sitting at and typing on a computer, so he recommended simple adjustments to my posture and desk setup and reminded me to get up and walk around several times during the day. He also recommended a memory foam pillow to adjust the position of my head and neck while sleeping. He suggested we meet again in a year unless the pain worsened. I liked this doctor, confirmed him as one of the best neck surgeons in Rhode Island, and decided not to seek a second opinion.

I made the adjustments he had suggested and although the initial pain subsided for a while, it never went away completely and some new symptoms popped up. I still suffered from headaches and neck and arm pain, and most nights I woke up with numbness and tingling in my fingers. I also started to experience a new symptom that was both frightening and embarrassing. I frequently tripped over my own feet and lost my balance even when standing still.

Less than a year after my first consultation, the surgeon ordered a new set of X-rays and this time, maybe due to my unsteady feet, Marc came with me for the follow-up visit. When the surgeon reviewed the newest X-rays, he turned to me with wide eyes.

"The amount of degeneration I see in less than one year is remarkable. The fluid and space around your spine is decreasing and, if left untreated, could cause irreversible damage."

When the doctor asked me to walk in a straight line, I failed the test. He recommended surgery as the primary option and believed he could correct the current nerve damage. Because Marc met the surgeon and saw the X-rays himself, he supported my decision to have the surgery.

The doctor explained how he would perform the surgery—an anterior cervical decompression and spine fusion—and I wished he had not been so honest or descriptive. He would enter through the front of my neck, move all the stuff (you know, my esophagus, trachea, carotid artery) to one side to expose my spine, remove the eroded discs, perform a bone graft, and stabilize my neck with a titanium plate-and-screw device. My brother Arthur had also been given a similar diagnosis and surgical recommendation but I had heard he refused to have the operation after he learned how the surgeon accessed the spine.

Certainly the procedure sounded disgusting—and risky—but I never hesitated to have it. Much like when I had back trouble, I wanted to fix it, eliminate the excruciating pain, and move on with my life. And although having breast cancer caused no physical pain, I wanted it removed immediately—and forever. Because I had been through so many operations before this one, even hearing the gory details of how the surgeon intended to fix my neck didn't scare me. I had survived the embarrassment of having male and female doctors poking and staring at every single crevice of my entire body over the course of so many years that I now voluntarily flashed my naked body toward anyone willing to view it. By this time in my breast cancer journey, I felt proud of my survival and of my reconstructed boobs. And my fear of needles? Gone.

Much like my state of mind before my previous surgeries, I felt peaceful the night before my neck operation. But unlike the other surgeries, neither my parents nor my sister would be by my side when I woke up. I had to remind myself of the strength I had inside me and that I had inherited their wisdom to help me make the best decisions.

Marc and I walked into the surgical waiting area of the hospital, and as I scanned the room, my eyes met those of a previous coworker who had also been a close friend of mine. I introduced her and her husband to Marc, and she and I felt better knowing the two guys could keep each other company while they waited for us. I turned to my friend in the gurney across from me before the nurse wheeled me into the operating area. "See you on the other side. I mean, in the recovery room," I said.

When I woke up, I asked about my friend, but the nurse could only report that my friend's surgery had not finished yet. I dozed off again and woke up in my hospital room. Although unable to turn my head, I felt no pain, and I smiled when I saw someone out of the corner of my eye who resembled Marc. "Can I have my glasses?" I asked.

"Here you go, 'tupid. How do you feel?"

I raised my hand to my neck and felt the bulky foam neck brace I needed to wear for a couple of weeks to stabilize my neck. I blinked my eyes several times and rubbed my right eye. "I don't feel any pain, but what is that?"

"What's what?"

I removed my glasses and pointed to the inner corner of my right eye. "Look in my eye. Is there something in there?"

"I don't see anything. Why?"

I removed my glasses, stared at the lenses, and saw nothing. "I see a black blurry thing in my eye. Can you clean my glasses?"

He found a tissue on the nightstand, cleaned both lenses in my glasses, and handed them back to me. I kept my eyes closed while I put them back on and thought, please be gone, but when I opened my eyes and blinked, the annoying black amoeba-like blob remained in the bottom left corner of my right eye. When I looked up toward the ceiling, the blob stayed still. When I looked left, right, or down the blob stayed still. When I mentioned it to the nurses and my surgeon, no one could see it. They had no idea what it could be and shrugged it off. "I'm sure it will disappear. Be patient."

After one night my surgeon discharged me, and other than having to mash all my food in a blender like we had done for my dad after his stroke, I thought the recovery from risky neck surgery may be a cinch. Given the okay from my surgeon, I walked daily and felt great except for that black "floatie" in my eye that never moved. Two weeks later, at three o'clock on a Friday afternoon the weekend before the Fourth of July holiday, I finally decided to call my optometrist.

I had been going to the same eye doctor since before my divorce six years earlier. Unlike most doctors, he picked up the phone right away after I briefly explained my situation to his receptionist. After I repeated that I'd had neck surgery two weeks before and woke up with an amoeba in my eye, he insisted I come into his office that afternoon. So, just two weeks after my anterior cervical discectomy and fusion, I found myself on the way to the optometrist.

Within minutes of examining both of my eyes, my optometrist declared, "It looks like you have a detached retina."

"Oh, okay, how does that happen?" I asked.

"It's common for someone with severe nearsightedness like yourself, but most often it occurs with some sort of trauma," he explained.

"I see, no pun intended." I giggled to calm my nerves. "So, how does it go away? Does it just fix itself over time?"

"Well, no, you need to see an ophthalmologist, now—like, today—who may actually recommend you have surgery right away."

"Surgery? Are you kidding me? I just had surgery two weeks ago." I felt tears filling my eyes.

"I know. I'm sorry, but it's the right thing to do. Let me call to ask when they can see you." He left me alone in the room.

I sat shaking in the exam chair and staring at the eye chart on the wall in front of me. I searched for my cell phone at the bottom of my purse and called Marc.

"Hi, I have a detached retina and . . . I may need surgery." I sniffled.

"What? Are you kidding?"

He must really think I have become a royal pain in the ass.

"I wish. I can't drive home." I hoped he would offer to pick me up.

"Crap. I have a meeting I can't get out off." Marc never even offered another option.

My doctor came back into the room and announced, "They can see you now."

I spoke into the phone, "I'll call Cynthia, I guess."

"Okay, but let me know what happens."

I looked at my eye doctor. "Really? It's almost five o'clock. Can't this wait till Monday?"

"No, unfortunately, it can't, but the office will stay open and the surgeon will wait for you."

I called Cynthia, my brother's ex-wife, because I could always depend on her—for anything, no matter what.

When she arrived at my optometrist's office, she gave me a soft hug and I began to cry. She drove us to the eye surgeon, located about fifteen minutes away, sat by my side in the waiting room, and held my hand as we walked into the examination room. Cynthia sat in a wooden chair against the wall and I planted my butt in the big black eye exam chair and stared at her as I clenched my teeth and jaw.

"You know, after having breast cancer, it's like I'm not afraid of anything. I mean, I never even flinched at the neck surgery. But eye surgery? This scares me to death."

She smiled and inhaled. "I know, but you need to have it taken care of. They have the best doctors here." Cynthia was so calm and always the voice of reason. I thought about how lucky Faith and Andrew were to have her as their mom.

When the doctor entered the room I looked at Cynthia. *I mean, really, are you sure they are all the best here?* First of all, I had never needed emergency surgery for anything so I had always had time to research the procedures and the doctors before making a decision. Second of all, this *eye surgeon* wore coke-bottle glasses. I mean, really? He looked like a complete nerd. Cynthia looked at me with wide eyes and smiled.

When he spoke, he had a squeaky mouse-like voice and I wanted to either laugh or get up and leave or both. But when I told him about my recent neck surgery, he said, "I had that same surgery." I immediately felt a strange bond with this geeky guy.

He flashed a bright light in my eyes to examine my retinas and then asked me if the floatie had changed much in the past two weeks since I had first noticed it.

"No, it's been the same size and annoyance since the day of my neck surgery."

"Well, if you can limit your eye movements over the weekend, I see no reason why the surgery can't wait two more days until Monday." He explained the type of surgery he would perform—a scleral buckle. It entailed a silicone band be placed around my eyeball, like a belt, to indent and support the area of the tear.

"Limit my eye movements? I like to do Sudoku puzzles before I go to bed."

"Me, too, but absolutely no Sudoku puzzles are allowed between now and Monday."

"Really?"

"Really. Just think about how you solve the puzzle by scanning up and down the squares—no, don't think about it because you'll actually make the movements."

Part of me preferred he perform the surgery right then and there so I wouldn't need to stress over it all weekend. What if just the thought of not moving my eyes made me move them?

Having to wait over the weekend had been a very good thing. Our neighbor and friend Phil, who, with his wife, had bought my sister's condo, worked as an eye surgeon in Massachusetts specializing in cataracts. He visited with me the night before my surgery, and although I cringed while he gave me the surgical details, I much preferred to know what to expect than to be surprised.

Of all the surgeries I had ever had, eye surgery sucked the most. Although I'm sure I asked for general anesthesia, my surgeon worked on my eyeball with local anesthesia. I received a tranquilizer that should have relaxed me and made me sleepy, but how could I sleep with my eyeball in a vice that prevented it from closing? I heard my doctor talking to the assisting doctor and the nurse. I heard the music they had playing from a radio in the corner of the operating room. And at one point, I flinched and he asked, "Can you feel what I am doing?"

I must have answered, "Yes."

"Okay, I need to numb your eye a bit more then." I watched him stick a needle in my eye. *Hey, I didn't say "cross my heart and hope to die, stick a needle in my eye."* I didn't feel him poking around after that needle, but I certainly didn't relax during the entire surgery.

Marc met me in the recovery room and helped me get dressed. He pulled back the curtain and said, "Look who's here to see you." I covered my mouth when I saw my neighbor Phil. "Hi, Linda. How are you feeling?"

"I'm fine. What are you doing here? I mean, didn't you have to work today?"

"I wanted to check on you to be sure everything went well and I see it did. I just spoke to your doctor. You're going to be fine."

I couldn't believe this man had taken time out of his very busy surgical schedule to drive to Rhode Island to check on me, and then I realized: it's Phil, of course he did.

His wife and three daughters were just as compassionate. After the surgery, the vision in my right eye ended up twice as bad as my left eye so I needed to keep my right eye closed while wearing my eyeglasses. When the girls heard this, they made eye patches out of construction paper for me to tape onto the right lens of my glasses.

I fully and easily recovered from my intricate neck surgery, but needed an extra two weeks out from work to recover from the disgusting eyeball surgery. The lingering eye pain and vast difference in my vision caused a perpetual headache, and I kept my eyes closed more often than open. Whenever I had complained about being too busy at work, my sister always told me, "Enjoy any downtime you get because I'm certain you will be busy again and then wish you had more time off." So I tried to just live in the moment and let my body heal. And when I looked back on what I had endured in the two years since my sister had died and how I had managed to pull myself through every challenge, I summoned my inner wisdom and heard Lori's voice: "Bring it on."

Lori's wisdom and eyes would really have proved useful to me those days because I was trying to find a house to eventually decorate. With or without emotional or sexual intimacy, Marc and I were still friends and had always talked about buying a house together. He had finally sold his house a month earlier and had never liked all the rules associated with condo living. As a single girl living alone, I loved the security and maintenance-free perks of owning a condo. But I also liked the idea of having a big yard with room for vegetable and flower gardens that my dad would be proud of. I depended on Marc to teach me about owning and caring for a house. We agreed to make a few cosmetic updates to my condo before Marc's Realtor listed it on the market. In the meantime, I had become obsessed with finding the perfect house for us in Bristol, where we had lived together for the past six years.

On a Saturday afternoon in September, while Chalupa and I surfed the Web (yes, she loved to chase the mouse pointer) for real-estate listings and planned our itinerary for the next day's open houses, Marc worked behind me, rehanging the office door before my own condo's open house. His cell phone rang while he banged in a nail. He looked at the number and said, "Oh come on." He sighed and answered the call. "Hello?"

I heard a woman yelling at the other end. Marc didn't respond, but I still heard the female voice ranting. He slammed his cell phone shut and secured it back into the plastic holder that hung on the belt loop of his Levi's.

"Who was that?" I asked.

"I don't know, sounded like an angry Italian woman," he claimed.

The phone rang again. He stepped into the hallway to answer it. "Who is this?" I heard him ask the question calmly as he walked down the stairs to the first floor and then farther down the stairs to the basement and garage. I tiptoed to the first floor and paced the kitchen floor, thinking of an excuse to follow him to the basement. Chalupa jumped on the kitchen counter as I grabbed a half-empty bag of garbage from the trashcan and slithered down the stairs. I stopped on the other side of the door to the garage and my heart raced as I heard him whispering to the angry woman. Marc had stepped outside so I stuffed the trash in a garbage can and, when I heard him slam his phone shut again, I rushed upstairs to the kitchen.

As he climbed the stairs, his cell phone rang again and when I heard the voice mail indicator I knew he had ignored the call. While I poured myself a glass of ice water, the house phone rang. Holding my water, I walked to the living room phone and the caller ID indicated "Private," a type of call I never answered. Then I thought it might be Mickie calling to confirm the number of support group members attending next week's dinner.

"Hello," I said with a smile.

"Is this Linda?" said a woman's voice.

"Yes, who's this?" I tried to recognize the voice.

"Are you Marc's wife?"

"Yes," I lied.

"This is going to sound strange, but I have some news I think you should know."

"Uh huh."

"But I have to ask you, if you don't mind telling me, when were you married?"

"Two years ago. Who is this?" I took a sip of water and stared out the sliding glass door at the seagulls diving in the cove for their lunch.

"Oh, well, that's pretty interesting because I am his girlfriend and he's been seeing me for two and a half years."

"Oh really?" I turned my head to glare at Marc returning from the basement.

"What's the matter?" he asked.

"You tell me." I gritted my teeth and threw the phone at him. He climbed the stairs to the second floor with the phone in his hand.

I placed my water glass on a table, plopped my ass on the couch, and started shaking my head and squinting my eyes. I thought about the last two years and asked myself several questions. If this woman called him two years ago, while he was planning my surprise fortieth birthday party, why didn't he mention her then? Could this woman be telling the truth? I mean, about being his girlfriend—for a second time—since then? Could she be the reason Marc stopped having sex with me? Why the hell would he renovate my condo and buy a house with me if he wanted to be with her?

Marc walked back into the living room and didn't look at me as he put the phone back on the table. Then he looked at me and started to ramble.

"She is an ex-girlfriend from ten years ago. She has MS. She called me two years ago when her disease got worse. She has no family and asked if she could list me as her emergency contact. Her doctor's office called me yesterday because she missed an appointment so I called to check on her. She's a wack job. She called today to tell me not to bother her."

I leaned forward and grabbed my glass of water. "Oh." I'd always admired Marc for his compassion and generosity, so I believed his story.

"I feel bad for her. She has no job, no insurance. I can't just turn away when she needs help."

"Of course you can't. Well, I need to get back upstairs to finish the list of open houses for tomorrow." I smiled at him.

I never asked him why she had claimed to be his girlfriend for the past two and half years. I heard Marc call her a wack job and I believed him.

Chapter 26

My Sixth Sense

On the first Valentine's Day after my sister's death, Marc and I invited John to join us for dinner. John announced that he had met someone after Christmas and had been dating her ever since. Marc later revealed to me that John had plans to marry the woman. I would never want John to live a lonely life, but each time I saw him with his girlfriend, they reminded me how much he and my sister had been in love. Maybe that's why he chose not to tell me. I wondered if my sister would have chanted, "Bring it on," had she known her husband had decided to remarry. I had become comfortable drawing on my sister's wisdom in order to make decisions, but for the first time since her death, I encountered a situation that required me to act on her behalf and I felt paralyzed.

Before my mother's death, I thought the words "religious" and "spiritual" had the same meaning. Although my parents had raised me as Catholic, attending church did not remain a habit of mine after my wedding. After my mother passed away, I found it extremely painful to attend any event that took place in a church because I had such fond memories of my us attending mass together. I only knew that I felt more connected to my mother outside of church.

My mother and I had shared a special sequence of numbers between us—1-4-3. It meant I (1 letter) Love (4 letters) You (3 letters). While in college, one of my roommates had told me a story about a lighthouse keeper who sent love messages to his wife by shining the beacon of light in this pattern of pulses, 1-4-3. When I told my mother the story, she lifted her hand and raised one finger, then four, and then three while she mouthed, "I love you." After my mother died, it seemed that whenever I looked at a clock, whether on my computer, alarm clock, or dashboard, the time read 1:43. Even today, I always smile and whisper, "I love you, too, Mom."

I never received any signs from my dad after he passed away. I joked with my sister, "He's too busy golfing or maybe celebrating at the nineteenth hole." I wanted to visit a medium to see if either of my parents came through, and my sister had told me, "Don't be crazy. That stuff isn't real." I became obsessed with the TV show *The Medium*, and each episode fascinated me more than the previous one. I had wanted Lori to like it, too. I told her she was confusing mediums with fortune-tellers and tarot card readers.

I had been to both once or twice and the messages seemed fairly general and applicable to most anyone. I never wanted to know about my future anyway—I mean, with my fixation on project and risk management, can you imagine that insanity? But mediums intrigued me. How lucky that they were given the ability to communicate with the spirits of those who had once lived on earth.

I remembered I had seen a sign—I mean, a real-life business sign, like a billboard—for a medium with an office in the next town over from where I lived. I had pointed to the sign several times while riding with Lori. "Look, we should go see if she can reach Mom and Dad." Lori had mocked my suggestion, and because I preferred not to go alone, I never made an appointment.

About a week after I heard about John's upcoming marriage, I drove by the medium's office. In the pouring rain, I pulled into the parking lot and stared at the sign—Certified Medium—while I listened to the swishing of the windshield wipers. I scrambled to find a scrap of paper to jot down the medium's name and number.

The following day, I sat in my home office during the virtual lunch break that I always worked through, grabbed the neatly folded napkin from my purse, and googled the name of the medium. The planner in me had the urge to poke around Lynn's website before I called for an appointment. I pictured her looking like an angel or a ghost, and to my surprise, she looked much better than that. Lynn resembled the character from *The Medium*, Alison DuBois. She had blond hair, bright, wide eyes, and a big smile—and she was friendly. I stared at her title, "Afterlife Certified Medium Psychic," and then as if I could hear my sister saying, "That stuff isn't real," I read the definitions of psychic and mediumistic abilities Lynn had posted on the home page of her website. I breathed deeply as I learned how the two abilities were intertwined. A medium is "psychic *and* is able to interpret the communication connection provided by Spirit entities." Mediums do not believe in death; they believe life is continuous and unending. I turned my head toward my office window and shaded my eyes from the reflection of the sun glistening on the harbor and thought, Lori, I'm coming for you. I picked up the phone and dialed Lynn's number.

The first available appointment happened to be an hour before the annual holiday dinner Mickie and I had scheduled for our cancer support group, Sisters in Survival. We had discontinued our attendance at the support group where we had first met because every meeting consisted of the same four women who had been free of cancer treatments for at least a year. One Monday, Mickie called me before that night's meeting.

"Mickie, I love you dearly, but there's never any new people for us to help. I'm getting sick of hearing your story, and frankly, I'm sick of telling you mine."

Mickie agreed. "Me, too. Let's just go out to dinner."

We called the other two women and the four of us had dinner the following week. Within three years, Mickie's dinner group had grown to include fifty or more women who had been diagnosed with all types of cancer. Some had been cancer-free for more than twenty years while others were newly diagnosed. I helped Mickie organize the monthly dinners at nearby restaurants. Lori had attended two or three gatherings, and shortly after she died, Mickie asked me to take the lead on the Sisters in Survival. Mickie continued to negotiate the dinner reservations and recruit new members, while I coordinated the email and phone communications to keep track of the attendance. Forty cancer survivors planned to gather at the holiday dinner the evening of my first visit to the medium.

I didn't know what to expect when I walked into Lynn's waiting room. It looked like a traditional doctor's office except more peaceful due to the subtle scent of incense. Lynn escorted me to a dimly lit room with two upholstered wingback chairs and a small table that held a lamp, a box of tissues, two small glasses of water, and a cassette player. As Lynn placed a new blank tape in the player, I sat back in the chair, inhaled a few deep breaths, and listened to the subtle sound of running water from a tabletop fountain in the far corner of the room.

I leaned forward in my chair as Lynn opened the session with a prayer that welcomed the Spirits and asked them to come through for me. She sat back in her chair, closed her eyes, and kept them closed for what seemed like an eternity before she shared her first vision. She told me she heard the sounds of a marching band, possibly on the Fourth of July, and tons of people in and outside of a house.

"The band is in the background."

Her eyes remained closed while she fidgeted in her chair. I shook my head from side to side as I looked back on all the Fourth of July parties my sister and her husband had hosted.

Lynn rubbed the goose bumps that had formed up and down her arms. She opened her eyes and looked up to the left and then to the right. "One at the time," she said to the Spirits. She turned to me and said, "They are all over me. Do you have any idea what the music may mean?"

"My sister lived on the parade route in Bristol, and she entertained up to seventy or eighty people each year. She served breakfast at seven o'clock, lunch after the parade, and dinner for those who stayed to watch the fireworks. She always hired live entertainment—a magician or juggler or something— for the kids because the four-hour parade couldn't be enough." My eyes filled with tears as I realized how accommodating and thoughtful my sister had always been.

I fanned myself in an effort to stop myself from crying. "Anyway, my mother loved the sound of a marching band and when she didn't feel up to baking in the sun at the parade, she sat in my sister's air-conditioned condo with the windows open, and listened to the bands in the background."

Because Lynn's office was located in the next town over from Bristol, her vision might seem suspiciously general to someone like my sister, but Lynn had no idea where I lived or where my sister had lived for the past fifteen years. I had never given Lynn one ounce of information about anyone in my family—dead or alive.

Lynn closed her eyes and put her head back against the chair. "She looked a lot like you." Lynn lifted her head and looked at me. "Was she older than you by quite a bit?"

"Yes, nine years older than me." I sensed my mother and sister fluttering above me, like two hummingbirds eating nectar from a bird feeder.

Lynn indicated that she saw a revolving door to a hospital and told me this usually suggested many trips to the hospital by one or many people. She asked me if Lori had passed very young or if she had been sick for a long time.

"She was forty-nine when she died. She lived with breast cancer for seven years, but when I got the call that she had passed away in her sleep, the morning after we celebrated her birthday, I was in shock."

"She is much sadder about her passing than your mom and dad are about their own passing."

"Maybe because she was so young." My eyes filled with tears and I reached for a tissue. "Mom was the one who had been most in and out of the hospital. Well, Mom and Dad, I guess." I patted my eyes dry.

Lynn told me she saw a room full of flowers. "Lori is telling me to say there are flowers coming for you. You'll be carrying them or given them in a personal way."

I thought of all the flowers I received once everyone had heard of Lori's passing, and although Lynn's vision may seem applicable to many of her clients, I remembered my dream of Lori giving me permission to enjoy the flowers and I decided this message was meant only for me. I laughed. "When Lori died I must have received fifty bouquets of stunning flowers. I never had the same appreciation for plants and flowers as my parents or Lori so I felt guilty surrounded by so many flowers, especially because my sister had died."

As I listened to the reeling of the tape recorder, I asked Lynn if Lori had anything to say about her husband. And then I received the message I secretly wanted to hear. "Lori is saying that you are not ready to let it go, but she is. He needs to move on in his life. She's cool with this relationship. Doesn't matter how you feel about it, get to know her a little." I only heard Lori's voice saying, "Get over it."

"You have to go into the house—meet him at a party—with an open heart."

"Friday night." I gasped and shook my head in disbelief. If I had any doubt about Lynn's validity, or that of any medium, this one message changed my mind.

"Oh, you'll see him Friday night?"

"Yes, at a Christmas party." Marc and I had been invited to a Christmas party at Bob and Susan's house, and Susan had let me know ahead of time that John would be there with his girlfriend.

"Lori wants me to tell you, when you meet and greet on Friday night, she *will* be there. She's telling me something will happen—a light or maybe a candle will flicker when the two of you are together. You're going to recognize that Lori is there with you. She makes me feel you will see signs. Something to do with a ring."

"Could it be an earring?" I fondled my left ear.

"It could be. Ring. Earring. Are those her earrings?"

"Yes." I breathed deeply and exhaled. "I couldn't wear them for the first year after she died because I felt guilty."

"Oh no. Don't feel guilty. That is a way to honor Spirits. They love when we wear something they left for us or make a recipe they gave us." Lynn took a sip of water. She pointed to the other glass. "That's for you. I don't know if I told you that earlier."

I told Lynn about another dream I had that carried a message similar to the flower dream. In the dream, I wore Lori's diamond earrings to a party that John attended with his girlfriend. When I saw my sister arrive, alone, with bare ears, I covered both my earlobes with my hands. She shouted from across the room, "No, I don't need them anymore. Wear them!"

"Lori's telling me her earrings are bigger now. She's laughing." I laughed out loud, too, as I remembered Lori losing her hair for the third time and asking John for or maybe strongly suggesting he buy her bigger earrings to divert people from staring at her bald head.

"The ring may be a diamond. You may need to brace yourself for what is going on with your brother-in-law. Perhaps a ring has been exchanged?"

"Perhaps." I bit my lower lip and looked up toward the ceiling.

"Find a place in your heart for this, Linda, okay." She paused to listen to the Spirit.

I stared at Lynn, waiting for Lori's advice. "This is what Lori wants. Learn to accept. His girlfriend is good to him. He's not going to marry her unless he knows you are okay with it—especially you—since you are so much like Lori."

Lynn asked if I had any specific questions.

"You already answered the main question I had." I leaned back in the chair. "Well, wait, I've always felt my mother and sister close by, but I wonder about my dad. Do you see him? Hear him?"

"Yes, he's here, just quiet."

I shimmied to the edge of my chair.

"Men are just not as good with showing their feelings. Wait until the summer when I think he may be a bit more vocal. Did your dad have a vegetable garden?" She folded her hands and rested her elbows on the arms of the chair.

Any skeptic would have told me that question was ridiculous because all Italian men have vegetable gardens. When Lynn said I would acquire a lot of vegetables this summer, I shrugged, not knowing what that could mean. "Well, Marc and I have been searching for a house, and we want a big yard for a garden, maybe a pool or a fish pond."

"Your father says you're driving him crazy. Have you looked at a lot of houses?"

"Yes, we're all over the place. Some weekends we only look at land to build a house and other weekends we visit two or three open houses that are vastly different from each other, especially when it comes to having a garage. I want at least a one-car garage, Marc wants three—one for his car and one for his motorcycle and other toys."

"Your dad wants you to get very clear about what you both want in a house and then narrow the search and, most important, if it doesn't have a garage, but has everything else you want, Marc can build a garage."

"Okay." But I knew the biggest conflict would always be that I wanted a newer house with all the latest and best bells and whistles, and Marc only cared about the house's structure and insulation.

"There's a gentleman here with a message for Marc—wait, is there a Peter, too?"

"No, not that I can think of," I tried to think if Peter could be someone from high school or maybe someone Lori had known. "No, I can't think of anyone with that name, Lynn."

"Okay, well this gentleman is just confirming that he agrees with your dad about Marc being able to build anything."

After she had received hugs from my family, Lynn shut off the tape recorder, handed me the cassette, and closed our session by saying thank-you and good-bye to the Spirits. As I clutched the cassette tape in my hand, she escorted me to the front door and I stepped outside as she closed the door behind me. I reached inside my purse to find my car keys as Lynn opened the door again.

"Linda, wait, they have asked me to tell you one more thing."

I looked up from my purse with my heart racing. "Oh?"

"They want you to know you aren't going to die the way they did."

I pressed my right hand, and the cassette tape, on my heart. "Oh my God." I tried to catch my breath.

"Are you okay?"

"I think so. Thank you." I placed the tape in my purse and gathered my keys again. I ran my fingers through my hair and took a deep breath. "Thank you, Lynn."

"You're welcome." Lynn closed her office door.

I stood still for a minute and shook my head, trying to digest this last message she had delivered from my mother, father, and sister. I had never told Lynn that I had survived breast cancer nor that, on a daily basis, I forced fears of a recurrence out of my mind.

I waved at the closed door and walked toward the exterior door of the office building when I noticed the heavy sleet falling and the icy road. I sat frozen in my car, waiting for the heated seat to warm my butt and thought, if I'm not going to die the way they did—from cancer—then how would I die? Ever since my mother had died, I no longer feared my own death because I knew she would be there to greet me. And I had accepted I would die in the same way as my mother and sister had died—as a result of a cancer recurrence—since they had shown me what to expect and how to die, that way, with dignity and grace. I drove a few feet out of the parking lot and then slammed on the break and panicked. Lynn's last message to me echoed in my head and I thought, if not from cancer, then could I die in a car accident, on a stormy night, two weeks before Christmas, on my way to a holiday dinner with fellow cancer survivors?

I paid close attention to the road as I drove, but had no idea how I arrived at the restaurant. Mickie noticed the blank but enlightened stare on my face. "How did it go" she asked.

I shared the highlights of what had just happened with the medium and Mickie gasped when I shared the last message. "I knew it. I've always had that same feeling," she declared.

Brenda had always thought the same thing. "I just have a feeling, Lin," she'd say whenever I had a slight ache or pain. "It's never coming back," she'd assure me. I just shook my head from side to side because now I knew I had proof from the angels.

By the time dinner was over, the sleet had stopped, but the roads were slick. I drove home with a new sense of peace, excited to tell Marc what the medium had communicated. Chalupa met me at the door and I found Marc asleep on the couch with the TV on. As soon as I clicked the "off" button on the remote, he woke up. "Hey, what'd you do that for?" he asked.

"I thought you were sleeping." I sat on the arm of the couch, by his feet.

"How was dinner?"

"Fine, but did you remember, I met the medium today?"

"Oh, yeah, what'd that kook have to say?" He sat up and turned the TV back on. Without his full attention, I recited fewer highlights from the session and jumped right to the last message I had received.

"How does she know that?" he asked.

"She just told me what my parents and Lori told her to tell me."

I emphasized what Lynn had told me about Lori being at the upcoming party Friday night but Marc didn't buy it. "She actually said a candle will flicker? Come on, 'tupid."

I stood up to walk upstairs.

"Of course a candle will flicker," Marc added to drive the knife just an inch or so farther into my chest.

Marc may have believed the medium had fed me a crock of bull, but he also must have sensed my anxiety about what could happen at the party because he stayed by my side as soon as we stepped foot on Bob and Susan's seashell-covered driveway. Bob greeted us at the heavy wooden front door, decorated with a boxwood wreath, and Marc and I followed him into the foyer. Susan smiled as she walked toward us and I handed her a small hostess gift before giving her a hug.

"The house looks stunning, Susan." She had always claimed she learned decorating tips from Lori. We walked by the dining room table that held poinsettia plants and white votive candles placed in between platters of various types of hot and cold food. When we reached the wide open kitchen lined with dark wood cabinets, Bob guided us toward the wine bar. I raised my glass and took a sip before I spotted John and Jane standing at the edge of the sunroom off of the kitchen. Marc and I walked toward my brother-in-law and I gave John a gentle hug without spilling any of our wine. I stood back and we all raised our glasses.

About an hour later, the four of us met again on the half moon–shaped couch. I watched and listened to many guests standing around the grand piano and singing Christmas carols being played by a man wearing a tuxedo. I glanced at the fish tank nestled into a wall that separated the living room from the den as I eavesdropped on Jane speaking lovingly to John. She excused herself to refill John's plate with goodies from the buffet, and I moved closer to John and placed my hand on his.

"She takes care of you." I glanced toward Jane and then stared at John with wide eyes.

"She does." John agreed.

"I know you want to marry her. And I want you to know it's fine. You should marry her." I patted his hand. "I know Lori would approve. She would want you to be happy."

Shortly after our chat, John and Jane walked past me as they were leaving the party and John put his hand on my shoulder. "Thank you."

I touched his hand with mine and took a deep breath. "You're welcome." Marc put his hand at the top of my back and a weight lifted from my shoulders . . . and from my heart.

Marc and I wanted to find Bob and Susan to thank them before we left. I stood by a small table on my tiptoes, searching for our hosts in the kitchen. I pressed my heels back to the floor, looked down at the top of the table, and gasped. Under a delicate Tiffany lamp, someone had placed a black mesh purse with a bright yellow sunflower in its center. I thought of the basket of sunflowers at my sister's burial and the sunflower painting I had received for my fortieth birthday. I brought my right hand to my heart and then to my mouth, and looked at Marc.

"She's here. Oh my God, she *is* here." Marc rubbed my back and shook his head from side to side.

I walked to the kitchen with tears in my eye to find Susan. "What's wrong?"

I walked her back to the table and pointed to the purse. "Do you know whose bag this is?"

"Oh my, Linda. I have no idea." Susan stared at me. "I knew I felt Lori here while I decorated the dining room table tonight."

It started to snow just as we walked to our car. Marc opened my car door for me and handed me my seatbelt before he closed the door. After he started the car and turned on the heat and heated seats, he turned to me.

"Wow. Now I know what you meant. Of all the flowers to be on that purse, right? I mean, even I know it should have been a poinsettia for this time of year."

"Exactly. Who wears a purse decorated with a summer sunflower in the middle of the winter?"

Chapter 27

Surprise!

Two weeks into the New Year, Marc and I received a photograph of John and Jane announcing they had exchanged wedding vows, at midnight on New Year's Eve, while they cruised on the Panama Canal. It took me a few days to call John to wish them both the best of luck. When I hung up the phone, I realized I had called solely on my sister's behalf because I really wasn't ready to let go of my images of Lori and John together and in love.

Later that month, Marc and I took a Sunday drive by his old house to see if any changes had been made since he had sold it. We always loved his neighborhood and wished we could find a house there since we weren't having any luck in Bristol. Marc remembered a friend of his had recently bought a house nearby and that he and his fiancée were renovating, so we took a detour to check it out. We stayed long enough for Marc to salivate at the sight of exposed electrical wires, interior wall partitions, and buckets of paint before we drove home on the same road we had taken to get there. But this time, we both noticed a bright red "Open House" sign on the front lawn of a house. Marc slowed the car.

I stared at the house. "What a cute house. Did you see that sign on the way here?"

"No." The house sat on a corner lot so he drove around to have a better look at it and the yard from all sides. "What the heck, let's go in."

"There's no garage."

"I know, but look at all that land." Marc had a glimmer in his eyes.

He parked the car on a side street and walked ahead of me as we stared at the Cape Cod–style house with its natural shingles and white trim. We reached the crushed stone driveway leading toward the side door and a Realtor opened the door and welcomed us into a small, enclosed entryway. We then stepped into a large kitchen filled with light maple cabinets, brick-red paint, and black granite countertops. I stood with my back to the white porcelain farmer's sink and stared at the open floor plan that led to the outdoor deck and dining and living rooms. Marc admired the tall cathedral ceiling with skylights above the center island that allowed tons of natural light into the kitchen. I leaned forward and my eyes landed on a corner window seat covered with cushions and fluffy pillows. Trying to hide my excitement—a lesson Marc had taught me after every open house we visited—I approached the window seat and leaned forward to peer out the windows, into the backyard and, much to my instructor's dismay, I gasped at the site of a waterfall flowing into a fish pond surrounded by a flower garden.

"Isn't it beautiful?" the Realtor said.

"Yes, my dad had a fish pond. They can be a lot of work." I smiled at her and thought Marc would be happy I had thrown in a negative.

The Realtor turned our attention to the dining and living rooms as she explained that the original home had been built in the 1800s. About five years ago, the sellers had added the kitchen, large mahogany deck, laundry room, and master suite onto the first floor. The moment Marc heard the age of the original house, he asked to see the heating and air-conditioning units in the basement, but I only wanted to see the rest of the living space. We followed the Realtor to the basement and once Marc reviewed the house's engine, he announced that we could see the rest of the house, and I knew that meant he had approved the mechanical stuff.

I fell in love with the master bathroom with its corner Jacuzzi tub surrounded by windows. I gasped again—fully aware I may catch a scolding fit for a child—when I noticed Mexican-style accent tiles behind the tub that perfectly matched a set of tiles Marc and I had purchased on our last vacation to the Mayan Riviera.

We finished the tour and congregated around the kitchen island where I looked away from the Realtor to hide my strong love for this house. Marc handled the discussion about the price and other boring topics unrelated to the bells and whistles that made this house perfect to me, such as the average monthly heating and electrical costs and the age of the roof. I wished he would just make an offer right then, but we walked to the car in silence. When we had both closed our car doors, I looked at Marc. "I love that house."

"No kidding." He lifted an eyebrow at me. "I do, too, but I thought you wanted a garage."

"I did, but there's something about that house that feels like home . . . like my childhood home . . . and that fish pond— it's as if my father dropped this house here within the past month. I mean, I never saw this house when you lived on this road, did you?"

"No, I never noticed it."

Marc made an offer on the house the next day and within two weeks we had a signed deal and an April closing date. When I told our friends about the house I first reminded them of the message from my father that the medium had given me in December. If my friends were on the fence about believing in mediums after the sunflower purse made an appearance at a Christmas party, they crossed over when they heard my father had been behind the house with a fish pond, but no garage.

Some friends asked me to host a Spirit party at the new house so I called Lynn for some available dates. The first date she offered me was April 6—the anniversary of my mother's death. But even my mother had to know the house would never be ready for entertaining by then. I asked Lynn for a date closer to June or July. "I have August second available." *My sister's birthday.* I closed my eyes and booked the party.

Marc, still not ready to admit he believed in the medium's ability to contact the dead, left for the day while five of my friends, including one of his three sisters, each received a thirty-minute reading with Lynn. Each guest experienced at least one magical moment and then my turn arrived. It had been about a year since I had last visited Lynn. I settled into a chair across from her and she began with the familiar prayer to welcome the Spirits and ask them to come forward.

"Your sister has been full of energy today—throughout everyone's readings—and wants me to thank you for having this party. She thinks you had it for her." Lynn rolled her eyes and smiled.

"It's her birthday today."

"Well, that explains it, doesn't it? Your mother wants to say something before your sister monopolizes the rest of the conversation. Your father has taken up residence in your backyard, behind the pond."

I took a deep breath. *Of course he has.* I remembered the two of us sitting together on his wooden bench and feeding the fish in our own backyard.

"They found this house for you, Linda. And they kept the price high until you two finally discovered it."

I leaned forward, placed my elbows on my knees, and folded my hands in front of my mouth. Marc's Realtor had helped him make the best offer when she shared the house's price history and told him it had dropped a week or two before the open house we had attended.

"They are all happy you and Marc have settled here." She squinted. "Can you show me that again," Lynn asked the Spirit.

I leaned back in my chair and crossed my legs in front of me. I had just started to feel more settled in the house, too. I had accepted an offer on my condo a couple of months earlier and once the deal closed two weeks from then, I would have money to invest in this house. Marc and I agreed he would refinance and make it official by having both our names on the mortgage and the deed.

"Someone or something is expanding . . . a wedding or a baby? There are lots of flowers. Did you and Marc get married?" I shook my head from side to side. "Or any plans to get married?"

"No." I wondered if that question came directly from my mother or father.

"Okay, I'm not sure about this. I'll leave that so I don't misinterpret, but there is some sort of a surprise coming."

She may have left it, but I only thought about who could be having a baby considering that Marc and I had no plans to get married.

"Lori likes this room. She loves the picture you have on the wall. She had mentioned it during another reading, I think, with your friend Brenda."

I wondered which of Marc's framed prints Lori would have liked because I never liked any of them.

Thirty minutes had passed very quickly, and although I received confirmation that Marc and I had chosen the right house, I wanted more time with my parents and Lori. Lynn handed me the cassette from my session and gathered her tape recorder. She followed me down the hall, but as I descended the staircase, she stopped in front of my office.

"The house really is lovely, Linda. What's in this room?" Lynn pointed at the door to my office.

"Oh, that's my home office."

Lynn walked into the small room with golden yellow walls and olive green carpeting. "Lori likes something in this room. The picture is in this room, not the room we were sitting in."

I placed my hand on my heart and breathed deeply. "Of course." I walked into the office and pointed to the painting with Lori's face in the center of a sunflower.

Over the next two weeks, Marc and I moved the remaining furniture and boxes from my condo to the house. After my closing, we stopped at a local restaurant to celebrate. I held the check in my hand and smiled at Marc.

"I should be able to give you my share toward the house next week. Have you called the banker for an appointment or should I?"

"What's the rush? I'll call the guy next week." I wondered why he thought I might be rushing when we had been planning this for months.

By October he still hadn't made plans to refinance. I had just finished packing up my laptop and work files in the office and walked downstairs when I heard Marc on the phone in the living room.

"Do you know of any vacant apartments for rent?" he was saying.

I proceeded down the stairs and he rushed to hang up the phone. When I asked who needed an apartment, he yelled at me, "I can't believe you were eavesdropping on me." Then he told me Sharon had run into some trouble and needed a place to live.

"Sharon?"

"Yeah, remember my friend with MS?"

"Oh, really? You mean your ex-girlfriend, don't you?" I glared at him. "Why didn't you tell me you had heard from her again?" It had been more than a year since she had called my condo and announced she and Marc had been dating for two and a half years.

"I didn't want to bother you with this."

"You didn't want to bother me with this? You thought it was better to sneak around? You've obviously been in touch with her all this time!" I screamed.

I felt more furious with myself than him. I grabbed my car keys and bit my lip to stop myself from crying. I stomped past my cat and she scurried under the couch. I slammed the side door and retreated to my car. I had never confided in any of my friends—not even Brenda—about the first time the bitch had called me. Part of me felt embarrassed to reveal my stupidity and part of me didn't want my family and friends to worry about me. I drove about a mile away from the house and pulled into an empty parking lot before dialing Brenda's number. I stopped crying long enough to tell her what Sharon had claimed a year ago, but then I lost it before I could explain what had just happened. "He's obviously having an affair with her, Bren!"

"Lin, I can't believe that. I mean, maybe she really is nuts," Brenda whispered, more likely because she was trying to calm me down than for fear someone might hear her.

"But Bren, I have to leave for a business trip in the morning."

"That's good, actually, I think the distance will be good for you." She assured me everything would work out for the best.

"What if he has the bitch stay in our bed, or even upstairs, while I'm gone?" I felt like a complete fool for being so naïve for so long.

When I returned from my short road trip around the neighborhood, Marc apologized for not telling me about Sharon but I couldn't let it go. I walked around the house—especially in our bedroom and bathroom—and documented the placement of every single knick-knack so I could investigate any suspicious changes when I returned from my business trip.

Marc called me the following night. First he told me how much Chalupa missed me, and then he let me know he had rented an apartment—above his best friend's garage—for the bitch. My jaw dropped as I sighed into the phone. "Are you serious? Ya know what, I can't talk to you right now. I'm in the middle of a meeting that I can't get out of." I could have gotten out of my own meeting, but I didn't want to and I still remembered the time he had left me at the eye doctor searching for someone else to help me.

Sure, I felt better knowing Sharon hadn't stayed in our house, but I still wanted to know why he felt the need to take care of her. And then, for a brief second, I wondered if she had been the reason Marc had delayed refinancing his house and adding me to the mortgage and deed.

As I look back now, I remember the weeks that followed that specific business trip, and I realize that Marc and I had become more distant during those six days than we had been in the previous six years combined. I actually felt like the fifth wheel. We watched Patriots football at his best friend's house almost every weekend, and every week I became nauseated just by the sight of Sharon's car parked in front of their house. Marc and his friends acted as if nothing had changed between us and seemed to accept this ridiculous living arrangement. In fact, one time, I actually thought Marc might invite Sharon down to watch the game with us.

The night before Thanksgiving, while we prepared to host Marc's family for dinner the next day, I blurted out, "She must be why you don't want to refinance the house. Why don't you just tell me so I can get out of your way?"

"Don't be 'tupid," he replied.

I still felt like the outcast in a high school clique. I made myself sick anticipating the day Marc asked me to move out so he and Sharon could be together.

I had just taken a baking dish out of the oven while Marc stood behind the washing machine, fixing the dryer vent, when our house phone rang. I threw the red oven mitts on the counter, picked up the handset, and stopped breathing when "Private" showed up on the phone.

"Hello?"

"Hi, Linda. It's Sharon . . . you know, Marc's girlfriend."

"What do you want now?" I really wanted to add "bitch."

"Would you please tell him to leave me alone? You really need to have sex with him again because I don't want to have sex with him anymore."

I handed him the phone and dropped to the floor.

"Forget it, you're nuts." Marc hung up the phone. He walked around from the back of the clothes dryer and stood staring down at me while trying to explain why she had called.

"She knows she's not welcome in that apartment and would rather just stay on the boat again."

"What?!" I snapped at him. "She stayed on our boat?!"

"Yes, back in September, before I found her the apartment, but then it got too cold out."

I put my hand up. "Shut up." I glared at him. "I'm done. You need to get your priorities in order. I'm going to put on a pretty little smile for your family tomorrow, but after that, you need to make a choice or I will." He tried to touch my arm and I pushed him away.

After a chilly Thanksgiving dinner (and I'm not referring to the temperature of the food or the air), I stood outside on the deck with Marc's oldest sister. "Is everything okay with you and my brother?"

I had kept my sadness and shame a secret for so long. "No, not at all." I told her about Marc's relationship with Sharon.

"Oh jeepus, not again." She bowed her head.

"Again?"

Marc's sister confessed that Sharon had caused Marc's divorce. I covered my mouth and thought I may pass out.

I turned my head toward the fish pond and stared at the water flowing downward. Marc had always claimed that his ex-wife had been the cheater. His sister shared that Sharon had acted like a psycho, and then she disclosed how Sharon had deliberately cut the pads of Sophia's paws, hoping the bloody floor would get Marc's attention. I thought to myself, how the hell did I get myself into a real-life version of *Fatal Attraction*? Does his family think this living arrangement is normal, too?

Just two weeks before Christmas, Marc traveled to New York City for his school's annual board meeting. After the conversation with his sister, I dreaded sleeping in the house alone, and my fear caused me to keep a knife under my pillow—to protect my kitty cat. On the day I expected Marc to arrive home, I had just finished working in the home office when my mind turned to the events with Sharon over the past three months. I gave into my urge to sneak around Marc's computer and opened his work email. I never had to enter a password; the application simply displayed the emails from the last time Marc had signed in. I searched for emails to or from Sharon and a long list appeared in front of me. I started with one dated around the same time as my last business trip. I stared at the words in black and white and felt the vomit rising to my throat. I closed my eyes and squinted before fully opening them again and thought, holy shit, you must be kidding me.

Sharon wrote, ". . . some more rocking the boat would feel good. . . ." to which Marc responded, "Yeah, the boat thing would be fun tonight. . . . I'm on a loose pulley."

I looked at the date of the email and realized the timing referred to when I had been out of town. Tears stung my eyes as I glared at my sister's face in the sunflower. Is this my surprise? I turned back to the computer and read all the emails before and after this one. I mean, this must be a joke, right? But each time I read the original email, my nausea worsened and my tears flowed heavier—thicker—stronger.

I pushed my chair away from the desk, sunk deeper into its seat, threw my head back, and screamed out loud. I heard my cat's bell jingle as she bounded up the stairs. She paused in the doorway and stood still as she stared at me.

Chalupa slowly approached me and rubbed her entire body against my shin. I leaned down to pat her head and she licked my fingers. I fell backward into the chair and she jumped into my lap and gazed into my soaked eyes. Watching her watch me made me sob heavier. I had known for a while that I had to get out of this house and out of this relationship, but what about Chalupa?

I turned my attention back to the hurtful email, bit my thumbnail, and sighed. I realized Marc and I had turned into roommates the moment I told him I wanted a double mastectomy. I always ignored our lack of intimacy while he assumed the role of the supportive friend—such as when Lori had died, and when he threw a huge surprise birthday party for me, and even when he gave me my very first pet—because, even with the absence of sex, I still thought he loved me. Chalupa had settled into my lap as I shook my head from side to side and continued to stare at the computer screen. I thought back to the previous year—after my neck and emergency eye surgeries—and how I had noticed his impatience with me, and the lack of love and compassion compared to when he had nursed me through my chemotherapy. I had ignored my suspicions of his infidelity, even after the wack job announced they had been dating for two and a half years. I had accepted being roommates because I never considered he would completely betray me. I had trusted him.

When I turned back to the words in black and white, I wondered what time Marc would be home. I reached for the phone while Chalupa jumped off my lap and onto the floor. I dialed Marc's cell phone. "When will you be home?"

"We're on the train now. Should be there in a couple of hours. Why?"

"Because I won't be here when you get back."

"What?" I hung up the phone without answering him. He called my cell phone several times and I ignored it.

As I walked to the basement to get my luggage, I called Brenda and had trouble getting the words out over the tears.

"You can stay with us," she said.

"Thank you, Bren. I knew you'd say that. I'm going to call Frankie, and I'll call you back if he kicks me to the curb."

I rolled the suitcase into our bedroom and called my brother.

"Hi, Frankie. I have a problem." I sniffled.

"What happened?"

"I'm leaving Marc. I hate to even ask, but can I stay with you guys for a little while?" I tossed my favorite sweaters into the suitcase. I had a little déjà vu, too, thinking about how I had called my sister for a place to stay after Dean had asked me for a divorce.

"What? Yeah. Of course. What's going on?" He sighed and it sounded like he had expected this would happen.

"Thanks. Can I explain later? I'll be there sometime tonight."

I threw the phone on the bed, picked up my kitty cat, and kissed her head as tears streamed down my face. I placed Chalupa on the bed and she jumped into my suitcase. I placed her back on the bed and she jumped back in. I giggled and cried at the same time—a little more déjà vu as I pictured Sophia acting the same way while I tried to pack for Florida when my dad had been hospitalized. I could have taken Chalupa with me, but wondered if she and my brother's dogs would get along. I filled my suitcase with whatever I could fit. I picked up Chalupa one last time, zipped up the suitcase, and wheeled it to the kitchen. She clawed at the suitcase while I filled her food and water dishes. I grabbed my coat and car keys, closed the door behind me, and never looked back.

Chapter 28

No Regrets

I drove to Frankie's while in the biggest funk of my life. I cried out in disgust and shame as I interpreted the events that had been unfolding throughout my entire relationship with Marc—taking advantage of that wonderful thing called hindsight—and how I had ignored the fact that we were living without physical and emotional intimacy for the last six years. But had I really ignored it? Or had I just accepted our lack of intimacy because Marc had always made me feel safe. I knew we had grown apart, but in a million years, I never would have pegged Marc as a liar or a cheater, nor had I anticipated he would put my life in danger. And yet, for all the shock and anger I carried, a burden had been lifted when I finally allowed myself to admit that I would not live that way anymore. As I thought about losing the protection of having Marc in my life, I felt fortunate to have family and friends willing to offer me a safe place to stay while I figured out my next move. And then I cried out with frustration at the thought of packing and moving again, this time after only eight months.

Frankie had told me he would be home from a trip the following day, but his wife, my nephews, and their two dogs all waited up for me to arrive. The only questions came in the form of loud barks, wagging tails, and sloppy dog kisses. Dinner time had already passed, but Deb set the kitchen table with two wine glasses and three bottles of my brother's homemade wine.

"Frank called and told me which wines to grab from the cellar and said to have whatever you need." Deb poured us each a glass of white. "The boys are upstairs in Dan's room. Nick wants you to stay in his room." Maybe my brother told Nick what had happened, or maybe the reason never mattered to my nephews. They only knew that their auntie needed a place to stay and that's what family does for each other.

"No, he shouldn't have to do that for me." My heart melted at how thoughtful and selfless my young nephews had become. "Are they still awake?"

"Yes."

I took my glass, climbed the stairs with the two dogs at my heels, and knocked on Dan's bedroom door.

"Come in, Auntie," both boys said.

"Hey." They were playing a video game together. "Nick, I don't want you to have to move for me."

"It's okay. I want you to be comfortable. We're family. It's fine." His eyes never left the computer screen.

"Okay, well, thank you." I called for the dogs to leave the bedroom and closed the door behind me. I glanced into Nick's room, recognized my parents' mahogany bedroom set, and felt as though someone had planned for me to stay in this house, in that room, and on that bed.

I returned to the kitchen and sat with Deb for a few minutes before getting my suitcase from the car.

"Are you okay?" she asked.

"I think so, yes. I mean, I think I will be."

I told my sister-in-law what had happened in September, and then again at Thanksgiving, and what I had found just a few hours earlier. She simply shook her head. "Are you sure?"

"You tell me." I pulled out the printed emails from my purse and slapped them on the kitchen table.

Deb raised her eyebrows. "Okay. Wow. I never would have guessed this about him. What a jerk."

"Me either." For a split second I wished I had refrained from displaying Marc's dirty laundry with my family in case we reconciled, but I knew I had no intention of staying with him. I still wanted to give Marc credit where he had earned it. "But Deb, I'll always be grateful for how he took care of me. It doesn't excuse this, but I guess it just proves that everyone comes into our lives for a reason. I mean, my ex-husband could not have taken care of me like Marc did."

"That's the truth. You can stay here for as long as you need. I have to go to bed."

"Thanks. I have four days left to work this year and then I'm on vacation until after New Year's. I plan to find a place to live by then." I had no plan, but just the act of voicing my goal for the first time gave me the determination to make it happen—in two weeks' time.

I grabbed my suitcase from my car, dragged it upstairs and into a corner of Nick's bedroom, and opened it to get my jammies. I picked up the journal I had placed on top of all my clothes, dropped my body to the floor, leaned back against the frame of my parents' bedroom set, and read the last entry I had written ten days earlier, in the waiting room of my oncologist's office—four days after Thanksgiving. I had written ". . . I need to leave . . . I just need to get out . . . ," so maybe finding the emails between Marc and Sharon just gave me the permission I thought I needed. If nothing else, the emails certainly gave me the courage, anger, and confidence to deal with Marc when he returned home and realized I really had left.

Marc had called my cell phone a couple of times since I had hung up on him earlier. Until I felt ready to talk to him, the caller ID saved me from crying, from saying something I may regret, and from being lied to again. But caller ID only postponed all of these things. Eventually, as I stared at my open suitcase and the framed photo of Chalupa I had thrown in there at the last minute, I knew I had to answer my phone.

And as much as I wanted to yell at Marc, I knew I had to be quiet while Deb and the boys were sleeping.

"I just got home and you're not here. Where are you?" he asked.

"Somewhere safe." I knew he hadn't believed I would leave.

"Why? What happened? What the hell is going on?"

"Nothing new. I sleep with a knife when you're not home. How crazy is that? I'm afraid that psycho is coming after me or my cat." My voice quivered.

"That's sick. Well, I'm home now and she's not doing that."

"Yes, *she* is sick. I cannot believe you knew how dangerous and psychotic this bitch was and you let her into our lives. It's too late."

"Too late? Where are you?"

"I'm at a hotel." *Who's lying now?*

"That's just great. I bought this beautiful house and you leave?"

I wanted to scream, are you serious? The house is beautiful because I made it that way—with the newly designed custom curtains and window seat cushions and pillows I just bought for the kitchen and dining room, but I restrained myself.

"The house may be beautiful, Marc, but we don't have a relationship there. You do your thing, I do mine. You made your choice. She won. Just tell the bitch she won."

"What? I won't be with her."

"Do you have any idea what she told me on the phone the night before Thanksgiving?"

"No, but she's a psycho." He laughed.

"Well, she's not too crazy to say something I thought only you and I knew. How did she know we don't have sex?"

"Because . . . I told you she's a conniving psycho."

"Once again—you knew she was a psycho and yet you let her into our lives—you let her into *my* life."

"I just don't understand. You were fine on the phone yesterday and now, all of a sudden, you're gone? There must be someone else!"

"How dare you." I composed my thoughts so he wouldn't know I had read his emails. "You're the one who has someone else! And who are you kidding? This didn't just happen. We've been roommates for years and you've been lying to me about your girlfriend the whole time."

"Wow, you're talking to me like one of your business conversations, with no emotion."

"Yeah, well, maybe I'm emotionally bankrupt. I feel nothing right now. I trusted you. I honestly believed you loved me—no matter what." I started to cry. When the phone connection became overpowered by static, I hung up on him and shut my phone off.

I changed into my flannel pajamas, put my head on the pillow, and curled up into a fetal position. Then I wished I had taken Chalupa with me so I could feel her warm furry body tucked into that space between my belly and my heart. I placed a box of tissues on the bed and cried myself to sleep that night.

The following morning, I set up my work laptop in my brother's office. My nephews had gone to school and Deb had some Christmas shopping to finish. Sometime after lunch, my brother pulled into his driveway and the dogs jumped from their slumber. They barked as we walked to the kitchen door to greet Frankie, who looked more like my father each time I saw him. I felt embarrassed to tell him what had happened between Marc and me. I knew I could take care of myself, but I wanted my big brother to protect me. I wanted my big brother to be my big sister.

"Lin, how are ya?"

"Okay, you?"

Frankie hugged me. "What happened?"

I shared the same story I had told Deb the night before and Frankie had the same reaction. "Are you sure?"

He followed me into the living room and we sat on the couch while I pulled the printed emails from my purse. "That bastard, and you just sold your condo."

"I know, but I don't regret that. I loved living closer to Lori, and that place helped me heal from Dean and breast cancer—and neck and eye surgery. God, what a mess I've been. I was ready for a move. It'll be good for me to find something new."

The following week, armed with my spreadsheet and Brenda, I looked at five condominiums in Providence and documented the characteristics, benefits, and downfalls of each one. I could work in the Providence office. Maybe I needed to be around people during the day rather than my cat. I narrowed down my condo options to the two within walking distance of my office so I wouldn't have to pay for parking. I dismissed one condo when the sales manager insisted I declaw my cat. But even before I heard that crazy request, I knew I wanted to live in the condos at the Westin Hotel. It was a thirty-two-floor tower attached to the newest mall in Rhode Island, which included my sister's favorite store, Nordstrom's. I mean, what woman wouldn't want that?

The condo's marble and granite interior, common areas, and the views from the twenty-first floor made my jaw drop. Additionally, a concierge provided twenty-four-hour security. By the end of the week, I had signed the lease on the dotted line and began to feel a little more independent—and safer. My decision was partly influenced by a friend and his partner who had been living on the twenty-third floor and loved everything about luxury living in the city.

Cynthia and her fiancé, Bob, as well as Faith and Andrew had Christmas Eve dinner with us at Frankie's, and although I missed not having Marc with me after seven Christmases together, I looked forward to just being with my family. By then, everyone knew Marc and I had split up, but I couldn't wait to tell them where I was moving. Faith's eyes lit up at the mention of the mall and Cynthia was relieved that I would be safe. I made a mental note to make an appointment with the medium to hear if my parents and Lori had an opinion on my new digs.

I woke up on Christmas morning to the smell of coffee and cinnamon monkey bread, a yummy family tradition Deb had created when my nephews were very young. Still wearing my pajamas, I walked downstairs and toward the den. My brother's family—dogs included—were sitting around the Christmas tree and waiting for me so we could exchange gifts.

"Here Auntie, come and sit here." Dan patted an empty spot on the couch near him. Although Dan and Nick were thirteen- and fifteen-years-old, respectively, I had forgotten what I loved most about being a kid on Christmas morning.

Later that day, instead of Marc and me leaving for a warm climate destination like we had for the past seven years, I planned to spend the day alone at his house packing up my life—again. I gasped when I saw Marc's car in the driveway because he had told me he would be at his sister's house. We had talked on the phone and through emails, but I hadn't seen him—or Chalupa—since before I had left over a week ago. Chalupa ran to the door and, with her stiff tail pointed at the ceiling with just that little curl at the end, she meowed at me and rubbed up against my ankles. I sat on the kitchen floor and she rubbed up against my entire body. Marc walked into the kitchen from the master bedroom looking like he had just showered.

"I thought you were going to your sister's?"

"I didn't feel up to it. And you have a lot of work here so I thought you could use the help."

"Thanks, I guess I could use it. The movers will be here in five days." *Wow, he's certainly not begging me to stay, is he? Damn right, you'll help me.*

"Oh yeah, where are they taking the stuff?"

"Mostly storage, and I'd rather not say." I had no interest in hearing his opinion about where I chose to live. And my life was no longer any of his business.

He turned to the kitchen sink to wash a serving dish before I packed it and I heard him sniffling. When he turned around, his eyes were red and it was clear he had been crying.

"What's wrong?"

"I just can't believe it's come to this." He sobbed. I found it very hard to muster up any compassion for him. "Well, I have your Christmas gift here."

"Oh? Really, let's not do that this year."

"I bought it in New York like I do every year and I want you to have it." He handed me the Tiffany blue bag with the Tiffany blue box. He had given me so many pieces of Tiffany jewelry that the previous Christmas he had actually repeated a gift. Of course, 'tupid me had never considered that maybe he had bought that gift for someone else. As we stood in the kitchen, I held the blue box in my hand for what seemed like minutes before he insisted I open it. I inserted my fingers into the blue velvet pouch and revealed a silver bracelet with a heart on it—the heart matched the necklace that Marc had already bought me—twice. I thanked him and returned the bracelet to its pouch.

As I turned back to the box I had been packing with books, I thought about where we had spent Christmas together the previous year. Of all the Caribbean vacations we had taken, our trip to Turks and Caicos had been my favorite. Well, my favorite place for the white sand beaches, the crystal-clear water, and the fresh fish, but favorite memories of the way Marc had treated me? Not so much.

Three days into the vacation, my damn period had started. I had been suffering with extremely heavy, painful periods for a few years—probably the beginning of menopause. As I keeled over in pain, I couldn't even utter the words "menstruation" or "menopause" around Marc without him cringing in disgust and blocking his ears. We had signed up for a snorkeling excursion before I started feeling so sick and afterward I didn't think I should swim around the ocean with a bunch of blood-sniffing sharks. You should just skip over the rest of this paragraph if you, too, cannot handle the words "menstruation" or "tampon." The blood flowed so heavily on the day of the excursion, I had to change my super-size tampon twice in the registration shack before we even stepped foot on the boat. During the entire ride, I wanted to vomit and could only think about bleeding through my tampon, maxi pad, bathing suit bottom, and shorts. But Marc bonded easily with the other passengers and the captain, so when I refused to snorkel in the Caribbean he didn't make me feel like too much of a loser. He saved his ridicule and insensitivity for that night when, instead of hailing us a cab, we walked more than a mile to the market to buy more tampons.

As I packed one of the candleholders Nick had given me for Christmas last year, I only hoped my nephews would grow up and become great men who treated women with respect.

As planned, I moved into my new condo five days after Christmas, and if my nephews' behavior on New Year's Eve reflected how they would grow up, I had no worries. Frankie and Deb had planned to celebrate with friends overnight at a hotel in Providence and my nephews insisted I not be alone on New Year's Eve. So with their sleeping bags in hand and the board games that had become our favorites over the previous two weeks, I celebrated the New Year with Nick and Dan. I treated them to dinner at a restaurant of their choice at the mall, and then, without ever having to walk outside, we walked back to my new condo, where my nephews treated me to several games of Life! We were blessed with a huge, but beautiful snowstorm that evening. Bundled in hats and scarves, we stood outside on my long, narrow balcony twenty-one floors above the city and listened to the sounds that marked my new beginning.

After a couple of weeks living alone, I decided that I wanted my cat back. I had initially worried she'd be unhappy as an indoor cat—in downtown Providence—but I just had to give her a chance. Unfortunately, Chalupa was not the last rope that bound me to Marc. Since he had decided to sell our boat, I needed to tolerate his voice until the spring when we were more likely to receive offers.

By March, Chalupa and I had settled into our new life in the big little city. But I had one challenge I wanted to overcome—something I needed to prove to myself. Marc and I had taken so many vacations together and I needed to confirm that I could still go on vacation—alone.

I left a message for my travel agent. "I need to get away for three, maybe four nights. It needs to be warm. It needs to be safe. I am traveling alone."

She called me within an hour and raved about a brand new resort in Montego Bay, Jamaica. The hotel's availability worked perfectly with the dates my boss had suggested I take off before the next huge project required me to travel to New York City every week. At the time, I only felt comfortable with Marc watching Chalupa. Once I confirmed his willingness to help me, I called the travel agent back. "It's perfect."

On my six-hour journey to Jamaica I relaxed with a couple of cocktails and read Steve Harvey's entire book *Act Like a Lady, Think Like a Man*. After two long-term and failed relationships, I needed to know why I kept choosing the wrong men. After Dean and I divorced, I had written the words to describe the next man I would love: polite, courteous, sensitive, funny, respectful, handsome, smart, and responsible. I also wanted a man who had experienced some sort of tragedy—lived through extreme sadness, loss, or pain—and had become a stronger, better person because of it. When I met Marc, he satisfied every requirement I had written down. He had even lost his mom to breast cancer. During my second cocktail and the eighth chapter "Why Men Cheat," I identified another characteristic I had forgotten to include on my list of requirements for finding a partner: integrity. I questioned if maybe I trusted people too easily or too quickly. If I chose to be skeptical of everyone I met going forward, that would make for a very lonely life, no?

When I read the second to the last chapter, "How to Get the Ring," I realized that maybe I had been dishonest with Marc, too. According to the author, there were three possible reasons why Marc hadn't seriously asked me to marry him, and as I read the reasons, I realized each one applied to us in some way. Two of the reasons pointed to Marc. Reason #1: He was still married to someone else, and I thought, well, maybe not in a legal sense, but he certainly still felt tied to Sharon. Reason #2: I was not really the one Marc wanted, and I thought, no shit, really? Reason #3: I never required Marc to marry me. The truth was, I never cared if Marc married me because I wasn't in love with him anymore. I fell out of love with him six years ago, when we stopped being intimate. I fell out of love with him when I had my breasts removed and he made me feel ugly. I fell out of love with him when I realized he never loved or respected the person who lived inside me.

I heard the landing gear come down, closed the book, and stared out the window. I could see clear to the bottom of the ocean as the plane made its landing. I walked into the airport and noticed only couples standing around me in the baggage claim area. On the bus to the resort, I met and spoke with Liz and Jeff. They were celebrating their first wedding anniversary.

Palm trees and hot pink flowers that looked like azaleas lined the driveway to the resort. The doorman wheeled my cat-scratched red luggage, and I followed him into the lobby with my eyes and mouth wide open. I stared at the lavish modern décor of the open and bright lobby. Tiles of black-and-white shiny marble covered the floor. There were several clusters of leather couches and chairs upholstered in my favorite earthy colors. Sparkling glass beads cascaded from every window and chandelier. I walked to the main lobby bar while housekeeping finished getting my room ready. Liz and Jeff asked me to join them and, not wanting to impose, I left two stools between us.

The concierge walked toward me. "Your room is ready, ma'am." We walked to the elevator and he escorted me to my room on the third floor.

I stared in amazement from the moment I opened the heavy, dark brown wooden door. To the right, there was an entire wall of dark brown sliding doors full of closet space and a stocked snack bar. To my left, light green frosted glass enclosed the gray marble bathroom with mirrors on every wall. Straight ahead, I saw the king-size bed smothered in white cotton linens, a dark brown velvet duvet cover, and dark brown, deep red, and rich purple velvet pillows in many shapes and sizes. I took one step down to the sitting area that held an upholstered couch, a funky modern chair, and a simple desk. And then I caught a glimpse of the balcony and the rattan swing that hung from the ceiling. My room overlooked the stunning ocean, a vast area of bright turquoise pool water, palm trees, grass huts, and maybe the best part of the entire resort: full-size brown rattan beds with ivory cotton mattresses, each covered by a gazebo and heavy cotton canopy. At that moment, I fully embraced the feeling of freedom and I liked it.

I answered a knock at the door and, standing before me, was a young Jamaican man with a huge smile showing his bright white teeth.

"Hello. Welcome. I am your personal butler and here to do whatever you need. May I help you unpack? Iron your clothes? Draw you a bath?"

"Seriously?" I raised my right eyebrow.

"Yes, ma'am.

"I'm fine, thank you." It reminded me of the television show *Lifestyles of the Rich and Famous*, and I realized some people rely on a servant to fulfill their every need. But I had traveled alone to relearn how to rely on myself.

The next night, I dined alone at a small table in the Italian restaurant. I scanned the entire dining room and never felt the least bit ashamed. In fact, I felt liberated when I realized every table hosted two or more guests except for mine. As I walked back to my room, I passed Liz and Jeff, who asked me to join them for a nightcap. I admired her outfit—a vibrant, abstract patterned dress, four- or five-inch high-heeled sandals, and the biggest hoop earrings I had ever seen (and I had seen a lot of earrings given that my family owned a jewelry company). Her entire ensemble fit her perfectly and made me feel like an old maid with my khaki capris, tank top covered with a white cotton sweater, and bronze mule sandals with a one-and-a-half, maybe two-inch heel at most. Only I knew my outfit screamed "sexy" compared to the oversize jeans and Dansko clogs I had worn for the past seven years with Marc. I shared the story of Marc's betrayal with Liz and Jeff.

"I'm so sorry. That must be very difficult for you. We see you writing in your journal during the day. Is that what you're writing about?" Liz asked with a curious smile.

"Well, that and all the other tragedies of my life. I hope to write a memoir someday. I was divorced once before, lost my mother and sister to breast cancer, lost my dad to cancer, and I had breast cancer myself."

"You are a very brave woman," Liz said.

The next morning, I jumped out of bed early to get the best spot on the beach. I opted for a bright yellow padded lounge chair under a grass umbrella closest to the water. I reached into my beach bag and pulled out my turquoise blue journal and my iPod, which I had loaded with new songs just for this trip. I stared out into the endless ocean, fully content with sitting still, listening to music or the sound of the waves, smelling suntan lotion, and just breathing. These choices were all mine and I didn't feel the least bit guilty about not wanting to fill every second of every day with some activity—kayaking or parasailing or walking the beach—like Marc had done when we vacationed together.

I opened my journal to a fresh clean page and thought about my intention—this was how Hannah, my writing teacher, motivated her students to journal at the beginning of each class. I wrote my intention in the form of a very important question: What do I love about Linda? I briefly closed my eyes and listened to Andrea Bocelli on my iPod. Then I opened my eyes and wrote my answer:

> I love my openness to try new things
>> and to share what I learn.
>
> I'm compassionate.
>
> I'm kind.
>
> I'm sincere.
>
> I strive to be a better person, to learn
>> something new every day.
>
> I love that I am aware of me.
>
> I love that I can be perfectly still, alone, quiet.

I realized it was my habit to turn to sleep when I needed to escape my sadness. But after I described what I loved about myself, I wrote, "I want to be awake more than I'm asleep." And even when my body required sleep, I wrote, "I want to be awake to enjoy it." Then I wondered how I could make that happen and I realized it was those naps on the beach. I loved the feeling of peacefulness at the beach late in the day, after most people had already left, about an hour or two before the sun set. That time of day when I loved to lie down on the blanket, wiggle my body into the sand, and take a nap. I imagined that space in time when I almost doze off, but then I'd hear a wave crash, a seagull squawking, or a child laughing. It never mattered what sound stirred my senses, it only mattered that I kept my eyes closed, breathed deeply, melted into my surroundings, and smiled.

The next day, I decided to test out the canopy beds by the pool. I pulled out my journal and began writing. I noticed Liz and Jeff lounging on a bed on the other side of the pool. They waved me over and asked me to join them for a drink. "We haven't been able to stop thinking about you after our chat yesterday, Linda," Liz said. "We wondered, have you been on any excursions while you've been here?"

I shrugged my shoulders. "No, I wouldn't dream of leaving the resort alone."

They looked at each other, and Jeff said, "Go ahead, ask her."

"Have you heard of the Luminous Lagoon?"

I shook my head.

"It's about a thirty-minute ride from here and then a twenty-minute guided boat ride to a place where the water glows."

"Well, it actually glows when people swim in it and aggravate the organisms below the surface," Jeff explained. "It's the place where saltwater and freshwater meet. There are only four places in the world that have this and Jamaica is considered the best place to experience it."

"Right. We would love to go with you. So you can make your own glow, Linda. There are openings for all three of us this evening. Will you come?"

"Sure. I'd like that. It sounds like a once-in-a-lifetime experience." I smiled.

Looking back now, my entire Jamaican adventure proved to be a once-in-a-lifetime opportunity.

I had found Linda.

All these years, I was writing a list of what I wanted to find in a man, but my decision to embark on this solo journey inspired me to only examine myself.

For the first time, given the distance and my own private butler on a Caribbean island, I had gained the insight—the wisdom—to connect all the dots. I truly believe I had to experience everything in my life prior to Jamaica for it to have had such a powerful impact on me.

I deepened my belief that everything in my life had happened for a reason.

I saw my life as a full circle. And just like the rim of a bicycle wheel is connected by spokes under tension, I started to see my life's center hub and I realized—my life is beginning to have a purpose.

I defined my core values—integrity, compassion, courage, and openness and dedication to personal improvement. And maybe, most important, I vowed to never compromise my values and regained the confidence I once had to live my authentic life out loud.

I returned home late on a Saturday evening and had the entire next day to transform my mind from vacation mode to work mode again. I ate breakfast and unpacked my suitcase before taking a shower. I stepped out of the glass-enclosed marble shower and reached for a fresh brown fluffy towel. I dried my body before I wrapped the towel tightly around my head and tossed my head back, letting the towel hang against my neck. Standing naked in front of the mirror, I stared at my chest and realized how much I missed my breasts. I had always wondered if this day might come.

Marc and I had been dating a little more than a year when I received my breast cancer diagnosis. He had listened to my fears and the reasons I wanted a double mastectomy, but he never truly agreed with my decision. After I created a cast of my own breasts, I reveled in pure peace the night before my mastectomy. I needed that surgery to reduce my fear of the breast cancer recurring. I never considered—nor would I have believed—that my decision to remove my breasts would tear us apart.

As I stared at myself in the mirror, I wondered if I had made the biggest mistake of my life. Could that arrogant plastic surgeon who told me breasts were important to men have been right? Would I ever find a man to love me again? Without natural breasts? Even after breast reconstruction, I had never felt sexy again.

My father had labeled my marriage to Dean a mistake, but I believed then—and still do—that the concept of "making a mistake" makes no sense. I don't regret marrying Dean because he helped me realize what I needed to find in my next relationship. And I don't regret selling my condo and staying with Marc because he took care of me when I needed someone most. He also taught me that I should find a man with integrity the next time around. Once again, I had confirmed my philosophy that I had confirmed so many times before: Everything in life happens for a reason, we're just not always given the reason at the same time as the thing. You see, I still believed there must be something or someone better out there for me—the authentic me.

I dried my hair, applied a small amount of makeup, and dressed into my comfortable brown velour sweat suit, no bra, and an ultrasoft tight T-shirt. I had no feeling in my breasts but I felt the soft T-shirt up against my shoulders, back, and stomach. I had a few hours before I could pick-up Chalupa at Marc's so I fixed a hot cup of tea with honey and opened my laptop to work on my Match.com profile. I needed a tag line, so I chose something I honestly believed: I am a work in process. I still believe that: I strive to learn at least one new thing every single day and have my life change in some way because of it.

Chapter 29

I Have Someone I Want You to Meet

I never considered myself obsessed with finding another man, but I enjoyed having the wide variety at my fingertips. I preferred writing over talking on the telephone—maybe because of the Backspace key or maybe because I needed to know if the guy could spell and use proper grammar, or maybe because email seemed safer than the phone.

I made an appointment with the medium, hoping to receive some guidance from my angels. As always, Lynn opened the session with a prayer to welcome the Spirits and asked them to come forward for me. Lori arrived right away.

"She is excited you came to see her. She says in another time you two would have been shopping for the upcoming holiday."

The previous week I had treated myself to a personal shopper at Nordstrom's to help me find some hip clothes for my new life in the city and I had sensed my sister in the dressing room with me.

I smiled at Lynn. "I went shopping alone for my Easter outfit last week."

"Are you living in the same house?"

"No." She really knew how to cut to the chase, didn't she?

"Lori is telling me that you need to live for you. Not for anyone else. You need a shoulder to cry on and he had not been that person. He wasn't as loving as you need." I sat still, wanting to hear more.

"You may need to be on your own for a while. There was something about Marc that was changing you. You were acting the way he wanted you to act—robotic—instead of who you really are. You need to find yourself before moving forward. No hurry. Lori says she will find the next one for you. Are you still in contact with Marc?"

"Yes."

"Who is doing most of the calling?"

"Both of us. We're still trying to separate things . . . car insurance . . . house bills . . . the cat . . . the boat . . ."

"You may be moving again. Are you on the second floor?"

"No, the twenty-first."

"She wants you lower. In a house. Near the water. Close to family." I thought I wanted to live in a house again, too, but not alone. I had liked living in a condo while being single because it spared me the maintenance headaches.

"Are you dating someone now?"

"No, just emailing with one guy on Match.com."

"Lori says he's not the one. There's someone else making his way to you. You don't know him yet. A relationship too good to be true. Your mom is here now."

I smiled.

"She agrees with everything Lori said and she, too, wants you to live in a house, not a high rise. She wants you to take more walks. In nature. She is concerned you are not getting outside enough."

I shook my head from side to side. I missed my ability to walk directly outside from my condo. I mean, I liked my balcony, but I wanted to put my feet in the grass without having to change into a decent outfit, ride an elevator, make pleasantries with the concierge in the lobby, and walk across the street to a park adjacent to the bus station. Of course, at the park, I never wanted to take my shoes off because of all the pigeon poop and homeless people lying on the ground.

"Anyway, Lori is happy you are on your own and still surrounded by people who love you. You need someone equal to you. Someone who will allow you to be yourself and whom you will allow to be himself, too." Cynthia had given me the same advice when Dean and I divorced. She had said I needed to find someone who lifted me up and inspired me to be a better person.

"Lori and your mom want me to remind you that there are people on earth who love you and you need to lean on them." Then Lynn relayed one last message from my mother and sister and, being someone who always has to plan ahead, I knew it wouldn't be easy. "They want me to remind you to take it one day at a time."

I really did try to take it one day at a time, but that never lasted long. It takes a long time to find a piece of property to buy, negotiate a price, and schedule a closing. My obsession to plan every little thing in my life would not let me just live in the moment and, by April, I needed to have a plan if I was going to buy a home in January.

I still heard my father telling me to make a list and narrow down my options—just as he had told me when Marc and I looked for a house together. So much had changed since my first divorce when I last looked for a home on my own—when my sister was alive and I only wanted to live near her. Because I worked from home now, not even my job tied me down to one area, so I started thinking about all the cities where my company had offices. And then I realized my mother and sister were right. I needed to lean on my family and friends who had supported me unconditionally throughout the past ten years. Staying in Providence, the central city in Rhode Island, allowed me to keep in contact with all of my family and friends, including my friend and best nail tech, Gina, for the past eight years.

"Okay, put your foot in there." Gina removed my toenail polish and pointed to the basin filled with warm water. Actually, Gina had filled the basin with boiling water and we had been repeating this same ritual for the past eight years. I put my foot in the basin.

"It's too hot."

"Really? Is it?" Gina added cold water to the basin while I touched the water with the tips of my toes. "How 'bout now?"

"Okay, that's better."

"Good. So are you still seeing that guy?" Gina jumped right into the important stuff.

"Tom?"

"Yea, I guess so. The one who went to school with your sister?"

"No, oh my God, it didn't work out after I realized he had lied to me."

I had met Tom on Match.com and we discovered he had attended high school with my sister. His uncle also owned a jewelry business so we discovered that my dad and his uncle had been friends. Tom seemed like a stand-up guy, working as a computer teacher in a high school and giving golf lessons at a local public golf course. Our numerous connections made me believe this may be the guy my sister had sent me.

We exchanged emails and regular phone calls for weeks before he finally suggested we meet. "Well, I've been waiting to see you until after I have knee surgery this Friday," he said on the phone.

"Oh, wow, I'm sorry to hear that. Is there anything I can do to help you?"

"You're sweet, but I'm all set. I will be in touch when I come out of anesthesia."

That Friday, I waited all night to hear from Tom, and at nine o'clock I decided to text him. He responded that there had been a complication with his surgery and he needed to stay in the hospital overnight. We spoke on the phone the next day.

"I'm so sorry. Do you need anything? I could bring you food or whatever you want."

"Oh great, our first date would be in a hospital with me wearing a johnny." He laughed.

"Well, that would certainly take the pressure off me to look good."

The following Wednesday, Tom finally asked me out on a date.

"Are you sure you're up to it?" We had been pen pals and telephone friends for more than a month, but I still felt a little nervous to meet him. I thought, what if he's the guy Lori wanted me to meet? What if he's the one?

"Yes, I'm fine, and I'm excited for us to finally meet. I know this great restaurant. We'll figure out the details later this week, okay?"

When I heard the knock at the door, I took one deep breath and really hoped my face would hide my thoughts. Tom's face and entire body looked bigger than his picture on Match.com. He wore khaki twill pants and a light-colored Hawaiian shirt that hung outside of his pants.

"Am I dressed okay?"

Who am I kidding? My darn face can't hide what I'm thinking.

"Yes, of course, come in, come in." I waved him inside, thinking I better not embarrass my sister by acting rudely.

He shook my hand and placed a bottle of white wine, still bearing its price tag, on the granite countertop right beside the "get well" gift and card I had bought for him. After our long late-night phone calls, part of me expected at least a hug or maybe a kiss on the cheek. Chalupa jumped onto one of the barstools and startled him.

"She's harmless, just nosy."

Tom ignored my cat. "I have no idea if this is good wine or not. I want you to have a glass—now. Let's open it. Sit down. I want to talk to you about something." He babbled and I became confused.

"Um, do we have time?" I thought our reservations were in a half hour, but he nodded and pointed to the bottle of wine.

"Okay, can I pour you a glass, too?"

"No, I can't drink yet. I'm still taking medication." I grabbed the gift I had bought him, brought him a glass of water, and joined him on the couch. Chalupa rubbed against his leg, sensed his disinterest, and walked into the bedroom.

"Here, I bought you a small 'get well' gift. Open it," I insisted so the attention would be on him and not me or whatever he wanted to talk about.

He opened the card and two Sudoku puzzle books—two of the exact same books —and he looked puzzled himself.

"I bought one for you and one for me. I thought we could have races." He smiled and laughed out loud. I hadn't met anyone who loved Sudoku puzzles as much as I had, and we each bragged about the level of the puzzles we were able to complete.

"Sweet. Thank you. You're very thoughtful." He took a small sip of water.

"So, there is something I need to tell you." Tom said.

"Okay." I folded my hands on my lap as an attempt to calm my nerves.

"I didn't have knee surgery." He looked over my shoulder at the skyline rather than at me.

"Oh?" I scratched my right eyebrow.

"I have always had a bit of a weight problem. At one time I weighed close to three hundred pounds."

Being naïve, I assumed his height could probably carry that weight without him looking as huge as that number sounded on its own.

He continued. "So, the surgery I just had was . . . I had gastric bypass."

Come on face, don't let me down now. "Oh . . . so, you lied to me?" I frowned.

"Well, yeah, I guess so, but I didn't want to scare you away or make you think I was huge. I wanted to have the procedure done first . . . to look better . . . to feel better."

"I see." I sipped my wine.

"It took me this long to ask you out because, well, prior to the surgery, I had to be on a strict diet, and I haven't been able to eat solid food since the surgery."

I wished he would just stop talking. "Um, I'm sorry, and why are we going out to dinner tonight?" I tilted my head to one side.

"No, it's fine, really. Tonight is the first night I can have solid food. And . . . well, you can still eat."

I took another sip of wine. *Don't embarrass Lori.*

"Really. I want us to have dinner together."

When we arrived at the restaurant, I encountered his second, and then his third lies. It turned out he had never made reservations so we sat at the bar. I ordered a glass of red wine and . . . so did Tom. So much for being on medication, although he insisted he could have one glass of wine and he had wanted to save it for dinner. We scanned through the menu together, looking for the best mushy food he could eat, but he chose to order something else.

After dinner, we sat in the driveway of my condo building and I got another handshake before he drove away.

I agreed to a second date the following Saturday and suggested we see a movie—no food. He insisted I choose the movie so, without much thought, I picked Julie and Julia. I only knew it had something to do with Julia Child. Tom asked if we could order a little something to eat beforehand so we each ordered an appetizer at a local restaurant on the way to the theater. Before the food arrived, he explained the challenge he had earlier that day. After he had driven by a Burger King billboard he found the nearest drive-through and ordered a Whopper. I was sure this story wouldn't end well and I looked around, wishing the waiter would interrupt us. Tom had taken just one bite of the Whopper before he had to pull over to the side of the road—to vomit. It reminded me of the times I had to pull over to the side of the road for my sister to vomit—after chemo—and then I thought, you know what, Lori, this ain't the guy.

After we found seats in the movie theater, he asked, "So, who's in this movie?"

"Meryl Streep." I smiled and found it strange that he hadn't heard about the movie.

"Really?" He frowned. "I cannot stand that woman."

Seriously? Who the hell hates Meryl Streep?

"Really?" I said. "We don't have to see this. We can see something else, seriously. I'm not even sure what it's really about except that she plays Julia Child."

"No, it's okay. It'll be fine. No worries," he said, but I had trouble believing him and I worried through the entire movie.

It had never even occurred to me that because Julia Child had been a chef that the movie would have something to do with food. And I never considered that every single scene may include food. The Julie character played a blogger who obsessed over Julia Child and she challenged herself to make every recipe in Julia's first cookbook while blogging about it. I loved the movie about food and writing. Tom, though? Not so much.

Over the next couple of weeks, Tom and I gradually stopped calling each other and our emails stopped without either of us offering an explanation.

Gina laughed as I shared the full story of Tom. I finally realized I had had enough distance to see a little humor in it, too, but wished Tom or I had properly mastered the "this isn't working out for me" conversation instead of walking away without an explanation.

"Well, I have someone I want you to meet." Gina smiled from ear to ear.

"Oh." I rolled my eyes. "I'm not sure I can do this dating thing anymore." Besides Tom, I had emailed with a few other guys who all turned out to be something other than what they had advertised in their profiles.

"No, I think you should meet this guy. His mother has been a client of mine for years. I love her. And her husband . . . such a nice family. He's divorced and his kids are so cute. He's a lawyer."

"What's his name?"

"Peter." It took me a few seconds and then I remembered what the medium had once asked me: Is there a Peter? Seriously?

When I heard Peter's last name, I shrugged. "Oh, he's Italian, too? Okay, I'll meet him."

The following week, I walked into my Tuesday night writing class and Hannah whispered, "Come here." I approached the long table where she had all her stuff sprawled out as she typed on her laptop.

"What's up?"

She pointed to the back door of the classroom. "I heard about Peter." She winked at me. Then I remembered Gina telling me that Peter's law office was in the same building as Hannah's writing class.

"Did Gina tell you?"

"Yes, I had an appointment yesterday. We have to start class now, but come earlier next week and I'll introduce you to him."

"Okay, sure." Wow, my friends really wanted me to meet Peter, didn't they?

The next night, I wondered why Gina would be calling me since I just had my pedicure a few nights ago.

"What happened last night?" She sounded a little angry.

"What? Nothing. What are you talking about?"

"Peter thought he was going to meet you last night. He stayed late at his office. What happened?"

I had no idea what she meant and then I remembered the whole conversation with Hannah and that she offered to introduce me to Peter next week.

"Oh my God, you have to call him. I thought you would meet him last night. He's going to think you're not interested."

"Really? Me call him? Give him my number."

"He's on Facebook, send him a message there."

"Well, okay, I guess so." I agreed because I realized this meant I could see his picture before meeting him.

"Let me know what happens . . . please."

I carried my laptop from the counter to the couch, signed into Facebook, and searched for Peter. "Oh wow." I said out loud. He had the kindest face, cutest smile, and most sincere eyes I had ever seen on any guy, ever. I wondered if he had posted a recent photo so I poked around his profile and found a picture from the previous year of him with his kids and he looked the same—promising.

I wrote (and rewrote) a short Facebook message explaining that we had a mutual friend and that I had no idea we were supposed to meet the previous night. I wrote that I had never intended to stand him up and even suggested maybe meeting the following week. Within an hour, he answered my message, saying he completely understood the mix-up. And he scored more points for using correct spelling and grammar. The next day, we exchanged a couple of emails to schedule a time to meet. It wasn't his weekend with the kids but he planned to take them trick-or-treating on Halloween night and hoped I would agree to meet him afterward.

I called Gina to tell her Peter and I had set a first date.

"Oh my God, I have had a feeling about this for a very long time."

"What do you mean? How long?"

"Well, since last November, at the spa's open house. You came into the spa with Marc and, after you left, Peter came in with his family. After he left, I told my cousin that you two would be a perfect couple."

"What? Are you serious?"

"Yes, she thought I was nuts because you were both still in relationships with other people, but Linda, I swear I felt like the message came from your sister."

Chapter 30

Meet Pete

I parked my car, turned the key, sat back, and took a deep breath. Although I felt excited I wondered why the hell I had agreed to go on another date. Maybe because Peter seemed to already have many of the qualities I now looked for in a man and I was feeling hopeful. I tilted the rearview mirror in my direction to check my makeup one more time. I opened my purse and took out my facial bronzer for some extra color on my cheekbones, forehead, chin, and a little on my cleavage. I reapplied some clear lip gloss and tucked everything back into my purse. I took another deep breath, opened the car door, stepped out in my black three-inch wedge heels (a little upgrade I had made after Jamaica), and closed the door. As I locked the door, I took one last look at my reflection in the window. "This is what you get," I whispered as I massaged my head, trying to pump up the volume of my fine blond hair.

Surrounded by two- and three-story houses in a poorly lit residential area, I stared at the ground as I approached the door to the bar. I looked up slightly and saw a guy parking his car and wondered if it could be Peter. He stepped out of his car and we both approached the bar entrance at the same time. "Linda?" he inquired softly.

I smiled, relieved that the photos were very accurate. "Yes, Peter?"

He smiled, shook my right hand, and placed a gentle kiss on my left cheek. I blushed under the bronzer.

Peter held the door open for me as I walked into the bar and noticed some people dressed in costumes. I looked back at him shyly, hoping he would choose a place for us to sit. Through the dim amber lighting and thin crowd, we eyed an intimate spot in the back corner of the bar. Peter pointed to a couple of empty leather chairs. "Is this okay for you?" he asked.

I nodded, sat down, and looked around to check out some of the characters seated around us. "What a great place this is, Peter. I had no idea it even existed. Have you been here before?"

He took off his leather jacket and sat down. "Once or twice before, maybe a year or so ago." Peter looked right into my eyes. "Admittedly, never on Halloween. I'm sorry. Is this too weird for you?"

"Not at all. I love to people watch. It's perfect." I liked that he cared enough to ask me my opinion instead of assuming I must agree with him the way Marc had done for so many years.

The walls were completely covered with dark, intricately carved wood. Two enormous mirrors etched with naked female figures hung behind the bar, and for a brief moment I thought about my own naked body and wondered how Peter may someday react to it. Van Morrison's "Moondance" played softly in the background. I removed my coat and settled back into my chair.

Peter stood up by my side and placed his hand on the back of my chair. "What can I get you to drink?"

I shrugged my shoulders. "Um, how about wine?"

"Red? Or white?"

"Red is great. Cabernet is good."

Peter placed a hand on my shoulder and walked toward the bar to order from the bartender. He returned with two glasses of red wine. "It's Franciscan, one of my favorites." He sat down, leaned in closer to me, raised his glass, and gazed into my eyes. "Cheers."

"Cheers." We both twirled the wine around in our glasses, took a big whiff, and then our first sips.

"Very good." I liked that he showed an appreciation for tasting wine.

"Have you always liked wine?"

"My father made wine with my grandfather, and I've been making wine with my father for a few years now so, yes, I guess so." He smiled.

"My dad made wine, too, from grapes. One of my brothers still makes it, but from juice. I was really too young to fully appreciate the process at the time my dad was making wine, but I wish I could learn from him now."

"There's plenty to learn from my family," he said, and I thought about all the Italian traditions our families must have in common.

"Did you and the kids have fun trick-or-treating?"

"We did. My eight-year-old daughter still likes for me and her mother to go trick-or-treating with her. My twelve-year-old son, on the other hand, would rather be with his friends."

"It's nice that you spend time with them even when it's not your weekend. You must have a good relationship with your ex."

"Yes, but only for the sake of the kids. Who really wants a relationship with their ex?"

"True. I'm fortunate to hardly ever see my ex-husband, partly because we never had children and partly because we just don't frequent the same hangouts or stores. Same is true for my ex-boyfriend. Although we were never married, we lived together for seven and a half years." I spoke very freely and never felt like I had offered too much information about what had happened with my exes.

I looked down to check on my plunging neckline and again wondered when would be the right time to tell Pete I had survived breast cancer and had had a double mastectomy. Part of me wanted the topic on the table, front and center, because if he couldn't accept my past and my appearance, I saw no reason to have another date or even another glass of wine. But the other part of me really liked his kind voice and eyes and didn't want to risk his rejection just yet.

"So, tell me about your work."

"I always have such a hard time explaining what I do for a living." I placed my glass on the table in front of us.

"Try me."

"I'm a project manager in the technology department at a bank. I manage teams that implement new software applications. Although, most of my work revolves around converting loans every time we buy another bank." I paused, picked up my glass, and took a sip.

"Do you travel a lot?"

"It varies. My boss is in North Carolina, so staff meetings are normally held there. I've had to travel a lot to New York City lately, but whenever it makes sense, I schedule my project meetings in Providence."

"How about you? Do you like being a lawyer?"

"Yes, so far," he said and I tilted my head with a curious face. "It's my second career," he added.

"Oh. What did you do before that?"

"I was a photojournalist for a local newspaper in New Hampshire."

"Oh, wow, very different. What made you switch gears?"

"I've always dreamed of being a lawyer."

I giggled. "Really? Me too. I just never pursued it. Good for you."

"I am proof it's never too late." He winked at me.

"I'm forty-five." I winked back.

He shrugged. "You never know what's out there waiting for you."

"Well, I do like to write and hope to write a book—a memoir—someday."

"I can't wait to read it. I like to write, too. How long have you been taking classes with Hannah?" I thought, here's a guy I just met who can't wait to read the story of my life, as opposed to Marc, who never asked about my childhood or family history and never cared about what I wrote in my writing classes.

"Um," I looked up at the ceiling as I calculated the years, "I guess about three or four years. Since my sister passed away."

"I'm sorry to hear that . . . about your sister, I mean. She must have been young?"

"Thank you, yes, forty-nine." I frowned. "She died of breast cancer. I lost my mom to breast cancer and I am a survivor, too. I'm not sure if you knew that or not."

"I heard you had lost both of your parents and your sister—I mean, I cannot even imagine the thought. And I know you are a survivor . . . from what Gina told my mother, you are pretty incredible." He asked if I wanted another glass of wine.

"Sure." I blushed a little as he stood up and walked to the bar. My gut, or my chest, told me that I had to tell Pete about my surgery because I had no doubt he would show compassion.

I smiled at him when he returned with two glasses of wine and handed one to me. I took a sip as he sat down. "So, how long ago were you sick, Linda?"

I liked that he felt comfortable enough to ask me. "Um, 2002, so, seven years ago, now. Wow. I don't think of that too often. Given my family history, I decided to have my breasts removed and reconstructed."

There, I had said it.

"And I think my decision saved my life," I added.

"You're a very brave woman." He raised his glass and we both took a sip as we stared at each other.

Before I knew it, the music had become much louder and we were surrounded by many people wearing costumes, including Batman, Wonder Woman, and a bride and groom. The bartender turned the lights brighter to signal last call and Peter and I decided to call it a night. He put his jacket on and then helped me with mine. With his arm around my waist to guide me, we walked side by side to the front door.

"Watch your step. I'll walk you to your car."

"That's okay, I'm fine. Thanks very much. I had a really great time tonight."

"Me, too. I hope we can do it again sometime."

"Me, too."

He leaned in closer to me and placed a soft kiss on my right cheek. I smiled. I actually smiled all the way to my car. We both waved as we drove in opposite directions.

Almost at the same time as when I entered my condo, I received a text message: "Thank you for a nice evening. Hope to do it again soon."

I whispered and typed the words, "Me, too." I felt a little flutter in my belly.

About a week later, I felt that same flutter in my belly the day I realized I may need a lawyer. At the beginning of that month, I had put a deposit down on a condo on the other side of Providence. I had applied for a mortgage with the bank that had employed me for the past eleven years and they approved it, pending the review of several condo documents.

Pete and I had stayed in touch via email after our first date, but between both of our schedules we found it difficult to plan our next one. When we finally arranged our second date—which, when I think of the hours we shared together, really had been our second, third, and fourth dates—he picked me up at eleven in the morning and dropped me off at seven that evening. We spent the entire day in Boston—walking, eating, shopping, laughing, talking, and eating more. Pete suggested dinner at one of his favorite Italian restaurants in the North End, and we shared wine and all the same foods we both loved.

Being with Pete seemed easy—we finished each other's sentences, had the same sense of humor, and our Italian heritage taught us both the importance of family (and food and wine).

The following day I left for a week-long business trip in New York City. Pete and I talked casually on the phone every day, but on the third day away, I heard from my bank—my employer—that they had denied my mortgage. I called Pete in a panic. The bank had discovered pending litigation between the condo association and the builder. Pete's soothing voice calmed me down on the phone, and a couple of days after I had returned home we met for a drink. Pete wanted to hear more about my real estate issue and give me some options.

That night, as Pete and I said good-bye in the parking lot, we had our first kiss. "I can't believe I waited this long to kiss you," he said

"Me either. Thank you for calming my nerves again."

Over the next few days, I requested my deposit be returned and when the seller refused, I got angry and defensive. Without me asking, Pete jumped right in and rescued me. He reviewed all my documents, consulted with another lawyer, spoke with both Realtors, and successfully retrieved 95 percent of my deposit. Throughout the entire ordeal, Pete explained everything to me and never made me feel stupid. He acted fairly, with compassion and integrity. I started to call him the BLE, or best lawyer ever.

I thanked Pete for recovering my money by treating him to a special and, what had turned into a very romantic, dinner. Given his appreciation for wine, I chose a restaurant known for a gourmet seven-course dinner with wine pairings. The server and the table location can really make or break any restaurant experience, and we lucked out with a cozy candlelit table and a very knowledgeable and personable waiter.

After dinner, Pete and I held hands as we strolled back to my condo. Chalupa met us at the door, but then quickly returned to the bedroom while Pete and I relaxed on the couch. Okay, maybe making out is not really relaxing. I mean, it is relaxing, but I'd be dishonest if I said we had just sat and talked. All of a sudden, however, Pete sneezed uncontrollably. "Bless you," I said after each sneeze. "Are you okay?"

His sneezing attacks had happened before, but never this bad. "I'll be okay. Unfortunately, I think I'm allergic to your cat," Pete said with a pout. That night, Pete left so he could stop at the drugstore for allergy medication on his way home. From then on, he medicated himself before visiting.

I continued searching the state for other condos to buy, but it seemed my answer was right under my nose or, in this case, above my head. That January, I signed a deal to purchase a two-bedroom condo on the floor above me. I had really become accustomed to the upscale living space in the heart of the city, and for the time being, I liked that the location was closer to my family and Brenda. While I loved living in the city, I noticed Chalupa hadn't been as content. She wasn't getting enough exercise and had gained a lot of weight. Pete's allergy may have influenced my decision a little bit, too, but he never suggested I give up my cat. And the fact that I had been traveling so much and constantly hiring pet sitters made me realize how unfair and maybe a little unrealistic I had been to take her with me in the first place. Thankfully, although Marc had been a jerk to me, he loved animals and agreed to take Chalupa back. It broke my heart, but I knew how much she loved snooping around the backyard and chasing birds and other critters. When I moved upstairs, Chalupa would move back in with Marc.

Pete and I were really happy together and he made plans to introduce me to his parents and his sister. We all met at a coffeehouse to listen to live music. I sat next to Pete's mom, Janet, and although we weren't able to chat too much during the show, her sense of style and her gentle mannerisms reminded me of my own mother.

A couple of weeks later Pete asked, "So, I'd really like you to meet the kids. What do you think?"

"I think I'd like that. I'm a little nervous though. What if they don't like me?"

"I'm not worried about that at all, but you could meet Jake first, and if he approves, we'll move on to Julia." Pete smiled. "I'm kidding. But we'll just make it a casual meeting."

"Okay."

A couple of days later, Pete met me upstairs in my new condo while I waited for a furniture delivery. He had brought Jacob. I had never dated anyone with children before, but Jake was just three years younger than my nephew, Dan, so I felt like I could relate to him in some way. Very polite, a little shy, and like most boys his age, very focused on his electronic device. Pete later revealed he had bribed Jake by promising to visit Game Stop at the mall if he was good.

A few days later, we set a time for me to meet his daughter, Julia. The concierge called when they arrived and I waited anxiously at the door. Like Jake, Julia loved the condo and the fact that it was attached to the mall. A very pretty little girl, she reminded me of myself at her age, except for her dark hair and dark eyes. After she overcame her initial shyness, she wanted all the attention directed toward her.

In early March, I made dinner for Pete to celebrate his forty-first birthday. I must have bought him a present, but what I remember most are the words I spoke—actually the words I *returned* to him that night. On Valentine's Day, Pete had told me he loved me and at the time I wasn't ready to return the sentiment. On his birthday, we were hugging and swaying to music in the living room when I whispered, "Ti amo."

He stepped back to stare at me. "Really?"

"Si. I'm sorry it has taken me so long, but I'm sure of it now."

Pete smiled.

"I'm so scared though."

We spent all of our nonworking time together, with and without the kids, and our four lives had become more integrated. At first, the possibility of being a stepmother scared me to death. I had always loved spending time with my niece and nephews—okay, spoiling them a little bit—but I loved delivering them back to their parents, too.

"What's to be afraid of?"

"Having kids scares me."

"I love having you around my kids. I love having you around me. We'll be a team."

Over the years, I had consciously decided not to have children of my own (conceived, adopted, or otherwise produced) because parenting was a huge social responsibility and personal commitment. Kids need—and deserve—lots of attention and, well, I recognized my need for "me time"—and yes, that my obsession for planning every little thing may drive me (and everyone around me) insane. But I always remembered my mother's advice from her deathbed: "You two need to go make a baby." Honestly, I had often wondered if I would regret my decision to not have children.

When I met Pete's kids, I believed they were a gift, to me from my mother. Maybe I was ready to adjust my need for "me time." And maybe, like everything else in my life up to that point, my life experiences and beliefs had prepared me for the moment I met Jacob and Julia. Even having met a great guy, I still knew I never wanted to bear my own children—okay, the act of giving birth has always scared me to death, too, but I finally believed that the person I had become could make a difference in these kids' lives, and that they could make a difference in my life, too.

Months before I had met Pete, I booked an April vacation—a Caribbean cruise with Frankie's family. I couldn't imagine the cruise without Pete so I asked him to join us. I thought we needed some time alone to figure out if we had a future together.

This cruise, by far, was much warmer than the Alaskan cruise. And I am not just talking about the weather. Pete and I survived a vacation—with my family, on a boat, in a confined cabin. Our relationship really matured on that trip, and after spending every day and night together for seven days, it was hard to live apart when we returned home.

That spring, we casually started to look for houses where we could live together. I wanted to move back to where I had spent the last ten years of my life—near the water, closer to all the women in my cancer support group and to my sister's burial site—and Pete loved the idea of being closer to his family. In August, we fell in love with a home just a mile between Pete's parents and his sister, and, once again, I found myself packing and moving—the fourth time in two years. Okay, maybe it was me that said, "I want to die in this house." I loved the Nantucket-style house, its open floor plan, and the idea of having a swimming pool, but after moving three times in the past two years, I really hoped this would be the last time I packed and unpacked for a very long time.

The first year of living together as a family had been an adjustment for all of us, but I finally answered my own question of why the hell I had agreed to go on another date less than a year after I had left Marc. Because, once again, everything in my life happened for a reason. I had to meet Dean to fully appreciate Marc when he graciously cared for me during seven of the most difficult years of my life. I had to meet Marc to never again assume someone is moral and honest. And so far, I believed I had met Pete because my parents and my sister never wanted me to forget the importance of family, tradition, always striving to be a better person, and the meaning of unconditional love.

Chapter 31

A Dream Comes True

If you dream in color while you sleep, but your surroundings appear in black and white when you wake up, change your surroundings. Never give up on your dreams. Dreams don't lie. Dreams hold the secrets to your heart, and if you want what you see in your dreams, only you can make certain they become your reality.

As a young girl, when I had a crush on a boy, I would write our names and circle them with a heart. In high school, when I "went steady" with a guy, I always imagined us married and I would practice my signature—my first name and his last name—to study how my new name looked before I repeated it out loud to hear how it sounded. After college, but before I met Dean, I drew my engagement ring—a round stone set in white gold. When Dean and I designed my engagement ring—a square, princess-cut diamond set in gold—it mirrored my sister's engagement ring, not the one in my drawing. No matter what my age, I had always imagined that my wedding proposal would take place with some sort of light—maybe from a candle or the moon—and my boyfriend would become my fiancé after he asked me to marry him while down on one knee. But Dean and I were horizontal—naked and hungover—when he sort of shrugged his shoulders and said, "Yeah, I guess we should get married."

When my wedding became overshadowed by my mother's illness, for a brief moment I only thought about myself and how my wedding would be ruined. But when the day arrived, I only cared about my mother and the fact that she felt well enough to attend my wedding. I never imagined I might actually learn a life lesson from my mother's illness and death. Over time, and with a lot of therapy, my mother's death taught me that life really is short, and I secretly vowed that I would never again abandon my own self—my beliefs, my values, and my dreams. Through the years, when I've risked breaking that promise, my mother often sends me a much needed message—on a digital clock, around 1:43 in the afternoon—that reminds me "I(1) love (4) you (3)."

I never would have anticipated the events that occurred in the seven years after my mother passed away nor would I have guessed that my simple vow would be so hard to uphold. As subsequent losses hit me, like bullets shot from a machine gun, one after the other, I only wished for them to dodge me. Once my life had become less tumultuous, I was able to reconnect with the promise I had made to myself. I understood that every single experience—person, place, and event—in my life had exposed a purpose and prepared me for the next experience. To this day, whenever my reality deviates from my dreams, I just know there must be a reason.

Even before Pete and I moved in together, we talked about getting married. We both dreamed of an Italian wedding—I mean, actually being married in Italy. About a year after we had settled into the new house, in September, his parents treated the family to dinner for his mother's birthday. Somewhere between the grilled pizza and warm apple tart, his parents casually announced that they had been researching villas in Italy for a family vacation. At first, I thought, sure, everyone wants to rent a villa in Italy, right?

Then, on an ordinary Sunday in early December, in authentic Italian fashion, Pete's mom invited us, along with Pete's sister, Elaine, and her partner, for a special dinner of baccalà (salted cod) and olives, a recipe she had learned from her own mother. As always, she smiled from ear to ear from the moment we arrived. We had barely enjoyed a glass of homemade wine and imported Italian cheese when Janet seemed to rush us to the table for dinner. She had set the table with china, crystal, and cloth napkins—as if it were a holiday dinner. With a twinkle in her eye, before she even served the first course, she handed each couple a wrapped gift—a traditional Italian hand-painted ceramic serving bowl and a travel guide for Florence and Tuscany.

"Janet, I love this." I stared at the bowl. "It's beautiful, thank you. Sal, thank you."

Pete picked up the travel guide and looked at the front cover, then turned it over and scanned the back cover before squinting curiously while his mom smiled. "Your father and I rented a villa in Italy for the family."

I stared at Janet with my mouth open and then quickly turned my head toward Pete's dad, then back to Janet. I put my hand on Pete's right leg while looking at him and mouthed, "Really?"

Janet smiled widely, immediately reminding me of my mother. "Really. For two weeks in June."

She handed us a printout with the description and photos of the villa they had reserved with a deposit. I shook my head from side to side in disbelief as I stared at a stone farmhouse built in the 1500s with an infinity pool overlooking the vast Tuscan hillside. I had always dreamed of visiting Italy—and Tuscany had been at the top of my list. I felt drawn to the vineyards and the landscape filled with earth tones of green, orange, yellow, and brown, all under a powder blue sky full of puffy white clouds.

A few weeks later, when I broke the news to Brenda during our yearly Christmas visit, she smiled broadly. "Oh my God, us, too!" She and her husband had booked a trip to Italy in June, to celebrate their twentieth wedding anniversary. They had planned to start in Rome before traveling south to

Sorrento. Rome had also been on my list, just much further down on the list than Tuscany. I had never been interested in history and, let's face it, Rome is ancient. But I wanted to see the Vatican, the Spanish Steps, and the Trevi Fountain.

"Maybe we can meet you in Rome." I looked at Pete and he shrugged.

"Sure, we can make that work."

"Leave it to us, Bren. We hardly see each other in Rhode Island, but we'll meet for dinner in Rome." We both laughed.

As our trip to Italy became more of a reality, so did the possibility of Pete and me getting engaged there. I had inherited my mother's and sister's jewelry, but I had only worn my mother's watch and my sister's diamond earrings, and only after I had dreamed that she gave me permission. All the rest of the baubles wasted away in a plastic container in my closet. But I had always wanted to reset my mother's engagement diamond and wedding ring to have as my own—as an everyday ring. I shared my idea with Pete.

"I love your sentiment." He gently touched the side of my face with his fingertips.

I held onto my dream of having an engagement ring with round stones, and only after having lived through the past thirteen years could I fully cherish the concept of a "past, present, and future" design that used three diamonds to represent each portion of time. I still believe that I am a work in process (just like I had claimed in my first Match.com profile)—my past and present experiences will always influence my future—and I always want my future to include Pete.

About a month before our trip, Pete and I made an appointment with a local jeweler who'd been born in Austria and trained in Milan. I had hired him to make two other rings for me over the years. I introduced Pete to Klaus and we all gathered in front of his computer. I handed Klaus the silk pouch that held my mother's diamonds and shared my design idea for the setting. He showed us several possibilities and I pointed to the two I liked the best. Klaus added the correct size diamonds to each setting on the screen, and once Pete and I were able to see the two side by side, we each chose the same ring.

"Do you need me to come in to try it on before you finalize it?" I asked Klaus. This was something I had done for both of the other rings he had created for me.

Klaus looked at Pete, who shook his head from side to side.

"Um, no . . . that won't be necessary," Klaus said with his Austrian accent as he measured the size of my left ring finger.

I looked at Pete and he smiled at me. "It will be a surprise."

"Really?"

"Really."

The next few weeks were filled with tasks to prepare us for the trip. Two days before we were leaving, Pete and I were accomplishing some errands together when I realized that maybe I should have nagged him about the three pairs of pants he needed to have hemmed for the trip. As a project manager, I lived by the saying, "your lack of planning does not constitute an emergency on my part." I never would have taken my pants to the tailor on Saturday if I needed them for Monday.

Feeling embarrassed for him, I wanted to wait for Pete in the car while he went into the shop to plead his case, but part of me felt curious about how this would turn out so I followed him into the shop.

"We won't know unless we ask," Pete said.

He stood confidently behind the service counter and I hid behind him.

I stared at the black-and-white tiled floor and cringed when the seamstress asked, "Okay, when do you need them?"

"Well, we're leaving for Italy on Monday afternoon, so will Monday morning work?"

She looked at me with an understanding smile and I shrugged my shoulders.

"I will have them for you today. We close at four. Say three thirty?"

Pete looked at me as if to confirm his brilliant negotiation skills, but mostly to ensure this new task could be inserted into our preplanned schedule of errands.

"Of course. That's perfect. Thank you so much."

"You're welcome. I sense I may have saved this trip." She winked at me.

Next, we walked to the jeweler. I needed a battery for one watch and the bracelet of another watch I wanted shortened. They agreed to have them both done within the hour so we decided to have lunch at a French restaurant next door. After we ordered, I pulled out my pad and pen to check the status of our tasks and plan the remaining stops, making certain to add the newest task of picking up Pete's pants from the tailor.

After we finished eating and had picked up my watches, we drove to the bank. Although we had installed a house alarm, we had both decided to store my unworn jewelry in a safe deposit box. We followed the teller into the vault to retrieve the key and the box. Then Pete and I walked into the very small room where customers privately access their boxes. I had all the jewelry in individual cloth pouches within a small paper shopping bag. When I flipped the bag over, all the pouches fell onto the table and we both saw something fall on the rug.

"What's that?"

"Oh my God." I bent down to pick up the charm. "You're not going to believe this."

"I thought I had lost this." I rubbed the gold charm between my thumb and forefinger. "My sister's last trip was a Mediterranean cruise. She toured the Vatican and bought a silver medal for me and a gold cross for herself. After you and I moved to the house, I realized I had lost the gold cross and it's always irritated me. This is the gold cross." I held it up so Pete could see it.

"I guess Lori's coming to Italy with us."

After the bank, we picked up Pete's pants and I remembered to ask Pete about our cell phones. "So what's the status of our phones? Are they all set to work in Italy?"

"The rep I spoke to last week said we just needed the newest BlackBerry model. Do we have time to swing by there now?"

"Really? Sure." On the way, I called the store and found out they had already closed.

This chore had never made it to my list for that day, or any other day, for that matter, because I had assigned it to Pete. As the project manager, I guess I should have checked on the status of the phones more often, just as I had to for the pants that needed hemming. Personally, I wanted a phone only to update my Faccbook status and post some pictures from Italy, but it was critical for us to have a working phone so the kids could call their mother in the States while they were abroad.

That Monday, we had finished all the "day of departure" tasks and had a couple of hours to spare before picking up the kids from school, so Pete suggested we stop by the phone store. The store clerk informed us that the model they'd previously given to Pete would not work internationally, but thankfully he knew of one that would work. There just weren't any in stock at his store—or any other store in Rhode Island.

Smiling, but with blood beginning to boil on my insides, I asked Pete, "So now what?"

"We'll stop at Sam's Club on the way to get the kids. I know they have the iPhone, but if they have the BlackBerry we need, we can look at that, too. What time is it?"

"Okaaay." *Great time to be shopping for a new phone, honey!*

Although I don't remember our exact conversation as Pete drove to Sam's Club, I do remember laughing my butt off. Maybe the giggling developed from nerves, or maybe the laughter marked the exact moment I realized that this man could do just about anything wrong when it came to planning—which was my passion—and I would still love him to death. Making light of a situation that I would have kicked and screamed about years ago, actually felt great when I accepted it as a tiny bump in the road in the overall grand scheme of life.

We decided to buy an iPhone, and the best deal entailed that we switched providers, too. We just needed to activate the service—including temporary international service—and transfer all my data to the new phone.

"So, I can activate the service, but you need to visit the service provider store to transfer your data, photos, and contacts," the salesperson informed us—after it was too late to change our minds.

"Really?" I asked, trying hard not to sound aggravated, because, after all, our lack of planning was not her problem. I mean, who does this? Who waits until two hours before their first trip to Italy to buy a new cell phone?

Pete had moved on to shopping for phone covers and other accessories when I shared the latest update.

"Okay, there's a store down the street. No problem. What time is it?" he asked ever so calmly.

As I walked back to the counter, the salesperson said, "I can't activate the international plan here so you would have needed to visit the store anyway."

We had roughly forty minutes before we needed to pick up the kids, but I thought, perfect, no problem, this must be our lucky day, as we entered an empty store except for two salespeople eager to help us. I placed my new iPhone box on the counter and Pete explained. "We need to activate international calling on her service plan and transfer her data from the BlackBerry to the iPhone."

"Okay, sure, no problem. Where did you buy the phone?"

"Sam's Club."

"And you have service with us now, right?"

"Yes, she activated my service at the store."

"Did she tell you about the waiting period for the international plan?"

"No. She didn't tell us that." I glared at Pete.

"How long is the waiting period?" Pete asked.

"For new customers . . . six months." *Did he just say six months?*

The much calmer and reasonable Pete explained our situation to the guy who completely understood our predicament—you know, that we were leaving for Italy in less than an hour and needed a phone that worked internationally. I had much to learn from Pete's calm approach because the salesperson escalated our situation to a manager and with about two minutes to spare, the salesperson said, "You're all set. Let me just get your iPhone."

Pete parked the car on a side street near the kids' school and we moved swiftly to the playground to meet Jake and Julia right as they walked through the door. Julia ran out first.

"Daddy!" She handed me her backpack.

"Can we get ice cream?" Of course the ice cream truck had conveniently parked behind our car. The three of them each purchased a treat from the ice cream man, but I still felt a little anxious—and maybe even nauseous—after the last-minute iPhone purchase, so I put their backpacks in the car and slouched in the front seat while they picked out their treats.

Pete sat in the front seat, handed me his Creamsicle—exactly what I would have ordered—while he buckled his seat belt, started the car, and looked in the rearview mirror.

"So, what do you say, anyone want to go to Italy this afternoon?"

The four of us had been living together for nine months, and before this two-week adventure to Italy, we had only vacationed in New Hampshire for two nights and had encountered no problems. Less than an hour into the seven-hour flight from Boston to Munich, with the smell of dinner rising from the trays in front of us, motion- and homesickness hit poor little Julia. Like most of us, Julia only wanted her mom to comfort her. I could relate because I wanted my mother, too. Pete played the role of both parents to soothe Julia, and when she felt better about an hour later, she asked me to take her to the bathroom. When we returned to our seats, I covered her with blankets and she fell asleep peacefully.

I thought we were doomed when I saw the tiny little plane we would take from Munich to Rome. Unlike the previous jet that had eight seats in each row, this one had four—two on either side of the aisle. Maybe our excitement outweighed any fear, but we all traveled that leg with smiles and no incidents. As Jacob and I stared at Rome through the tiny window, my heart expanded and my eyes filled with tears. I felt blessed by my new family and sensed my own ancestors with me as I listened to people speaking Italian.

I had heard many scary stories about driving in Europe, but nothing had prepared me for the Roman roads. Squished together in the backseat of the taxi with the kids, I held my breath and prayed my dream vacation would not be ruined by a car crash, train wreck, earthquake, or any other tragedy. I stared out the window, searching for the street sign bearing the name of our hotel as the taxi driver turned onto a narrow cobblestone street. I could have reached my hand out of the car window and touched terra-cotta pots filled with red geraniums, parked motorcycles, or diners seated at outdoor cafés. When he stopped in front of our boutique hotel, I inhaled deeply and exhaled with relief.

"Here we are." I looked at Julia and we both raised our eyebrows and smiled.

I thought we all would have preferred to take a nap before meeting Brenda, but I reminded everyone that we needed to adapt to the new time zone in order to overcome the jet lag. I texted with Brenda, and while she made her way back from Piazza Navona, we freshened up and changed out of the clothes we had been wearing for the past fifteen or more hours.

Brenda and I hugged tightly when we finally met each other in the hotel lobby.

"I just cannot believe we're here . . . together," I whispered in her ear.

"Me either. It's absolutely amazing."

We didn't allow the rain to dampen our dining experience at an outdoor table covered by a canopy. The four adults sat at one end of the table, with the wine, and the four kids sat at the other end, with the pizza! All of the kids had pizza except for Jake, who, for the past eight months, dreamed of eating prosciutto—lots of prosciutto—in Italy.

After dinner, the sun started to set as we strolled by the glistening Spanish Steps on our way to the famous Trevi Fountain. I heard the cascading water as we stood among hundreds of tourists taking photos, eating gelato, and tossing coins over their shoulders into the fountain. The traditional Roman legend says a coin tossed in the fountain promises a return trip to the Eternal City, but I had heard that that was only one third of the legend. The second coin promises you will fall in love, and the third coin promises marriage. We all posed for photos, tossed in our coins, and then searched for the best gelato in Rome. Still too stuffed with pasta and wine, I had just enough room for a dark chocolate truffle. Julia offered me a spoonful of hers, but I just enjoyed watching her eyes roll toward the heavens after her first taste of Italian gelato.

The next day, after we said good-bye to Brenda and her family, we savored cappuccinos and cannoli, leaving us just enough time to appreciate the iconic Coliseum before we headed to Florence to meet Pete's family.

The train station in Rome seemed to be ten or twenty times larger than Grand Central Station, but we interpreted the Italian language and illustrations on the ticket kiosks, purchased our boarding passes, and found the right platform where we waited for our train. When we arrived in Florence, we only had to find the location of the rental car we had reserved and then drive to Chianti.

We hailed a cab outside of the Florence train station and drove to the car rental location. None of us needed to understand Italian to recognize that the blue metal garage door covering the entrance meant that it had closed. Using my new handy dandy iPhone, we called Elaine and, God bless her heart, just hearing her voice calmed me down. Then she spoke directly to the taxi driver and convinced him to drive us twenty-two miles to meet them in the town center of Castellina in Chianti. When I finally laid eyes on their familiar faces, I felt relieved to reunite with Pete's family.

Perched on a hill, the town's center offered the most spectacular views of Chianti. With my eyes and mouth wide open, I shook my head back and forth in disbelief as I stared at rolling hills filled with vineyards, Italian cypress and olive trees, and rustic stone structures all under a soft, amber light. I hardly noticed how fast we were traveling along the extremely winding and sometimes steep roads.

When we turned onto the stone driveway lined on both sides with cypress trees, my heart started to beat faster and then—there stood the natural stone villa with terra-cotta tile roof. Elaine walked us through the kitchen and gave us a tour of the dining room and two sitting rooms on the first floor before helping us carry our luggage upstairs to the bedrooms, or suites. The top of the stairs opened up to a third sitting area with a fireplace that led to a covered porch. Janet escorted us down a long hallway, first pointing to her bedroom suite and then into Jacob and Julia's suite. Janet helped the children settle down and freshen up for their grandfather's birthday dinner while Pete and I walked down the hall to our suite. The view from every window exposed another glimpse of heaven and I truly felt the presence of my parents and sister with every blink of my eyes.

We all met in the dining room, but none of us could wait until morning to see the pool. We walked out the kitchen door and followed the lighted pathway lined with lavender and rosemary bushes, then up a short hill to the infinity pool—fully surrounded by an Italian stone patio, more lavender bushes, and olive trees—that overlooked a panoramic view of Chianti. I hadn't shaken my head from side to side so much since my sister had died.

The next afternoon, after Pete and I returned from Siena to rent the car we should have picked up the night before, we changed into our swimsuits and met the rest of the family by the pool. After about an hour of sun and swimming, Pete and I couldn't wait any longer to visit our first Italian vineyard.

We had a favorite vineyard in Rhode Island where we liked to enjoy a picnic of cheese, crackers, and fresh figs before napping on a blanket while overlooking the water, but we were both looking forward to finding our favorite Tuscan vineyard. Less than two miles down the road from our villa, we indulged in our first Italian wine tasting. We bought two or three bottles of Chianti to enjoy with the dinner we were having prepared by a private chef at the villa that night.

When we returned home, I rushed upstairs to our bathroom to pee, but mostly to take off the straw hat I had inherited from Lori. I loved that hat, but after just an hour, it gave me a headache and made my head sweat. Pete stood at the base of the stairs when I returned wearing my blue Boston Red Sox cap with the bejeweled "B" in red, white, and blue.

"Oh, you took off the cute hat?"

"Yeah, is it okay?" I made a frown as I bent my head and touched the top of the cap.

"Yeah, of course. That's cute, too. You're cute no matter what. Everyone is outside on the patio. I'll be out in a minute."

Surrounded by the scent of lilac and rosemary and the majestic cypress trees that lined the crushed stone driveway, I met the family on the stone patio. We snacked on the Italian cheeses we had bought at the local co-op and Pete's dad opened a bottle of the newest wine we had tasted that day. Jacob appeared from the side of the villa and stood below the stone wall that bordered the patio on all sides. "Linda, Dad wants to see you . . . um . . . down there . . . for a minute." He pointed to the wrought iron gate that led to another stone patio on the west side of the villa. Instead of meeting Pete from outside, I entered the villa through the kitchen and walked through the dining room to the glass door that led to the patio where he stood—I mean, where he paced.

I opened the door, "Hi, honey. What's up?"

"Have you seen the outdoor kitchen and dining table downstairs?" He knew I had seen it because we saw it together on the tour of the entire villa when we had arrived the night before.

"Yeah . . . but no . . . not in the light."

With his arm around me he guided me down the narrow stone stairway, beyond the outdoor kitchen and long tile table, to where the patio opened up to face the vast Tuscan landscape. No matter how many times I stared at the powder blue skies and huge, white puffy clouds that protected the cypress trees, bales of hay, precious olive and nut trees, and rolling hills filled with perfect rows of plump grapes in the distant vineyards, I had to catch my breath and wipe a tear from my eye.

Pete took my hand and gently pulled me closer to him.

He gazed into my eyes and said, "I hope you know how much I love you and I always will."

He got down on one knee and grasped my other hand. We both had the most beautiful view of the world right in front of us—and circling around us—the view of each other completely surrounded by what I knew heaven must look like.

My heart pounded as my entire body became filled with a sense of peace, contentment, and overwhelming love.

"Yes, I really do know. I love you, too." I took a mental picture of this once-in-a-lifetime moment. The moment I had dreamed of my entire life. The moment I thought might never come, but had never stopped believing was possible.

I stared at Pete while he opened the small box that held the ring made of the diamonds my dad had given to my mother more than sixty years earlier.

He took my left hand and stared directly into my eyes. "Will you marry me?"

I stood still, staring at Pete, while he waited anxiously for my answer.

"Si." I smiled and felt tears well up in my eyes.

He let out a huge sigh of relief and I realized I had made him wait for my answer a little longer than he had expected while I took my own sweet time branding the moment into my memory.

"Did you think I would say anything but 'yes'?"

"You haven't looked at the ring yet." He raised the box up a little higher.

I looked at the finished ring for the first time. It sparkled like no other ring I had ever seen.

Pete removed it from its box as I extended my left hand and watched him slip the ring on my finger. Two family's pasts, presents, and futures now on my left ring finger—on the finger believed to have the vein that ran directly to my heart. I had always felt my mother in my heart since she passed away, but wearing this ring renewed our mother-daughter connection. And I never even questioned whether my sister would have approved of this engagement. In fact, I will never forget what my first writing teacher, Hannah, helped me to realize: My parents and my sister weren't really gone, they each lived within me. I inherited my parents' and my sister's wisdom. Without their infinite presence and guidance, how else could I have survived through the darkness to reach this amazing light?

After all the negative events of my past, this moment could not have been any more perfect—standing with the man of my dreams, in the country that felt like home from the moment I stepped foot in it, surrounded by family—our pasts fully disclosed, our presents embraced, and our futures ready and eager to create—together.

A couple of days later, we made lunch reservations at another vineyard located on the same street as our villa. As Pete drove on a long dirt driveway, we passed fields of olive trees and an unexpected pool of mud filled with distinct black-and-white pigs, before we reached the wrought iron gate guarding Casamonti. Pete parked the car and, for some reason, I lagged behind him and the kids as they met the rest of the family and were greeted by the owners of the vineyard. When I finally reached the group, the female owner introduced herself to me. "Pronto. Io sono Anna Rita." My jaw dropped. I put my left hand on my heart and shook Anna Rita's soft hand as I admired her fair and smooth complexion. I turned toward Pete and Janet with tears in my eyes.

"My mother's name was Anne Rita."

Janet's eyes widened as she put her arm around me.

I looked at Pete. "I think I found my favorite Italian vineyard." He kissed my forehead.

One week into our trip, on the day after Father's Day, we drove to well-known vineyard in the Brunello region of Tuscany, in Montalcino. Before reaching the medieval fortress that protected the magnificent castle, we passed through quaint towns, industrial areas, and sprawling fields of green stalks not quite ready for harvesting.

"Is that corn? Or hay maybe?" I asked.

"I'm not sure."

And then, there it stood. A solitary bright yellow sunflower with a dark brown center blooming alone among a field of green. I grabbed Pete's hand.

"Wow, she really is here."

"All my dreams—and all my angels—are right here, honey."

Chapter 32

Perfectly Negative

The morning after we returned home from Italy, I sat at my desk in my home office, staring at the hundreds of work emails I had received over the past two weeks. I leaned back in my chair and dreamed of when Pete and I would live in Italy. Then I realized that the Tuscan adventure simply redefined what home truly meant to me and reminded me of the good fortune I had to experience life with the man I loved.

Although grateful to have had an amazing vacation, I always dreaded that moment when the much anticipated event—vacation, party, or wedding—had come to its end. It seems I constantly struggle to live in the moment, while, at the same time, plan the next adventure so we have moments to live in. That summer marked our first full summer in the new house. Pete, Jake, Julia, and I looked forward to warm and sunny days when we were able to hang out by our backyard pool, invite family and friends over for a barbeque, and then toast marshmallows in the fire pit.

That summer also marked nine years since I had been diagnosed with breast cancer. While most cancer patients welcomed the day of their oncology discharge, I insisted on seeing my oncologist every six months—for peace of mind. And, although I had not seen my plastic surgeon regularly since my mastectomy, I knew my breast implants only had a ten-year "shelf" life.

That September, I experienced the most annoying itch under my left implant that would not go away, and Dr. Liu suggested it may be a good time to replace the original saline implants with silicone. He couldn't guarantee that the new implants would eliminate the itch, but he provided me with a good laugh when he said he would give my chest a "good scratch" while he was in there.

With passion and excitement, he described all the "work" he wanted to perform, which included extracting fat from my stomach and grafting it into my décolletage—the fancy name to describe the area of my chest from my neckline to my cleavage—to create a more natural breast shape and remove the sensation and perception of having Major League baseballs as boobs. He also planned to re-create my nipples and retattoo the areolae. I had always just been happy to have something to fill the void in my chest, but his excitement wore off on me and I looked forward to getting this boob job.

Two weeks before my scheduled surgery, at my biannual oncology examination, Dr. Legare spent more time than usual running his hands around my left breast (the breast that had once rented space to cancer) and he recommended I have an MRI.

"Do you feel something?" I asked even though I did not want to hear his answer.

"Most likely scar tissue, but since you're having the implants replaced, it's a good idea to get a look at what's in and around that area ahead of time."

"Okay." I agreed mostly because I wanted to be thorough but I also wondered why my plastic surgeon hadn't ordered an MRI. I mean, if anyone needed to see what lurked around my breast implants, wouldn't it be him?

Then I thought, what's the big deal? But the truth is, after you've been diagnosed with breast cancer and no matter how much time has passed after you have finished all your treatments, the fear of a recurrence never, ever goes away. Since being diagnosed nine years earlier, I constantly had to balance being cautious and being a hypochondriac. My fear subsided each time I received a good test result, but aside from normal blood tests and an occasional bone scan, I had never endured a breast MRI. Maybe I needed the good MRI results so I could just enjoy being engaged—and eventually, married— to the man I loved. Or maybe I needed the good MRI results to confirm what the medium had told me five years earlier when she said I would not die from what my mother, my sister, and my father had died from.

A couple of days after having the MRI, while working upstairs, I answered a phone call from the hospital and my heart stopped the moment I heard my doctor's voice. I thought, this can't be good if my doctor is calling me himself instead of his assistant. Dr. Legare explained that the MRI revealed enlarged lymph nodes under my arms, on both sides. I felt sick to my stomach. I thought of the day my father's lymphoma had been diagnosed through the revelation of enlarged lymph nodes after his MRI.

"Symmetry is good, when we talk about cancer," my doctor explained, "asymmetric, or just on one side, can indicate something abnormal. So you can go ahead with your surgery, but the radiologist and I both want to follow up with a PET scan in, say, four or five weeks. There's no rush to have it done now."

"Okay." But waiting a month to have a PET scan—the newest test that could potentially find cancer in the tiniest crevices within my body didn't feel like a good idea to me.

And then when I learned that Dr. Liu preferred to know the cause of the enlarged lymph nodes before performing my surgery, I called my oncologist back right away.

"I can't wait four weeks. I mean, I need to know now. And my plastic surgeon won't do the surgery until he knows the cause of the enlarged lymph nodes."

"Okay, I see, I will transfer you to my assistant to schedule an appointment right away."

"Doctor, will you prescribe something I can take before the test . . . to relax me?"

"Yes, of course. I'll call it in this afternoon."

Two days later, on the day I should have been getting new boobs, improved cleavage, new nipples, and fresh tattoos, Pete drove me to have a PET scan. I smelled the familiar yet long-forgotten scent of death and illness as we walked through the hospital lobby filled with patients in wheelchairs and men and women dressed in multicolor scrubs. Even if Pete had visited sick people in the hospital before, I suspected he had never experienced the other, darker side of hospitals—what I thought of as the dungeon or bowels of the hospital. We rode the elevator to the basement and held hands as I guided him down the long corridor to the radiology registration desk. I gave the frowning receptionist my name and she handed me a plastic blue bracelet and, in a matter-of-fact voice, as if we were there to meet the wizard of Oz, she told us to follow the signs to nuclear medicine.

We sat in the waiting area and reconnected with what nonworking people watch on midday television, specifically Eva Longoria baking her Aunt Elsa's pineapple upside-down cake on *The Chew*. While my mouth watered for the sweet cake, a man walked into the room holding a large plastic container filled with a thick milky substance and a small plastic cup.

"Linda?" He scanned the room. I raised my hand to my shoulder and identified myself as the winner of the goop. Once I had finished gagging on the disgusting barium sulfate that tasted nothing like the pineapple nor the cherries in Eva's cake, the man returned to escort me farther into the bowels of the hospital.

"I should be about an hour?" I questioned the man while looking at Pete.

"You can pick your wife back up here in, say, an hour and a half, to be safe," he said to Pete. We never corrected the man's assumption about our marital status and I just wished I could ignore the negative images that invaded my imagination, such as the one where Pete and I could never be married because my cancer had spread to my bones, liver, lungs, and brain, and I'd spend the rest of my life decomposing from chemo and other chemicals.

I kissed Pete on the lips. "I love you."

"I love you. I'll see you soon," Pete said.

As soon as I entered the exam room, my eyes focused on the large leather recliner and I had the urge to vomit. I remembered all the times I (and my parents and my sister) sat in those recliners while being infused with chemotherapy dripping from the upside-down plastic bags. A male nurse asked me to take a seat in the recliner next to an older gentleman wearing a johnny and hooked up to an IV. Then the nurse explained the schedule of events.

"We'll inject the radioactive tracer in about thirty minutes and then you should be ready for scanning forty-five minutes after that. The test itself takes about twenty minutes, okay?"

I nodded, shivered and informed him, "I have a sedative. . . ."

"Of course," he whispered. "I'll have you take that after we get you injected with the tracer. That way the sedative won't wear off before you have the test, okay?"

I nodded and clenched my teeth.

Fifteen minutes later, the nurse approached me wearing rubber gloves and carrying packets of alcohol swabs, a tourniquet, catheter, and strips of tape.

"You can only use my right arm . . . and . . . you may have trouble finding a vein . . . sometimes they hide."

Even though nine years had elapsed, most of my veins had collapsed from needles needed for chemotherapy, anesthesia for all the surgeries, and routine blood work. "Most technicians have had good luck using my hand."

I looked away as he squeezed my bicep with a blue rubber band and poked at the potential veins in my right arm.

Despite his tender and gentle nature, the dizziness and nausea increased and I felt a hot flash brewing. He stuck the needle in one vein that looked promising, but after several pinches, he declared, "Well, that's not going to work." Then he prodded at my veins again and I reminded him. "I have some plump ones on the back of my hand."

"I'm sorry. I think I can get it this time. Are you okay?" he asked, but he never seemed to care how I answered him. He acted like a full-fledged vampire, determined to get blood from my arm at any expense.

The next thing I knew he had pushed my recliner as far back as it could go, placed cold compresses on my forehead and the back of my neck, and called in nurses and doctors for backup. I must have turned three shades of white and gray as my blood pressure dropped before I noticed several medical staff wearing stethoscopes and face masks hovering over me. I wished they would just give up on my limp veins, send me home to Pete, and forget about the scary test. I never wanted to know all the places in my body where the cancer must be lurking anyway. When my original nurse asked me for Pete's phone number I hoped he would ask Pete to pick up my pathetic ass now and take me home. But he only wanted to let Pete know my test would take longer than expected. They had allowed another patient—one who hadn't acted like such a baby—to go ahead of me while my blood pressure came back to normal and I regained some composure.

After a few minutes, I focused on a very pretty but reserved woman wearing a white lab coat standing next to me and placing tape on my right hand where she finally had success with the catheter. She leaned in closer to check my pulse and blood pressure. "There, feeling better now, I think?"

I just stared at her name—Anne—embroidered on her coat and I sensed my mother standing next to me.

"She'll be fine now," Anne told the male nurse as she turned her back to me and left the room.

When the door closed behind her, my nurse walked over to me with a plastic cup filled with water and smiled. "You can take that sedative now." *Right, nice timing, Dracula.*

Two hours later, Pete greeted me in the waiting area with a smile.

"Are you okay, honey?"

"Yeah, they just had some trouble finding a vein. No big deal." My veins had partially caused an issue, but they had nothing to do with why I almost passed out. And the worst part of the whole test—getting the results—had not even happened yet.

I had to keep busy to ignore the proverbial elephant that followed us around for the five days following the dreadful PET scan. The previous month, while on a tour of the Connecticut Wine Trail, Pete and I had fallen in love with one of the vineyards and signed up for a "Grape Nuts" membership. Every quarter we received three bottles of wine and a free wine tasting for ourselves and up to four other guests. A day or two before the PET scan, we received notice that our November wines were ready for pickup. The timing worked out perfectly for us and our new pet elephant.

We invited Pete's parents to join us for a Sunday road trip. The more time I spent with Janet and Sal, the more and more I became convinced these two blessings were my own parents—reincarnated. Maybe because we shared a common Italian heritage or maybe because my mother had cherished some of the same things Janet cherished— frequent, quality family time (especially with grandchildren), cooking and eating homemade Italian-inspired meals, reading, and always having a sense of style. And Pete's father loved to play and watch golf and make homemade wine as much as my father had.

Even today, whenever someone complains that their parents are driving them crazy, I remind them of what I have lost and encourage them to breathe deeply and inhale for every moment they are privileged to share with their parents.

As our car approached the vineyard, the four of us noticed the vines were empty and brown, but we still caught a glimmer of Italy as we stared at the endless rows of grapevines. The quaint and renovated New England dairy barn buzzed with visitors enjoying the warmth and charm of the vineyard. We each chose one of our favorite wines from the tasting and enjoyed a glass outside on the deck overlooking the vines. After we noshed on cheese and crackers and finished our wine, we decided to find a place for lunch.

At the end of the estate's driveway, Pete had the choice to go left toward the center of town or right toward Foxwoods Casino. We all agreed that Pete should take a right. He had never been to Foxwoods and I hadn't been since before my sister died. Lori and I loved to play bingo in honor of our mom, or just sit for hours mindlessly playing the slot machines.

MGM Grand had been added to the reservation since the last time I'd visited Foxwoods and it created a magnificent sight as we approached the casinos. I loved seeing Pete's amazement as he experienced the "wonder of it all" for the very first time. We visited MGM Grand and, after playing a couple of slot machines, we walked over to Foxwoods for lunch.

Although thankful for an extraordinary day that helped me to live in the moment and distract my mind from the PET scan, I started to do what I do best—plan for the future. On the ride home from Connecticut and for the two days leading up to the appointment with my oncologist, I had a silent conversation with myself—Could the medium have been wrong? I mean, could I be rediagnosed, and unlike my sister and mother who endured many years of chemo, maybe die quickly? Could it really be possible that after I had survived so much heartache and emotional pain—and had finally found true love—that this is it? Was my whole purpose on this earth to demonstrate that life's challenges can lead to rewards? I mean, is it like what happens in the movies, we spend two hours waiting for the happy ending and then the movie ends?

The Tuesday we would receive the results of my PET scan started like any other weekday morning. We woke up next to each other—smiling—and Pete kissed my shoulder. He made coffee, took a shower, changed into a suit and tie, and then drove to court. I showered, changed into a sweat suit, and walked upstairs to my office. But then Pete returned home for lunch (I was feeling so nauseous, I hadn't eaten anything all day) and then he drove us to Providence for the dreaded appointment.

And that's when the day began to feel like no other day I had ever encountered. I checked in with the receptionist and, much like I had tried to read the minds of the technician who performed the PET scan, I stared at each person behind the desk and tried to figure out the results of my test.

Pete and I found seats in front of the windows in leather chairs separated by a table with a lamp on it. I felt like I hadn't inhaled a full breath of air in more than a week, but I tried not to let Pete know how nervous I felt, so I just gave him a toothless smile. He never doubted that my enlarged lymph nodes were caused by the severe cold I had suffered just two weeks before the test.

"Honey, I just know, you're fine. Trust me." I wanted nothing more than to believe him. He seemed so certain, but I struggled between wanting him to maintain his innocence and wanting him to be fully prepared for the potentially bad news we were about to receive. I couldn't catch my breath whenever I thought about having to tell Jacob and Julia my breast cancer was back. I never even wanted them to know I had had breast cancer nine years before. They should never have to worry about these awful things. Pete disagreed with me and wanted his kids to be aware so they would know a success story—with a happy ending.

I heard a female voice call my name. "Linda?"

I looked at Pete. "Come on." We both stood up and walked toward the physician's assistant. She led us into the exam room, but instead of performing the normal routine—

weight, blood pressure, and johnny—she never smiled. She only said, "The doctor will be right in," before she turned and left the room. I tried to read her mind for the split second that she had looked me in the eyes. Surely, she had read the test results with the receptionists.

"Honey, sit down." I offered the only chair to Pete as I stepped up to sit on the exam table.

I smiled at my fiancé while trying not to let him know my body was shaking from the inside out. My teeth chattered from nerves, not temperature, and my palms were sweaty. I heard the doorknob turn before I saw my doctor walk into the room, followed by a resident. I held my breath and immediately thought, oh my God, today must be the lesson on how to deliver bad news to a patient.

A few weeks earlier, I had told my doctor how Pete proposed in Italy, but before I could proudly introduce them to each other, the doctor walked toward me, shook my hand as always, and blurted out, "You're fine. The scan is perfectly negative. In fact, it is the most boring scan I have ever seen."

At that moment, time stopped for me. Then I remembered to breathe. I stared at the doctor in utter disbelief. "You're serious?" He nodded and smiled.

"Oh my God, you could have called me sooner."

"I literally just received and read the report before I walked in the room."

I raised my hands to his neck as if to strangle him and he smiled. Pete stood up from his chair as I jumped off the exam table and we hugged. "We can get married now," I whispered in his ear.

I remembered that we weren't alone in the room, stepped back from Pete, and still holding his hand, turned to Dr. Legare.

"Doctor Legare, this is my fiancé, Peter. Peter, this is Dr. Legare." They shook hands and I realized I had just introduced two of the most important men in my life—one man saving my life for the other.

The professional and reserved oncologist who had treated me for the previous nine years smiled from ear to ear. "We can marry you two right here. My assistant is a justice of the peace." Surely, this doctor had to revel in the moments when he could deliver good news to his patients. He seemed to possess the same level of relief as us.

When Pete and I returned to the car, we both melted into the leather seats that had been warmed by the sun. Pete had tears in his eyes. "I was so worried about you."

"Really? You seemed so sure of yourself."

"I was, but . . . well, never mind. Can I just say I think we just heard the title for your book?"

"Perfectly negative?"

"Yes, perfectly negative."

I texted the test results to Brenda, Pete's sister, my brothers, Mickie, and a couple of my fellow breast cancer survivors. Neither Pete nor I returned to work that afternoon. We drove to a waterfront restaurant located a mile from our house, sat on backless stools at the bar, and ordered raw oysters and the best martinis with blue cheese olives either of us had ever tasted. We carefully raised our glasses and Pete said, "To being perfectly negative." I smiled at him, took a sip, and then kissed the man I should have trusted all along.

Exactly one week later, I answered an expected call from my boss—a weekly call to review the status of my projects and discuss risks and issues.

Without any of his normal pleasantries, my boss blurted out, "Linda, I'm sorry to have to tell you this, but your position has been eliminated."

Much like when I had heard "it's cancer," I never heard another word after my boss gave me his news.

But given what had occurred just one week earlier, I never progressed through the five typical stages of loss. I skipped the denial stage because I had known layoffs were being announced that day. I indulged in the anger phase for about a minute. I mean, how dare they? I'm the best they will ever have. I skipped the bargaining stage and all the "what if I had done that" or "what if I had said this." I never once felt depressed, but slid comfortably into acceptance—and I deemed this most recent loss the greatest gift of my life.

I called Pete. "Are you sitting down, honey?"

"Um, yes."

"I just got laid off."

"What? Really? I'm sorry, honey. Are you okay?"

"Yeah, actually, I am. I mean, given where we were last week, this is nothing, right?"

"Absolutely nothing like last week."

Within minutes of us saying goodbye, Pete had sent me the most beautiful email and confirmed I had been blessed with a man who not only knew how to write, but who also gets the gift of life—who gets me—who gets us:

> So, I refuse to look at this as entirely bad news. I'm sorry that you have to go through this, because regardless of the reason, it is a difficult thing.
>
> But . . . you are perfectly negative . . .
>
> In the meantime . . . Enjoy the weather. Take a walk. Paint. Write.
>
> Most of all, know that I love you, and anything that comes our way, we face it together.
>
> I love you,
> Pete

They say all good things must come to an end. Aside from wanting to know who the hell "they" are, I'm here to tell you that that cliché is most definitely—okay, maybe—not entirely true.

My parents had hammered that cliché into my head every time I kicked and screamed after they denied me something I wanted. And when I screamed, "That isn't fair, so-and-so gets to have such-and-such," my parents tried to pacify me or maybe prepare me for the future by saying, "You're right, but life isn't always fair," and always threw in, "All good things must come to an end," for good measure.

Hearing that cliché over and over again for thirty years caused me to anticipate a bad event after every good one and maybe even increased my pessimism, rather than living in and appreciating the good moment as it happened.

Hearing that cliché over and over again had programmed me to believe that negative events were just plain bad. Of course, there's nothing good about death, divorce, disease, or deceit when we're smack in the middle of it. But I now believe that given some space—sometimes many years—from the pain and the opportunity to look back, I can recognize how the knowledge and experience I gained shaped subsequent decisions I made. Today, I need less time to uncover a lesson being learned when faced with a negative situation.

In fact, I just don't believe anything in my life is negative anymore, which is why I don't believe that "all good things have to come to an end."

I believe everything happens for a reason (or to deliver a lesson)—and that it's all good. I believe even negative experiences will become positive, because, for me, living through the most difficult life circumstances has, over time, led me to recognize true love, outlined my path to survival, and revealed my life's purpose.

Words of Gratitude

I believe people enter and, sometimes, leave my life for a purpose. I am eternally grateful for each named, renamed and unnamed character in this book --- from my family, friends, doctors and nurses to my therapist, tailor and telephone salespeople --- for sharing one or more life experiences with me and having an impact on the person I am today and will continue to become.

To my angels, thank you for the unending support and encouragement I sense from you every day and for the determination you bestowed on me to share my story of resilience and hope with the world.

For over thirty years, I have been blessed to experience life (and the deepest, most healing belly laughs!) with my best friend, Brenda. It is her loyalty, optimism, and honesty that has motivated me to push through the most difficult times of my life.

I thank my friend, Alayne White, for the peace and beauty she enables me to enjoy and for introducing me to my first writing teacher, Hannah Goodman, a good friend who teaches writing workshops where I found my writing voice, courage, and confidence among the talented and inspirational writers Hannah attracts.

I am grateful for Lisa Tener for believing in me, guiding me to my writing muse and ultimately introducing me to Stuart Horwitz, my book architect, writing coach, editor, and friend.

Stuart, Stuart, Stuart (I'm shaking my head from side to side in disbelief), I am grateful for your creativity (I mean, it's the best sub-title ever!), patience, mentoring, unwavering encouragement, and connection to Chloe Marsala, Rudy Vale, Maria Gagliano Scalora, and Linda Feldman.

To my beta readers, Chloe and Rudy, thank you for your invaluable professional, candid, and thoughtful feedback that I often read to remind myself why I want to share my story.

To Maria Gagliano, thank you for our encouragement and for providing precise feedback to strengthen the logistics and character development within my story. I'm grateful for our common Italian heritage.

To my enthusiastic early readers – Allan, Arthur, Ashley, Brenda, Bob, Chloe, Cindie, Cleveland, Cynthia, Debby, Elaine, Faith, Frankie, Gina, Hannah, Heidi, Janey, Linda, Lydia, Maria, Mark, Mickie, Mike, Nick, Peter, Rudy, Sal, Stuart, Susan, and Tanya – thank you for your constructive feedback, sincere praise, and overall faith in my ability to inspire others with my story.

I thank Mark DaPonte at Mirage Design, for wanting to read my story and capturing its theme perfectly with a bright and cheerful cover design.

Words may never express how grateful I am to Gina Aguiar for her instincts regarding friendship, love, choosing the right nail color and, mostly, for playing matchmaker for me and my husband...the man who believes in me even in the moments when I don't believe in myself, encourages me to live my life's purpose and proves he loves me unconditionally – every day.

I absolutely have no regrets, hold no grudges, and am only thankful for the lessons I learn from every experience, person, and furry friend I encounter. My sincerest wish is that my story ignites the courage in you to face unexpected life situations and unlocks a new perspective that paves the way for you to move forward with purpose.

About the Author

Before becoming a life coach, Linda earned a bachelor's degree in Computer Information Systems from Bentley University, a master's degree in Business Administration from Bryant University, and certificates in project and risk management. She dedicated more than twenty years of her life to corporate America as a technology change manager. This business experience made her aware of how nothing in life stays the same. She mastered the technical, organizational, and communication skills necessary to successfully implement requested changes in people, processes and systems.

Linda is also a breast cancer survivor who lost her mom and sister to the same disease. In the midst of turmoil, she often wrote in her journal for comfort and healing. When Linda's employer eliminated her position, she seized the opportunity to satisfy her long-forgotten goal to write a book. She never imagined that her life would be the book's topic. But in the process of reading her old journals – filled with a decade of heartache – many revelations and life lessons emerged. In fact, this kind of education ... the kind of education that used Linda's life experiences to demonstrate key theories and practices ... earned her a burning desire to inspire others to overcome the myriad of difficulties life hands us. Once she had gained enough distance from each tragedy and she dedicated time to examine each event and connect all the dots, a nugget of wisdom emerged – "Everything happens for a reason, we're just not given the reason at the same time as the thing."

When Linda finished writing the last chapter of her memoir, the reason for her existence stared her in the eyes and ignited a fire in her heart. Linda's life purpose is to serve as an example of resilience. Her mission is to share how patience and an open mind provides a person with courage to move beyond any unexpected situation. She has chosen to achieve her mission through writing and life coaching.

One of Linda's short stories, "I Miss My Breasts," is published in *Chicken Soup for the Soul: Hope and Healing for Your Breast Cancer Journey.* She co-facilitates a cancer support group, Sisters in Survival, for women to gather and share their strategies for surviving cancer – and more importantly – surviving life.

Linda earned her Certified Life Coach credential from The Institute for Life Coach Training (ILCT) and she is a member of the International Coach Federation (ICF). She is also a Board Certified Coach with the Center for Credentialing and Education (CCE). What excites Linda the most about coaching is working with people who have encountered unexpected life circumstances and sharing thought-provoking, creative processes and tools so they may regain a sense of control, move forward with a new perspective, and uncover their life's meaning.

Linda lives in Rhode Island (USA) with her husband, two step-teens, and a Shih Tzu named Enzo.

www.lindacarvelli.com